Jerzy Grotowski s
Journeys
to the East

ZBIGNIEW OSIŃSKI

Jerzy Grotowski's Journeys to the East

Translated from Polish by
ANDRZEJ WOJTASIK and KRIS SALATA

Edited by
KRIS SALATA

Polish text edited by
IGA RUTKOWSKA

Routledge
Taylor & Francis Group

Holstebro – Malta – Wrocław
London – New York
2014

ICARUS Publishing Enterprise is a joint initiative
of Odin Teatret (Denmark), The Grotowski Institute (Poland)
and Theatre Arts Researching the Foundations (Malta)

Cover design and layout Barbara Kaczmarek
Typesetting Tadeusz Zarych
Index Agata Kaczmarek and Iga Rutkowska

Published by
Icarus Publishing Enterprise and Routledge
www.icaruspublishing.com
www.routledge.com

The Grotowski Institute
Rynek-Ratusz 27, 50-101 Wrocław, Poland

Routledge
2 Park Square, Milton Park, Abingdon, OX14 4RN, UK
711 Third Avenue, New York, NY 10017, USA

Routledge is an imprint of Taylor and Francis Group, an informa business

ISBN 978-1-138-77991-4 (paperback)
ISBN 978-1-138-77990-7 (hardback)

Printed in Poland by JAKS

CONTENTS

Contents

EDITOR'S NOTE

JERZY GROTOWSKI'S JOURNEYS to the East is an unusual scrapbook of facts, quotations, and commentaries documenting real and metaphorical journeys. Painstakingly researched by Grotowski's biographer, a distinguished scholar of his work, it is necessary reading for those interested in Grotowski's rich relationship with the East, but will also appeal to readers who would like to have a glimpse of the East from the 20th century Eastern European perspective – theatrical and otherwise. In that sense, the book opens a passage to the past, to the less known or forgotten pages of Polish theatre history, and to the lasting legacy of this most influential and enigmatic of artists.

While preparing this book for publication in English, I was concerned about the cultural and historical weight of such terms as 'Oriental theatre', 'Orient', or 'Orientalism', problematized in Western discourse by Edward Said since the late 1970s. I preserve these terms in the book as the marking of a historical narrative. I also hope that the meaning of these terms becomes quite clear in the text, and their tone, problematic from a postcolonial perspective, renders itself politically neutral in the context of Grotowski's intercultural search for objective aspects of ritual and performance techniques.

The basis for the English text was a preliminary translation by Andrzej Wojtasik, which I decisively altered in the course of rereading the Polish original and consulting with its author, Zbigniew Osiński. My goal was to prepare a version accessible to those less familiar with the nuances of Polish cultural, political, and historical contexts that surround Grotowski's journeys to the East. At the same time, I took care to preserve the style of the author's narrative and the integrity of the quotations. As a translator of Grotowski's texts, I am particularly aware of his aversion to 'interpretation', and thus kept my interventions in check, often favouring the flavour of the original syntax over merely the clarity of style.

All original titles mentioned in the body of the text and in the footnotes are followed by their English translation in square brackets. I also used these brackets for occasional editorial inserts. My own footnotes are clearly marked as well.

Finally, I wish to thank Dr Charles Poole and Lauren Hlubny, my two outstanding assistants, who dedicated countless hours helping me to prepare the English edition of this book.

Kris Salata, PH.D.,
ASSOCIATE PROFESSOR,
SCHOOL OF THEATRE,
FLORIDA STATE UNIVERSITY

HOW WAS THE BOOK
JERZY GROTOWSKI'S JOURNEYS TO THE EAST
CONCEIVED?

AFTER BECOMING ACQUAINTED with my book *Polskie kontakty teat-ralne z Orientem w XX wieku*, Eugenio Barba suggested that I select several chapters from it which directly refer to Grotowski and prepare for the Icarus Publishing Enterprise a book provisionally titled *Jerzy Grotowski's Orient*, or *Jerzy Grotowski's East*. I have known Eugenio since the early 1960s, the first years of the Laboratory Theatre in Opole, and I know well that his attitude towards Poland is entirely special. Andrzej Wajda perhaps best described it in his letter to me written on 22 September 2003, after the ceremony awarding Eugenio Barba an honorary degree from the University of Warsaw: 'For me personally it was a very touching moment demonstrating true and lasting friendship with our country through friendship with one man, Jerzy Grotowski.'[1]

After receiving this proposal, I asked Iga Rutkowska to read the book carefully and present her ideas on what could be done with it. Rutkowska participated in my seminar at the Faculty of Polish Studies at the University of Warsaw from 2005 to 2008, and is currently my assistant in the interdisciplinary seminar at the Department of Japanese Culture of the Polish-Japanese Institute of Information Technology. I knew that she was remarkably gifted, diligent, and filled with passion for research. I also knew that she was trained in three disciplines: anthropology, theatre, and Japanese studies. I also knew her book, which I read in autumn 2009 before my only trip to Japan.

In response to my request, Rutkowska proposed her approach to disassembling and reconfiguring the text. In principle, I accepted her idea, at the same time suggesting some edits and additions. In that way, together we worked towards the present version of the book. (Its final version had been further shaped with the editors.)

I hope that the participants of the interdepartmental seminar I conducted at the Faculty of Polish Studies at the University of Warsaw, as well as all others who are interested in such topics of research in cultural and theatre studies, adopt the issues and problems presented or only suggested in this book. Some of the seminar

---

[1] Andrzej Wajda, letter to Zbigniew Osiński, 22 September 2003, author's private collection.

sessions were led by eminent scholars, as well as young experts and students. I consider their contribution a valuable source of inspiration for me.

Finally, I would like to express my gratitude to all those without whom this book would simply not exist. I want to thank Eugenio Barba; Professor Anna Czekanowska; Professor of Indian Studies Maria Krzysztof Byrski; experts in Japanese Studies and consecutive ambassadors of the Republic of Poland in Tokyo Dr Jadwiga Rodowicz and Henryk Lipszyc; Japanese Studies scholars Professor Ewa Pałasz-Rutkowska, Dr Beata Kubiak Ho-Chi, and Dr Iga Rutkowska; Sinologists Professor Lidia Kasarełło, Professor Izabella Łabędzka, and Maurycy Gawarski; Dorota Buchwald and Monika Krawul of the Zbigniew Raszewski Theatre Institute; Afghanologist Szymon Skalski; employees of archives and libraries, especially the libraries of the University of Warsaw and my everyday favourite, the Library of the Literature Institute and the Institute of Polish Culture at the Faculty of Polish Studies of the University of Warsaw. Last but not least, I would like to thank the publisher.

Zbigniew Osiński
WARSAW, 20 DECEMBER 2010

I.
Nienadówka

THE FIRST TRACES of Grotowski's fascination with the Orient can already be found in his childhood. His mother's role in inspiring such interests was crucial. In Nienadówka, a village near Rzeszów, in south-eastern Poland, in spite of extremely difficult conditions under German occupation, Emilia Grotowska (1897–1978) would acquire books, assign them to her sons, and oversee their reading. A book that played a special role for Jerzy was Paul Brunton's *A Search in Secret India*, whose translation by Wanda Dynowska[2] was published in Poland shortly before the war as *Ścieżkami jogów* [On the paths of yogis]. This is how Grotowski described it to Andrzej Bonarski in 1975:

> Mother went to town – she walked on foot, or she walked or rode with someone – anyway she brought back a book titled *A Search in Secret India*, written by an English journalist, Brunton. He talked about the people he met in India, mainly about some unusual man, who in our civilization would be called 'yurodivy'. He lived on the slopes of Arunachala, a mountain considered as holy – the Mountain of Flame. His name was Maharishi. He had a peculiar custom. When someone came to him seeking an explanation about what is essential in life, how to bring meaning to life, or what is meaningful in general, [Ramana Maharshi] would ask him: 'Who are you?' But he would say it in the first person: 'Ask yourself "Who am I?"'[3]

[2]   Wanda Dynowska, known as Umadevi outside of Poland, was a writer, translator and propagator of Indian culture in Poland and of Polish culture in India.
[3]   'Rozmowa z Grotowskim' [A conversation with Grotowski], interview by Andrzej Bonarski, *Kultura*, 13 (1975), 1, 12–13; repr. in *Teksty zebrane*, ed. by Agata Adamiecka-Sitek, with Mario Biagini and others (Wrocław and Warsaw: Instytut im. Jerzego Grotowskiego, Instytut Teatralny im. Zbigniewa Raszewskiego, Wydawnictwo Krytyki Politycznej, 2012), pp. 588–605. An abbreviated version of the interview is available in English as 'Conversation with Grotowski', trans. by Boleslaw Taborski, in Jennifer Kumiega, *The Theatre of Grotowski* (London: Methuen, 1985), pp. 217–23. Here and later quoted after Osiński, *Grotowski and His Laboratory*, trans. and abridged by Lillian Vallee and Robert Findlay (New York: PAJ Publications, 1986), p. 13. See: Osiński, *Grotowski wytycza trasy. Studia i szkice* [Grotowski blazes the trails: Studies and sketches] (Warsaw: Pusty Obłok, 1993), pp. 11–55; *Pierwsza inicjacja Jerzego Grotowskiego* [The first initiation of Jerzy Grotowski]; 'On poprzez teatr bada świat. Rozmowa z Kazimierzem Grotowskim, profesorem Uniwersytetu Jagiellońskiego, fizykiem jądrowym, himalaistą' [He studies the world through theatre: A conversation with Kazimierz Grotowski, a Professor of the Jagiellonian University, nuclear physicist, and Himalaya-mountaineer], interview by Teresa Błajet-Wilniewczyc, *Notatnik Teatralny*, 4 (1992), 85–93; Kazimierz Grotowski, 'Portret rodzinny' [A family portrait], *Pamiętnik Teatralny*, 1–4 (2000), 9–36; Kazimierz Grotowski and Andrzej Michał Kobos, 'Wędrowałem za fizyką' [I wandered following physics], in *Po drogach uczonych. Z członkami Polskiej Akademii Umiejętności rozmawia An-*

The book proved very fertile for Jerzy, and as early as 1942 the nine-year-old authored a peculiar set of notes about entering into *direct perception*.[4] Moreover, thanks to his reflection on Brunton's book, the image of a 'divine madman' – *a yurodivy* – first appears for Grotowski, which later so powerfully reappears in many disguises throughout his life and in the performances of the Laboratory Theatre.

It is in Nienadówka that Grotowski met with a *yurodivy* for the first time, and because of Brunton's book he was aware that similar people also exist elsewhere in other cultures. This turned out to be one of the key experiences of his life. Thus it is also not by accident that in 'Nienadówka', the first chapter of his 1987 text 'Teatr Źródeł' [Theatre of Sources], Grotowski returns to the previously mentioned event and his reaction after reading Brunton's book. Actually, the later description of the event differs in some details from his 1975 account; it is also undoubtedly richer, thus worth quoting *in extenso*:

> The time I passed in the village was wartime. One day my mother set out to the city. No one could ever be sure if he or she would return from such a journey. These were the times of destitution. Yet my mother went to the city to buy books because she was convinced that some books can be like food. Then she brought two back – *The Life of Jesus* by Renan and *A Search in Secret India* by Brunton. Renan's book was forbidden by the Church, but my mother considered it an extremely important story about Jesus, and often repeated that, for her, it was the 'fifth Gospel'. Mother was practising the most ecumenical Catholicism. She emphasized that, for her, there is no such thing as the single truth of a single religion. It seemed quite logical, yet it always caused misunderstandings during confession. Besides, she was extraordinarily tolerant of people holding irreligious positions.

---

drzej M. Kobos [On the paths of scientists: Conversations of Andrzej M. Kobos with members of the Polish Academy of Knowledge] (Kraków: Polska Akademia Umiejętności, 2007), pp. 247–80. Editor's note: there are two different spellings of the name used in the book: Maharishi (as used by Grotowski, Barba, and commonly in Poland), and Maharshi (more commomly used in English). Most understandably, we preserved the longer spelling where it was used in quotations, but we use the shorter spelling, Maharshi, in the text. As this discrepancy may seem a bit confusing at first, it will help to prevent the reader from a greater confusion of actual people. Sri Ramana Maharshi should not be confused with the more recognizable Maharishi Mahesh Yogi (1918–2008), the guru to The Beatles and the founder of TM (Transcendental Meditation).

[4]   Jerzy Grotowski, personal conversations with the author, Wrocław, 4 March 1976, and Warsaw, 6–7 December 1976. [Editor's italics. The author doesn't explain the phrase here, but nevertheless addresses the meaning in the following paragraphs.]

Brunton's book was about a man who lived on the side of Mount Arunachala in India, and who saw in this mountain God as Mother. However, his experience would send him still somewhere else – he thought perhaps to Shiva, which means that the Mountain of Flame may be a male deity at the same time. This old man, Sri Ramana Maharshi, would say: if you ask 'Who am I?', the entire world living around you will send this question back to you, and your limited 'I' will disappear, and you will find something else. Later I learned that this something else was connected with *hridayam*, which means 'heart'; yet etymologically it means 'centre-is-this'. My first reaction to Brunton's book was a fever. Later I started to copy conversations of Ramana with his visitors. Then I discovered that I am not so mad as I thought before. I discovered that somewhere in the world there are people aware of such possibility. It gave me a considerable relief, but at the same time it somewhat put me in conflict with my Catholicism.[5]

The final fragment of the text quoted above refers to a peculiar ritual with a tree that Grotowski invented himself when he was seven or eight years old and became overwhelmed with 'the unreasonable temptation to become the priest of the apple tree'. It was actually not the wild apple tree that was important to him but the fact that while climbing it, and doing so in a different way than he climbed other trees, he felt as if the tree 'was transporting him somewhere else'. He kept it secret for a long time, for he thought it was something abnormal; only after reading *A Search in Secret India* did he somehow understand his own mystery.

While in Nienadówka, he also learned certain other forms of traditional rituals and cults:

> During this time, which was wartime, I had seen many corpses. Yet truly shocking to me was the butchering of a calf. The calf, with the throat cut but still alive, got away and ran around the yard, spattering blood. Why was I so shocked by this? [...] I have been told that humans are killed because they are 'enemies'. This word meant something devilish. In the case of butchering the calf, I myself participated in this strange game of nature since I was to eat its body. The other incarnation of nature was a bull kept next to the barn.

5   Grotowski, 'Teatr Źródeł' [Theatre of Sources], ed. by Leszek Kolankiewicz, *Zeszyty Literackie*, 19 (1987), 103–04. The translation is based on the Polish version of Grotowski's text from 1981. In many respects it differs from the one available in English under the same title, 'Theatre of Sources', in Kumiega, *The Theatre of Grotowski*, pp. 231–35, and in *The Grotowski Sourcebook*, ed. by Lisa Wolford, Richard Schechner (London and New York: Routledge, 1997), pp. 252–70, although some fragments are identical in both versions.

• *Kazimierz Grotowski and Jerzy Grotowski during the Nazi occupation,*
Nienadówka, 1941

• *Jerzy Grotowski and Franciszka Ożóg, Nienadówka, 1980*

The cows were brought to him to be mounted. The children from the village would observe it. It was neither rousing nor funny for us, but rather mysterious and even very serious.

I saw nature as the Mother giving life and death. However, I knew that the light of nature is transporting us to a different place.[6]

The antinomy of 'I saw' and 'I knew' is quite characteristic here. Grotowski's inclination towards antithesis, towards contradictions conveying his attitude towards humanity, the world, nature, appeared very early, already in his childhood, and in time it turned into an essential feature of what he would later call his 'originary standpoint' [*pierwotne nastawienie*]. Then he also came to an understanding of the paths of human logic, which ultimately resulted in his anti-discursiveness.

Nearly fifty years after his discoveries in Nienadówka, he described them as follows:

I also made many observations about people. Sometimes people came to our home to play cards. Then I would hide under the table. I noticed that the legs of the people playing cards talked about everything that was not said above the table. But even more, I noticed the complete nonsense of many human conversations. Somebody said, for example, that the cow has hooves, then somebody else said that his feet hurt, and then somebody else that when one falls off a horse, it hurts. In these conversations there was no continuity. They seemed to be pointless babbling.

Some years later I heard the expression 'Life is a dream'. I should say that I never understood this sentence in the sense that we are dreaming and then suddenly the awakening happens. I took this sentence precisely in the spirit of my childhood observations. Life is a dream in the sense that we are the prisoners of our babbling. Someone may call it 'internal monologues' or 'dialogues', yet for me this is just babbling.

All these experiences became a part of what can be called my originary standpoint.[7]

The sources of Grotowski's anti-discursive and antithetical attitude are simultaneously revealed here. These insights became constant presences in his work. For example, in the 1969 text *Teatr a rytuał* [Theatre and ritual], he formulated it in the following way – with reference to an actor of the Laboratory Theatre:

[6] Grotowski, 'Teatr Źródeł', p. 104. See: Grotowski, 'Theatre of Sources', in *The Grotowski Sourcebook*, p. 256. Editor's note: The above quotation comes from the early version of the text, significantly different from the later and 'final' version and its published English translation.

[7] Ibid. See the note above.

Yet in following the path of structure, one must reach that real deed – a process which contains contradiction. It was an issue of great importance to understand that these contradictions are logical. One should not strive for avoiding contradictions; quite the opposite – the essence lies in contradictions.[8]

And ten years later he confessed:

If you think that there are many contradictions in what I say, you are right. I am aware that I speak in contradictions, but please remember that in a basic sense I am a practitioner. And practice is contradictory. That is its substance. Thus if I am contradictory, I am – as a practitioner. I cannot theorize about my work. I can only tell about my adventure – with all contradictions it included and still includes. For example, when I say something that is not logical, I want to say that it is not a result of applying logic. I always speak in a pragmatic way. Yet should we say that because of that, it is illogical? When one *does*, one does not ask oneself questions about logic.[9]

In Grotowski's opinion, this paradoxical logic, based on the principle of complementarity 'and – and', rather than on the principle of exclusion 'either – or', somehow imitates contradictions residing in the very substance of his profession, his work, which he always understood in the medieval spirit, that is, as a vocation. This is connected with his special sensitivity to the direct experience of a particular man. This refers to the substance of an actor's and a director's work, as well as to experiencing history:

Spontancity is obviousness. The essence of the spontaneous now is obviousness. Not only for the one who *does*, but also for the one who is present. This is 'now' – *ordo aeternis*. It may last just a few seconds, yet it is much more important than long hours of work. And it may also last several hours, but seem as a few seconds... [...]

When we are immersed in the passage of history, then we are also unavoidably immersed in what is dirty and clean at the same time. When one says that his hands are absolutely clean – he is probably a criminal. If we participate in life, we take some options, and it is very seldom that we are fully aware of all aspects of a situation and – even more! – that we are absolutely impartial. If we are immersed in

---

[8]   Grotowski, 'Teatr a rytuał' [Theatre and Ritual], *Dialog*, 3 (1969), 71; repr. in Grotowski, *Teksty z lat 1965–1969. Wybór* [Texts, 1965–1969: A selection], sel. and ed. by Janusz Degler and Zbigniew Osiński, 2nd edn, revised and extended (Wrocław: Wiedza o kulturze, 1990), p. 79. Editor's note: All translations by Andrzej Wojtasik and Kris Salata unless otherwise noted

[9]   Grotowski, 'O praktykowaniu romantyzmu' [About practising romanticism], ed. by Leszek Kolankiewicz, *Dialog*, 3 (1980), 120.

a sea, we seek light – this is a historical consciousness. We seek light, making mistakes. We are entangled.

We reach some kind of cognizance when the 'linear time' is as if it does not exist. This is *ordo aeternis*, now, *hic et nunc*.[10]

And this could be a result of the full awakening of this 'organ for perceiving history'. Thus all this contains a certain vision of Man. 'Show me your Man and I will show you my God', says Grotowski after Theophilus of Antioch, a Christian writer who lived in the second century.[11] While interpreting the aphorism, he notices a corresponding image of man in works of Adam Mickiewicz:[12]

As Mickiewicz formulated it – I am quoting from memory – the point is 'the longing to be a complete human', 'a whole human', 'a human taken as a whole', which means the one who participates in history as a warrior and, at the same time, in the life of his essence – in short, 'one who devotes himself totally to the thing he does'. Such a man should have what Mickiewicz calls 'an organ of feeling'.[13]

It seems notable that Grotowski's reflective return to the 'land of childhood years'[14] and early youth took place in the late 1970s. Before, in the period of strictly theatrical work, this motif would have appeared much less frequently, at least in his published texts and interviews. Eventually, on 15 November 1979, while summing up twenty years of the Laboratory Theatre during a ceremony in Wrocław's Museum of Architecture, he referenced the town of his childhood:

The concept of 'frontiers' is a relative one: it is not the border area. In some countries the word used for what we traditionally call 'frontiers' is 'interior'. The role of 'frontiers' in Polish culture is an absorbing subject. [...] And there is after all an aspiring Poland... like my Rzeszów when I was growing up, when it was still a small town... So then, like in Wrocław, like in various foreign countries,

---

10 Ibid., p. 117. Emphasis original.
11 Editor's note: Theophilus of Antioch, a second-century bishop of Antioch (Syria), is the author of the oldest extant commentary on the book of Genesis. It is contained in his work *To Autolycus*, which is a reply to objections made to Christianity. The citation comes from Book I, Chapter 2.
12 Adam Mickiewicz (1798–1855), one of most renowned poets of Polish Romanticism. In 1961, in Opole, Grotowski directed *Forefathers' Eve* [*Dziady*] based on Mickiewicz's drama.
13 Grotowski, 'O praktykowaniu romantyzmu', p. 113. Emphasis original.
14 Editor's note: The author alludes to a well-known phrase from Mickiewicz's epic poem *Pan Tadeusz* (Epilogue, v. 68).

we should show *The Tree of People, In Dostoyevskian, Journey to the East*, and *Apocalypsis cum figuris* in this 'frontier' Poland.[15]

In his speech titled 'The Art of the Beginner', given on 4 June 1978, during a symposium organized by the International Theatre Institute in the Old Orangery of the Warsaw's Royal Baths Park, Grotowski took a position similar to Mickiewicz's, who claimed that 'For the Greeks [...] true poetry meant nothing else but doing. Ποίησις (*Poiesis*) in Greek means doing'.[16] The same image of poetry and a poet, obviously still in germ form, looms over some of the poems Grotowski wrote in his youth. It seems to be some kind of archetypal image. Yet it may be more important to realize that, in keeping with the ancient Greek etymology of the word 'poetry', Grotowski was a poet *par excellence* for his entire artistic life, even though – as far as I know – he published no poetry after his youth.[17] For him, poetry was not only associated with action but, in its deepest meaning, it was identified with *doing*; it was *doing* in itself.

---

[15] Grotowski, 'Teatr Laboratorium po dwudziestu latach. Hipoteza robocza' [The Laboratory Theatre after twenty years: A working hypothesis], *Polityka*, 26 January 1980, p. 10.

[16] Adam Mickiewicz, *Dzieła* [Works], XI: *Literatura słowiańska. Kurs trzeci i czwarty* [Slavic Literature: The Third and Fourth Course], trans. from French by Leon Płoszewski (Warsaw: Czytelnik, 1955), p. 22: lecture 2, 20 December 1842. See: Grotowski, 'The Art of the Beginner', *International Theatre Information* (Paris: ITI, Spring/Summer 1978): pp. 7–11.

[17] In 1976 Grotowski informed me that some of his poems were pseudonymously published in *Po Prostu* weekly magazine between 1956 and 1957. However, I could not identify them. See: Lech Śliwonik, 'Jerzy Grotowski – z rękopisów. (W trzecią rocznicę śmierci – 14 stycznia 2002)' [Jerzy Grotowski: from manuscripts (on the third anniversary of his death, 14 January 2002)], *Scena*, 6 (2001), 18–19; 'Listy do Ireny Jun' [Letters to Irena Jun]; Janusz Degler, 'Grotowski – poeta' [Grotowski, a poet], *Scena*, 1 (2004), 17–19 [Letters to Irena Jun]; *W stronę źródeł twórczości Jerzego Grotowskiego* [Towards the sources of Jerzy Grotowski's artistic work] (Rzeszów: MITEL, 2009), 'Uniwersytet Rzeszowski. Rok Grotowskiego 2009', '2009 – Rok Jerzego Grotowskiego' [2009: The Year of Jerzy Grotowski]: *Wiersze dziecięce. Faksymile dziecięcych wierszy Grotowskiego; Wpis do sztambucha ciotki Stanisławy. Faksymile wpisu do sztambucha ciotki Stanisławy. Rzeszów, 8 XII 1949; Poezje wybrane, Rzeszów 1949; Poezje wybrane, Rzeszów 1949; Faksymile tomiku poezji wybranych; wierszy; Pożegnanie barw. Faksymile i tomik wierszy; List do ciotki Stanisławy. Faksymile listu do ciotki Stanisławy. Katowice, 17 II 1960.* [Childhood poems. Facsimile of Grotowski's childhood poems; An inscription in aunt Stanisława's journal. Facsimile of inscription in Aunt Stanisława's journal. Rzeszów, 8 December 1949; Selected poems, Rzeszów, 1949; Facsimile of the volume of selected poems; Farewell to colours. Facsimile and a volume of poems; A letter to Aunt Stanisława. Facsimile of the letter to Aunt Stanisława. Katowice, 17 February 1960].

When he was sixteen, Grotowski fell seriously ill with a kidney disease that had resulted from a recent bout of scarlet fever. He was hospitalized and spent some time in a room among dying patients; doctors gave him a very little chance of recovery. Years later, one of these doctors could not hold back his surprise that Grotowski was still alive when they accidentally met on a tram in Kraków. Facing his condition, Grotowski imposed on himself a very strict discipline: above all he read voraciously, devouring stacks of books, and tried not to succumb to any situation. Finally he decided to live a normal life among healthy people. He calculated all the possible consequences of such a decision, taken openly against the doctors who insisted that he should always be cautious and take care of himself.[18]

That is when he began to live his, as he called it, 'conscious living with a deadline'. This – besides his understandably limited capacity for physical exertion – certainly strengthened his talent to focus on that one and only issue that interested him at the moment.

In 1950 Emilia Grotowska moved with her younger son to Kraków, where Kazimierz Grotowski, her older son, just received the post of an assistant in the Faculty of Physics at the Jagiellonian University. On 1 September 1950, Jerzy began his high school education. He graduated in May 1951 and was designated by the school as a 'leading student and activist' – such a distinction was a key factor in the admission to a university.[19] Obviously, he had to face the problem of choosing a major. Finally he decided on the acting school, which met the approval only of his mother and his brother. The rest of his family was categorically against it. For Grotowski himself, it wasn't an easy choice:

> When I passed my high school finals, I had to decide on what to study. I decided on three majors: the theatre school with an intention to continue in directing; the Medical Academy, for I was thinking of psychiatry; and Oriental Studies, with an intention to study traditional techniques of the East. Exams to the theatre school were held before the other two. And this was the only reason determining that I became, so to speak, the owner of a diploma authorizing me to work in theatre. If exams to the Medical Academy had been first, probably I would have become a psychiatrist; if exams

18 Raymonde Temkine, *Grotowski* (Lausanne: La Cité, 1968), pp. 56–57.
19 Editor's note: In Communist Poland, the so-called 'preference points' were an important component of the system of admissions to universities that accompanied preliminary examinations. Added to the exam grades, preference points enabled social advancement of young people from families of blue-collar workers and peasants. Grotowski's origins reduced his chances of being admitted.

to Oriental Studies were first, I would have studied traditional Eastern techniques. However, I am convinced that, regardless, I would have found myself in the same place I am now. Certainly, my vocabulary would have been different, for I am marked by theatrical experience; I am marked by my theatrical experience – even if I have gone beyond theatre. In fact, I suppose that I would have gone beyond traditional psychiatry or Oriental philology anyway.[20]

However, while applying for admission to the theatre school, he emphasized everything that could justify his decision in the eyes of the examination board: participation in amateur performances, numerous recitation contests, and awards he had received. His résumé attached to the application included a characteristic sentence:

> On the basis of my experience, obviously very limited, I arrived at the conclusion that the acting profession is the one in which I could find real happiness and full realization.[21]

Thus, one can say that everything actually happened by accident.

Jerzy Grotowski's family tradition, his experiences related to war, his school years and college days, his long-lasting illness, his experiences of 1956 and 1957,[22] the books he read, the people he met, his openness to other cultures, his countless journeys, and, finally, almost fifty years of professional work – in many ways related to theatre – had a decisive impact on shaping his attitude towards the world, nature, people, and values he subscribed to and practised, or – to put it differently – on shaping his worldview and attitude towards life.

A certain image of a man emerges from it, one I identified a long time ago as *senex et puer* – an old man and a boy in one – well recognized in the analytical psychology of Carl Gustav Jung and his school.[23] Here is a specific, yet at the same time paradoxical identi-

---

[20] Grotowski, 'Teatr Źródeł', pp. 104–05. Excerpts not included in the English version of the text.

[21] Grotowski's application for admission to the Acting Department at the State Drama School in Kraków, submitted on 3 July 1951. Together with other documents, it is stored in the archives of the Ludwik Solski State Drama School in Kraków. Filed under: *Grotowski Jerzy*.

[22] Editor's note: The brief period of liberalization and the end of Stalinism. More on the subject in the next chapter.

[23] This issue is discussed from a Jungian perspective in Maria-Luisa von Franz, *Puer Aeternus* (New York: Spring Publications, 1970); and John Hillman, 'Senex et Puer', *EranosJahrbuch*, XXXV (Zürich: RheinVerlag, 1967).

ty. As one can see, it goes far beyond theatre understood as a certain domain of artistic creation, or at least, as it is usually understood in our civilization and culture. Many years later Grotowski himself would say: 'Yet at that very moment I began my journey. And I had to start it finally. Everybody should start their journey.'[24]

His realization of life as a journey would accompany him permanently, combined with a nomadic lifestyle, a lack of family and permanent home. Grotowski established his first home only in 1986, in Italy. For him it was all about the painfully tragic feeling of the impermanence of everything, of the crumbling and disintegration of values: 'Impermanence is a sign of our time. Everything is like that.'[25]

In such a situation one has to defend things that carry real value, that contain significant meaning, that are creative and life-giving. This is also one of the important conclusions Grotowski drew from history – this is a result of having awakened his organ for perceiving history.

All these elements were once described by Simone Weil as 'uprootedness'.[26] She considered it as a basic condition for man's meeting the challenge of his vocation and his lot.

Grotowski returned to Nienadówka – where he had lived from age eight to twelve – only once, in the summer of 1980, when he was forty-seven and world famous. In a documentary made by an American team directed by Mercedes Gregory, he characterized the significance of Nienadówka as follows:

> So here from the town where I was born [in 1933], Rzeszów is 20 kilometres in this direction and I arrived here with my mother and my brother. Without having anything, just with empty hands, without money, in extreme poverty. And here I was born, in a way, a second time in this village. All essential motifs in my life started here. Before, it was destruction; after, it was something else.[27]

In the same film, Peter Brook concisely formulated the lifelong objective of Grotowski's work:

[24] Grotowski, 'O praktykowaniu romantyzmu', p. 115. Emphasis original.
[25] Ibid., p. 119.
[26] Simone Weil, *The Need for Roots: Prelude to a Declaration of Duties towards Mankind* (London: Routledge, 2003), pp. 41–98.
[27] Jerzy Grotowski, *With Jerzy Grotowski. Nienadówka, 1980*, conceived by Mercedes Gregory, dir. and ed. by Jill Godmilow, with an introduction by Peter Brook, cinematography by Maurice Jacobsen, produced by Mercedes Gregory for The Manhattan Project/Atlas Theatre Co. Inc, documentery film soundtrack.

For Grotowski, theatre is not a matter of art. It's not a matter of plays, productions, performances. Theatre is something else. Theatre is an ancient and basic instrument that helps us with one drama only, the drama of our existence, and helps us to find our way towards the source of what we are.[28]

---

[28] Peter Brook, 'Introduction to the film *With Jerzy Grotowski. Nienadówka, 1980*', in Brook, *With Grotowski: Theatre is Just a Form*, ed. by Georges Banu and Grzegorz Ziółkowski with Paul Allain (Wrocław: Grotowski Institute, 2009), p. 27.

II.
Central Asia

1.
MOSCOW, UZBEKISTAN, AND TURKMENISTAN

At the theatre school Grotowski did not lose his interest in the Orient. Just the opposite: he participated in meetings concerning such topics, systematically deepened his knowledge, met people involved in Oriental issues and maintained contacts with them. Among them were Professor Helena Willman-Grabowska (1870–1957), an Indologist and Iranist at the Jagiellonian University, and Father Franciszek Tokarz (1879–1973), a prominent expert on Indian philosophy, both of whom played an important role in shaping Grotowski's mature personality. Such contacts undoubtedly impacted his intention to change his major from acting to either Oriental studies or medicine with a specialization in psychiatry (he considered such possibilities even during his sophomore and junior years).[29]

In the spring of 1956, Grotowski took a two-month-long journey throughout Central Asia. According to his later accounts, he joined a team of Soviet geologists who were going to explore that region (however, no source materials confirm his claim).[30] It was

[29] Jerzy Grotowski, personal conversations with the author, Vallicelle, Italy, April 1988.
[30] I published a block of materials on this subject in the 2000 issue of the annual *Pamiętnik Teatralny*, 1–4 (2000), entirely dedicated to Grotowski: Osiński, 'Jerzego Grotowskiego doświadczenie Rosji. Rekonesans' [Jerzy Grotowski's experience of Russia: A reconnaissance], pp. 284–315; Osiński, 'Listy Jerzego Grotowskiego z ZSRR do Polski w latach 1955–1956' [Letters of Jerzy Grotowski from the USSR to Poland between 1955 and 1956], pp. 316–33; Osiński, 'Korespondencja Emilii i Jerzego Grotowskich z Jurijem Zawadskim w latach 1956–1975' [Correspondence of Emilia Grotowska and Jerzy Grotowski with Yuri Zavadsky between 1956 and 1975], pp. 334–46, repr. in an edited version in my book, *Jerzy Grotowski. Źródła, inspiracje, konteksty* [Jerzy Grotowski: Sources, inspirations, contexts], 2 vols (Gdańsk: słowo/obraz terytoria, 2009), II: *Prace z lat 1999–2009* [Works from the period 1999–2009], pp. 7–65 (the first text under a changed title, 'Jerzego Grotowskiego doświadczanie Rosji' [Jerzy Grotowski's experience of Russia]. See: Janusz Degler, 'Pierwsza podróż Jerzego Grotowskiego na Wschód' [The first journey of Jerzy Grotowski to the East], *Notatnik Teatralny*, 20–21 (2000), 9–13; Grotowski, 'Listy do Aliny Obidniak z oazy Bajram Ali (2 IV – 20 V 1956)' [Letters to Alina Obidiak from the Oasis Bayram-Ali (2 April – 20 May 1956)], pp. 14–28, repr. in Alina Obidniak, *Pola energii. Wspomnienia i rozmowy* [Fields of Energy: Reminiscences and Conversations], with an introduction by Janusz Degler, appendix: 'Listy Jerzego Grotowskiego do Aliny Obidniak (2 kwietnia 1956 – 12 lutego 1995)' (Wrocław: Instytut im. Jerzego Grotowskiego, 2010), pp. 192–97, and 'Listy

• *Jerzy Grotowski and his Kazakh friend in front of the Emir's palace in the Murgab oasis, Turkmenistan, 1956*

• *Jerzy Grotowski on a camel in the Murgab oasis, Turkmenistan, 1956*

Grotowski's first direct contact with the East. Soon after his return he published his impressions from the journey in *Dziennik Polski*, Kraków's daily newspaper, and several years later he shared these reminiscences with the readers of the monthly journal *Ekran*:

> During my 1956 journeys in Central Asia, between the old Turkmenian town of Ashkhabad and the western range of the Hindu Kush Mountains, I met an old Afghan man named Abdullah who performed for me a pantomime 'of the whole world', which had been a tradition in his family. Encouraged by my enthusiasm, he told me a myth about pantomime as a metaphor for 'the whole world'. 'Pantomime is like the world at large, and the world at large is like pantomime.' It occurred to me then that I was listening to my own thoughts. Nature – changeable, mobile, but permanently uniquely itself at the same time – has always been embodied in my imagination as the dancing mime, unique and universal, hiding under the glittering of the multiple gestures, colours and grimaces of life.[31]

It was by no means a theatrical mime in our Western understanding, but one of the people described by Mircea Eliade as being simultaneously a 'poet, musician, seer, priest, and doctor [who] seems to be the guardian of popular religious traditions, the custodian of legends several centuries old'.[32] Among the Kazakhs and Kyrgyz people, in the area where Grotowski was visiting, this kind of person is called bakhshi. The institution of the bakhshi has been there from time immemorial. Agnieszka Łytko brought it up in her paper 'Meddah (turecka forma teatru jednego aktora) w kontekście tradycji teatralnej Wschodu i Europy' [Meddah (Turkic form of one-man theatre) in the context of the theatrical tradition of the East and Europe], presented in Wrocław at the scholarly symposium 'Teatr Turecki – Dzisiaj. Jego źródła i tradycje' [Turkic theatre today. Its sources and traditions], where she wrote: 'Connected to the Central Asian tradition and called bakhshi (Turkmen *baqça*) or *ozan*, half-shamanized storytellers told heroic and epic tales, legends, and fables.' She continues:

> Ritual activity of the Asiatic shaman, a tribal ideologist, poet, and psychotherapist can be considered the first stage of development of the Turkic form of one-actor theatre. The Turkic peoples brought

---

Jerzego Grotowskiego do Aliny Obidniak z oazy Bajram Ali (2 kwietnia – 20 maja 1956, 1995)', pp. 198–214.

[31] Grotowski, 'Mim i świat' [A mime and the world], *Ekran*, 10 (1959), 9, quoted after Osiński, *Grotowski and His Laboratory*, p. 18.

[32] Mircea Eliade, *Myths, Dreams, and Mysteries* (New York: Harper & Row, 1967), p. 78.

this tradition to Anatolia along with the steppe culture. A shaman-
istic ceremony viewed as a spectacle can be considered a multi-act
theatrical performance of one actor.[33]

The man Grotowski met was probably evoking this archaic tradition.

In Muslim countries there is no autonomous art of mime as the
one developed in the West by Étienne Decroux and his two famous
disciples, Jean-Louis Barrault and Marcel Marceau. However, in
Central Asia one can still find representatives of the archaic ritual
tradition. Even if the interpretation given by Grotowski somehow
exceeded what he really saw and heard, it was significant anyway
since it revealed his interests, needs, and fascinations at that time.

Since April 1956, the twenty-year-old Grotowski, by then a first-
year student of Stage Directing at the Lunacharsky State Institute
for Theatre Arts (GITIS), had been a convalescent in a health resort
in Bayram-Ali (Baýramaly) in the Turkmen Soviet Socialist Republic (presently Turkmenistan). During his stay he wrote letters to Yuri
[Alexandrovich] Zavadsky and Zavadsky's wife, Irina Wulf.[34] On
10 April 1956, Emilia Grotowska wrote from Kraków to 'The Much
Respectable Yuri Alexandrovich', with deep gratitude and acknowledgments 'for everything you generously did for my son', including

---

[33] An unpublished typescript of a paper provided to me by the author. See:
Małgorzata Łabęcka-Koecherowa, Sławomira Żerańska-Kominek, 'Turkmeński
bachszy – bard Azji Środkowej' [The Turkmen bakhshi: The bard of Central
Asia], *Przegląd Orientalistyczny*, 2–4 (1993), 137–50; Agnieszka Łytko, *Meddah
(turecka forma teatru jednego aktora) w kontekście tradycji teatralnej Wscho-
du i Europy*, master's thesis written under the direction of Professor Tadeusz
Majda, University of Warsaw, Faculty of Modern Languages, Oriental Studies,
Department of Turkish and Inner Asian Peoples, Warsaw 1995.

[34] Yuri Alexandrovich Zavadsky (1894–1977), a director, actor and pedagogue.
In 1915 he entered the Studio led by Yevgeny Vakhtangov, initially as a stage
designer, then playing Anthony in Maurice Maeterlinck's play *The Miracle of St
Anthony* (1916) and Calaf in Gozzi's *Turandot* (1922). Between 1924 and 1931
Zavadsky was an actor of the Moscow Art Theatre (on 9 October 1920, the Soviet People's Commissar of Enlightenment Anatoly Lunacharsky declared it an
'academic theatre', and since then it has been called MChAT: Moskovskiy Hu-
dojestvenny Akademicheskiy Teatr [Moscow Artistic Academic Theatre (known
as MAT in English)]), working under the directon of Constantin Stanislavski. In
1924 he established his own Studio that operated until 1936 as Theatre-Studio.
From 1940 until the end of his life he was the main director of the Mossovet
Theatre in Moscow. From 1940 he worked as a pedagogue in the Lunacharsky
State Institute for Theatre Arts (GITIS). Jerzy Grotowski was one of his students.

• *Jerzy Grotowski on a donkey in the oasis in the Karakum Desert, Central Asia, 1956*

• *Jerzy Grotowski and a Turkmen girl in the Murgab oasis, Turkmenistan, 1956*

'the journey to Bayram-Ali, everything that my son saw, [and for] the hope for his health's improvement in the future'.[35]

Where did Grotowski go? In Turkmenistan, the route of his journey was marked by the Karakum Desert; the city of Mar in the centre of the Morghāb River oasis; the ruins of the city of Merv; Ashkhabad, the capital city; and, most of all, Bukhara and Samarkand in Uzbekistan. The last two of nine preserved postcards he sent during that trip to actress Irena Jun were dated 26 May 1956.[36] On the first he noted that he was writing 'on the way through Kazakhstan':

> For three days and two nights I have been going West, to the shores of the Aral Sea [Lake]. Yesterday the heat was awful, it was hitting my head like a heavy hammer. Today I woke up in a chill, the air crisp and cold. Perhaps it is still early morning and it will get warmer during the day. Nevertheless I have certainly left the subtropical climate. The scenery is changeless: steppe, deserts, sometimes rice fields, auls, the banks of the Syr Darya. Yesterday I passed ruins of old mosques and palaces.[37]

The second postcard, written on the same day, states: 'Western Asia; soon I will enter Europe.'[38]

After returning to Poland, in two issues of *Dziennik Polski* Grotowski published his report from the journey:

> Uzbekistan is a real Tower of Babel. A small territory bounded by the Aral Sea [Lake], the Syr Darya, the Amu Darya rivers, the Tien Shan range, and the Pamir-Alay Mountains is inhabited by Uzbeks, Russians, Tajiks, Eastern Iranians, Persians, Afghans [Pashtuns], Armenians, Arabs, Turkmens, Kazakhs, local Bukharan Jews, Polish Jews (called simply 'Poles'; there are plenty of them there, they settled in Uzbekistan during the war). Particular nations have become stratified through the centuries – with consecutive conquests. Traditions of each tribe were shaped in confrontation with other nations; from these fights emerged heroes praised in songs and epic folk poetry. Social relations were invariably shaped in accordance

---

[35] 'Korespondencja Emilii i Jerzego Grotowskich z Jurijem Zawadskim w latach 1956–1957', pp. 337–38.

[36] Irena Jun (b. 1935), Polish theatre actress, professor at the Aleksander Zelwerowicz Theatrical Academy in Warsaw.

[37] Śliwonik, 'Jerzy Grotowski – z rękopisów (w trzecią rocznicę śmierci – 14 stycznia 2002)', *Scena*, 6 (2001), 18–19; repr. as 'Listy Jerzego Grotowskiego z ZSRR, 1955–1956' [Letters of Jerzy Grotowski from the USSR, 1955–1956] in Osiński, *Jerzy Grotowski. Źródła, inspiracje, konteksty*, II, 51.

[38] Osiński, ibid.

with the dichotomy of the victors and the defeated, with a proviso that the victors of one century would be defeated in the next. However, the opposite phenomenon also could be observed: warring nations were also prone to assimilation. The great scholar Avicenna (Ibn Sīnā) is considered Persian by the Persians, Tajik by the Tajiks, and also Uzbeks to a great degree consider him their own. Navā'i – a great local poet of the past – wrote in Persian, Tajik, and Uzbek.[39] In such a situation the so-called national problem […] is especially complex.[40]

In 1996 I asked Grotowski about the circumstances of his journey to Central Asia. He answered that, as far as he remembered, it was Jerzy Jarocki, at that time also a student of directing at the GITIS, who urged him to go for treatment.[41] In that situation 'Zavadsky took matters into his own hands, using it as an excuse for me to leave Moscow'.[42]

According to the version related to me by Grotowski, one of the Poles studying in Moscow had denounced him at that time, and Zavadsky found out about it. To make the situation even more dramatic, some kind of High Commission from Poland was visiting Moscow at that time. Among the Commission's members was Professor Zofia Lissa, an eminent musicologist, who had a firmly established reputation as an avowed Stalinist. The point was to remove Grotowski from the view of the Commission, and thus, from the threat of punitive return to Poland. That was why he hid in a dormitory in Trifonovka, where he slept in Jarocki's room. Meanwhile, Zavadsky organized a trip to the health resort. Jerzy Jarocki presents the story in a slightly different way, and his account is much more complete than Grotowski's. Let us start with the issue of the trip to the health resort:

---

[39] Nizam-al-Din Ali-Shir Herawi (1441–1501), a Central Asian politician, mystic, linguist, painter, and poet, commonly known under his pen name Nava'i ('melodic' in Persian). He served as a vizier (public administrator and adviser) of Sultan Husayn Bayqarah. He wrote in Chagatai (an extinct language related to modern Uzbek and Uyghur) and Persian.

[40] Grotowski, 'Między Iranem a Chinami (2). Wieża Babel' [Between Iran and China (2). The Tower of Babel], *Dziennik Polski*, 22 November 1956, pp. 2–3.

[41] Jerzy Jarocki (1929–2012), one of the most renowned Polish theatre directors and pedagogues. He graduated in acting from Kraków's drama school and in directing from Moscow's GITIS. His directing debut was *Bal manekinów* [*The Mannequins' Ball*], based on Bruno Jasieński, in the Stanisław Wyspiański Theatre in Katowice, in 1957. He directed many famous theatrical productions in Poland, Germany, and Switzerland.

[42] Jerzy Grotowski, personal letter, Pontedera, Italy, 12 August 1992.

In the autumn of 1955 [the official date of registration in the student credit book was 23 August][43] Jerzy Grotowski showed up in Moscow with a referral to be admitted to the first year of Directing. A couple of days later he gave me a letter from his mother (addressed to me), and he did not want me to open it in his presence. I learned from the letter that Jurek was seriously ill with chronic nephritis, that doctors were very concerned with the advance of his illness, and that, in fact, the main reason for his arrival in Moscow was an attempt to get to the famous health resort located in the Karakum Desert in Turkmenistan, where supposedly the illness could be cured or treated.

Mrs Emilia [Grotowska] asked me – as a friend of Jurek from Kraków's Drama School, already settled in the GITIS – to help his case. Jurek brought with him appropriate diagnoses, medical records, and recommendations from Kraków's doctors. [...] N[ikolai] M[ikhailovich] Gorchakov promised to help with securing the spot at the health resort through his connections; also Jurek's mentor, Yuri Zavadsky offered his help.[44] I noticed that Jurek himself very actively and efficiently took care of this matter.

The task was, after all, not so easy. Reportedly, only two medical centres within our reach, thanks to their location and climate (dry and hot), would offer favourable conditions and gave hope for successful treatment: in Egypt and Turkmenistan. For that reason, the health resort in Turkmenistan was available only for the Soviet elite: for ministers, generals and, especially, distinguished Western communists, such as Dolores Ibaduri or Luigi Longo. Jurek had little chance; however, as it turned out, his situation was not so hopeless.[45]

The issue of Vsevolod Meyerhold's fate, of concern especially for the professors and students of the GITIS, is also cast in a different light by Jerzy Jarocki's depiction:

One must be aware that at the time when Jurek arrived, the campaign for the [posthumous] rehabilitation of Meyerhold had already

[43] According to Grotowski's student credit book at the Directing Depatment of the Anatoly Vasilyevich Lunacharsky State Institute of Theatre Arts in Moscow, academic year 1955/1956. The original is stored in the archives of the Ludwik Solski State Drama School in Kraków. Filed under: *Grotowski Jerzy*. Facsimiles of several pages of the book are available in Osiński, *Grotowski wytycza trasy*, photographs 5 and 6.

[44] Nikolai Mikhailovich Gorchakov (1898–1958), stage director, pedagogue, and author of books on directing, educated at the Third MAT Studio, where he was an actor and director between 1922 and 1924. He was admitted to the MAT in 1924. From 1939 onward he chaired the Directing Department of the GITIS.

[45] Jerzy Jarocki, 'Przystanek Moskwa' [The Moscow stop], *Notatnik Teatralny*, 20–21 (2000), 36.

been in progress – since the beginning of 1955. Letters concerning this issue were written to the Central Military Prosecuting Authority by B[oris] Pasternak, D[mitri] Shostakovich, S[ergei] Yutkevich, N[ikolai] Erdman and others. I want to mention this in reference to Jurek's often quoted stories in which he claimed that he was in danger of persecution because of mentioning Meyerhold during a lecture and that, following Zavadsky's advice, he had to hide for two months in my room in a dormitory at Trifonovka.

At that time one could ask about Meyerhold during lectures, and the answer would depend only on the courage, position, and taste of the teacher. In fact, Meyerhold was mentioned in legally published books, for example, in the selected works of [Alexander] Blok and the collected works of [Vladimir] Mayakovsky. One could find references to Meyerhold in the writings of M[ikhail] Narokov (*A Biography of My Generation*)[46] and V[ladimir] Davidov (*About Meyerhold and His Performances*).[47] Both books were published in 1956. Even then the special Commission for Studying the Artistic Heritage of Vsevolod Meyerhold was active. No one wrote about it publicly, yet it was widely discussed. For example, I knew that Gorchakov, my master, refused to participate in the commission's work; in fact, he died soon after, and Yuri Zavadsky accepted the invitation only ten years later, in the mid 1960s. I also remember that [Nikolai] Okhlopkov, either in the House of Literature or in the VTO during official meetings, shared his sensational (for that time) memories of Meyerhold.[48]

The reasons for Grotowski's stay in the dorm in Trifonovka were also, according to the testimony of his friend, quite different than those given later by Grotowski himself:

Indeed, Jurek stayed for a night at my place in Trifonovka from time to time, but never longer than for a couple of days and for completely different reasons. Sometimes we would return late at night after watching a film or a theatrical performance together, and my dorm was closer than his. Sometimes Jurek wanted to talk a bit. Sometimes we wanted to listen to the BBC or Radio Free Europe,[49] and there was an excellent radio in my room, brought by my roommates, two Germans from the GDR. The reception was ideal because, in Moscow, noise interference used for Polish language programmes

---

[46]   Mikhail Semenovich Narokov, *Biografiya moego pokoleniya* [A biography of my generation] (Moscow: Vserossiiskoe Teatralnoe Obshchestvo, 1956).
[47]   Vladimir Nikolaevich Davidov, *Rasskaz o proshlom* [A tale of the past] (Leningrad: Iskusstvo, 1962).
[48]   Jarocki, 'Przystanek Moskwa', pp. 40–41.
[49]   Radio Free Europe is a broadcaster established in 1949, financed by the US Congress. The Polish Section operated from Munich between 1952 and 1994.

was ineffective.[50] All these night visits were possible only when my third roommate, Andrzej B[rzeziński], was not there and his bed was available.[51]

After a two-month stay in Central Asia, Grotowski came back to Moscow. Let me quote Jerzy Jarocki again:

After his return from Turkmenistan, Jurek did not have much time to talk about his journey because he urgently had to prepare for the June exam session. He gathered the necessary books. He had to predict what he had to read and what could be summarized to him by someone else. He asked me to give him a few of such summaries. He would drill me about interests and inclinations of professors I had had contacts with before, and then he would disappear for a couple of days, skipping classes – reportedly, he slept because he studied at nights – and finally he passed all of his exams with flying colours.[52]

The schedule of the exams was as follows: May 29, *muzvospitanie* (musical education); two days later, Russian language; June 11, directing, examined by Zavadsky; later the same day *masterstvo* (technique, skill, craft), examined by Irina Wulf; June 16, Marxism-Leninism, examined by Erenfeld.[53] Soon after, Grotowski returned to Poland. Jarocki recalls:

This hectic exam session during our Moscow studies was accompanied by no less shocking political events. [...] On 25 February 1956, the Twentieth Congress began.[54] Three days later *Pravda* published a detailed report, yet the news was screened and sifted for months. At that time we learned about the personality cult, and incorrectness in ideological and economical estimations. [...] We learned about Stalin's crimes while listening to Radio Free Europe in my dorm on Trifonovskaya Street. In April [Władysław] Gomułka was released from prison; in June, Cyrankiewicz was 'cutting off a counter-terrevolutionary hand' in Poznań.[55] Jurek wanted to be in Poland.

---

[50] Editor's note: Authorities in the entire communist bloc used noise interference to block short wave frequencies used by foreign-based radio stations for broadcasting news and political commentaries aimed for the listeners behind the Iron Curtain.

[51] Jarocki, 'Przystanek Moskwa', p. 41.

[52] Ibid., p. 47.

[53] Based on the student credit book.

[54] The Twentieth Congress of the Communist Party of the Soviet Union (held between 14 and 26 February 1956), during which Nikita Khrushchev, the First Secretary of the party criticized the personality cult, *de facto* ended the Stalinist period.

[55] The author alludes to changes in the Polish political scene in the aftermath

He saw a bright future ahead of him. 'It is not theatre that is at stake now; one has to use the opportunity offered by the Twentieth Congress and the great thaw in Poland.' He tried to persuade me to quit my studies, to go with him to Poland and to join the political campaigns. [...] Jurek became madly involved in politics; I learned about it mainly from Polish newspapers and from brief telegrams: 'Could your brother put me up in Warsaw for a couple of nights? Hugs, Jurek.'[56]

He was fully involved; he advanced to the highest ranks in the new youth union. He had arguments with Gomułka and did not want to return to his studies in Moscow. Luckily a new department at the Drama School opened the same year in Kraków.[57]

In his application to the Directing Department of the Drama School in Kraków, Grotowski had to justify his request for an admission directly to the second year of studies: 'after my studies in Moscow for which I was selected by the Kraków's drama school and where I received A's in all practical and theoretical examinations'. The application was dated 7 July 1956; thus, Grotowski undoubtedly wrote it in Poland, and probably while in Kraków, so it was neither written in nor sent from the USSR, as I erroneously state in *Grotowski i jego Laboratorium*.[58]

2.

KRAKÓW

IN THE AUTUMN of 1956, 'the main forum of Grotowski's activity was [...] the Revolutionary Youth Union, which gathered the core of the youth movement organizations at several higher education institutions in Kraków, with the main meeting place in the Jagiel-

---

of the Soviet Thaw. Massive protests of workers dissatisfied with the living conditions in June 1956 in Poznań were labelled 'counterrevolutionary' and met with violent repression. The summer protests were followed by the 'October Events' and a relatively short period of liberalization, when the reformers' faction led by Władysław Gomułka took power.

56   Memoir of Robert Jarocki, the director's brother and well-known journalist, 'To żarliwie, to z ironią' [Sometimes with passion, sometimes with irony], *Rzeczpospolita*, 23–24 January 1999, weekly supplement +*Plus* –*Minus*, 4, p. 15.

57   Jarocki, 'Przystanek Moskwa', pp. 47–48.

58   Osiński, *Grotowski i jego Laboratorium* (Warsaw: Państwowy Instytut Wydawniczy, 1980), p. 26. Not included in the English version of the book.

lonian University'.[59] Jerzy Grotowski authored texts discussed among members of the organization. One of these texts included his thoughts on the philosophy of the East.

One year later, in Kraków's Old Theatre, Grotowski assisted Jerzy Kreczmar, who directed Henri de Montherlant's *Port Royal* – at that time a fashionable piece by one of the playwrights discovered by the Polish theatre only after the shift brought by October 1956 (the Polish premiere took place on 15 December 1957, in Kraków's Kameralny Theatre). Fortunately, a document from their collaboration remains – an offprint with Kreczmar's article titled 'Równoznaczność, wieloznaczność, znaczenie' [Equivalence, ambiguity, meaning],[60] prefaced with a meaningful inscription: 'I am offering this minor sin of European philosophy to Mr Jerzy Grotowski, a representative of Indian philosophy – to commemorate the collaboration of both philosophies on a philosophical play by Montherlant. 17 December 1957.'

These quoted words prove that Grotowski, a twenty-four-year-old directing apprentice, in some circles had a reputation as an ex-

---

[59] I quote after a note by Marian Stępień about Grotowski, included in his letter to me, dated Kraków, 4 July 1976. See: Osiński, *Grotowski and His Laboratory*, pp. 19–20; Marian Stępień, 'Październik 1956 na Uniwersytecie Jagiellońskim' [October 1956 at the Jagiellonian University], in *Październik '56. Odwilż i przełom w życiu literackim i kulturalnym Polski. Materiały Ogólnopolskiej Sesji Naukowej. Rzeszów, 23–25 września 1996 roku* [October 56: The Thaw and turning point in the literary and cultural life of Poland. Materials of the National Academic Session. Rzeszów, 23–25 September 1996], ed. by Adam Kulawik (Kraków: Antykwa, 1996), pp. 29–37; Osiński, 'Zmiany w uniwersyteckiej organizacji partyjnej w 1956 roku' [Changes in the university branch of the [communist] party in 1956], in *Polski Październik 1956 na Uniwersytecie Jagiellońskim. Materiały Sympozjum Naukowego zorganizowanego pod patronatem J.M. Rektora prof. Franciszka Ziejki przez Uniwersytet Jagielloński, Instytut Pamięci Narodowej i Konsulat Generalny Republiki Węgierskiej w dniu 10 listopada 2001 roku w Krakowie* [Polish October of 1956 at the Jagiellonian University. Materials of the Academic Symposium organized under the auspices of University President Prof Franciszek Ziejka by the Jagiellonian University, Institute of National Remembrance, and the Consulate General of the Republic of Hungary on 10 November 2001 in Kraków], ed. by Rudolf Klimek (Kraków: Universitas, 2004), pp. 181–87.

[60] The offprint is held in the Grotowski Institute Archive in Wrocław, Poland. Jerzy Kreczmar's text was published in *Fragmenty filologiczne. Księga pamiątkowa ku uczczeniu piętnastolecia pracy nauczycielskiej w Uniwersytecie Warszawskim prof. Tadeusza Kotarbińskiego* [Philological fragments: Book of remembrance in honour of Prof Tadeusz Kotarbiński's fifteen years of work as a teacher at the University of Warsaw] (Warsaw: published by students, 1934), pp. 35–52.

pert in Eastern, particularly Indian, philosophy. A news article published on 14 December 1957 in *Dziennik Polski* is another piece of evidence: 'The Student Club Pod Jaszczurami is organizing a series of open lectures on Oriental philosophy, given (every Sunday) by Jerzy Grotowski.'[61]

In 2004, almost fifty years later, Jerzy Huczkowski, who had been the first president and manager of the Pod Jaszczurami club, and later, for many years, served as a publisher and editor-in-chief of *Gazeta Antykwaryczna*, comments on the open lectures and their context:

> In 1957, when the clout and impact of the student movement were still held in regard by the government, the decision was made that students would be given a place for their forthcoming club in the building of a former bank inside the [historical] Pod Jaszczurami tenement house, situated at 8 Main Square. Under the banner of establishing the Club Spring '56 [Wiosna '56], we began to collect money necessary to redecorate and refurbish the building to make it suitable for club activities. Our [fundraising] activity was very successful, especially in the first period. The club was supported by the Regional Council of the ZSP (Polish Students' Association), with an office located in Kraków, on Floriańska Street. At a certain moment, the Council – in fact, always kind to our cause – suggested that, under the current circumstances, the name Spring '56 was no longer the best fit for our attempts to establish a club. It seemed natural to change the name to the Student Club Pod Jaszczurami, after the historical name of the tenement house. And that is what we did. Although the place was officially opened only in 1960, the club's programme was already running almost since we had been given the keys. There were various projects. Jerzy Grotowski was involved in most of them.
>
> The most popular and probably the first event organized by the Club Pod Jaszczurami was a series of open lectures on Indian philosophy given by Jerzy Grotowski, which attracted large audiences. The lectures took place in the rooms provided to us by Teatr 38, located in the back building of 8 Main Square. I also managed to involve Grotowski in an attempt to rebuild the theatre (at that time still in ruins, for the club was not renovated yet); however, this attempt was not entirely successful and Jerzy Grotowski pursued his theatrical aspirations in the Old Theatre, staging *Bogowie deszczu* [Gods of rain], by [Jerzy] Krzysztoń.[62]

[61] 'Odczyty. Pod Jaszczurami' [Lectures: Pod Jaszczurami], *Dziennik Polski*, 14 December 1957, p. 6, section 'Kronika krakowska' [Kraków's chronicle].
[62] Jerzy Huczkowski, 'Studencki Komitet Rewolucyjny w Krakowie i jego losy' [The Students Revolutionary Committee in Kraków and its story], in *Polski Październik 1956 na Uniwersytecie Jagiellońskim*, p. 26; repr. in Huczkowski,

In his reminiscences published in *Gazeta Antykwaryczna* soon after Grotowski's death, Huczkowski wrote:

> We met for the first time in autumn 1956. Grotowski returned from a year-long stay in Moscow where he had studied directing [...] and 'fell into' the October events. We met in the Students' Revolutionary Committee, although neither of us was a student anymore: he graduated in 1955 with an MFA in acting from the State Drama School [PWST] in Kraków, while I, in the same year, began to work with Professor Henryk Niewodniczański at the Institute of Nuclear Physics of the Polish Academy of Sciences. I also took a trip to the East, though not as far. I had been sent for an internship to Kiev, Leningrad, and Moscow. I returned in May 1956, a bit earlier than Grotowski.
>
> We were making a revolution. We were both involved in most of the events related to the rise and fall of the Revolutionary Youth Union [Rewolucyjny Związek Młodzieży], as well as in our attempt to create an independent entity within the Union of Socialist Youth [Związek Młodzieży Socjalistycznej] – the organization that had been forced upon us. Within it, we established the Political Centre of Academic Left (POLA ZMS), and initially, on its behalf, we were able to assume leadership of ZMS in Kraków. [...] In this final revolutionary episode of our ZMS activity, Jurek was our leader, the main strategist and tactician of the movement. [...] Soon we were dissolved though. To be precise, we signed a declaration that we were suspending our organizational activities and beginning 'organic work'; that we would go on, each of us in his own post, without giving up the objectives that had guided us before. The declaration was officially signed by all of us, with full names and personal data. In my opinion, Jurek had fulfilled his promise most completely. After all, he revolutionized the world theatre, didn't he?
>
> [...] Our paths did not part after the dissolution of the POLA ZMS. In accordance with the declaration mentioned above, I got involved in the establishment of the Kraków's Student Club, which changed its name from the provocative Spring '56 to Club Pod Jaszczurami. I was the chairman of the Club Council. Physically, the club did not exist; what did exist was a place for the club: a ground floor and cellars of the building located at 8 Main Square, continu-

---

Spotkałem Jerzego Gierdoycia. Listy 1993–2000 [I have met Jerzy Giedroyc: Letters 1993–2000] (Kraków: Universitas, 2011), pp. 164–65.

Jerzy Krzysztoń (1931–1982), noted Polish writer and playwright. His play *Bogowie deszczu* [Gods of rain], directed by Jerzy Grotowski, premiered on 4 July 1958. A production titled *Pechowcy* [The misfortunate] based on the same drama, and also directed by Grotowski, was staged at the Theatre of 13 Rows in Opole on 8 November 1958.

ously renovated. However, we organized various forms of activities there, in these ruins. The idea of open lectures on Indian philosophy was conceived there. Who was supposed to lecture? It was Jerzy Grotowski, who was fascinated with the philosophy of the East as much as he was fascinated with theatre.

I do not remember each of Grotowski's seventeen [in fact, sixteen] open lectures, yet the first one was attended by crowds. Soon, a playbill announcing the performance of *Bogowie deszczu*, based on the play by Jerzy Krzysztoń, directed by Jerzy Grotowski, was posted on a wall of the tenement house at 8 Main Square. Then I too began to share Jurek's [Grotowski's] fascinations with a strange theatre in which the stage action is accompanied by film and political essays. My file of artistic attempts from those years includes many works going in the same direction. Some of them were even intended as our joint ventures. We tried to stage one of Kafka's short stories just published in *Przekrój*.[63] This required establishing a theatre in the club. I organized a recruitment of actors. Jurek came to the first meeting, yet he was disappointed. However, he somehow wanted to make use of my enthusiasm and asked me to prepare a screenplay for a science fiction movie. He thought that because I was an 'atomist', I would manage it. Grotowski was quite interested in film then.

He discussed his various ideas to inspire me. Thus manipulated by Jurek, I went to Zakopane to dedicate myself to creative work. I stayed in the Dom Turysty Hotel, and did my writing, as far as I remember, in the International Book and Press Club café, on the corner of Krupówki Street, where I sat for several days. Unfortunately, the result of my work was entirely different than the one commissioned by the Master. The screenplay was a story referring more to sentimental songs and skits of Bim-Bom rather than to my atomistic provenance.[64] I gave it to Jurek to read, yet we both knew that this wasn't it.

Another time that I involved Jurek in my 'theatrical longings' was when composer Ireneusz Weiss and I had established a cabaret and asked Jurek for support as a director. He did not refuse. This time, however, he had some benefit from my work. Two actors of

---

[63] In 1956, *Przekrój*, a popular socio-cultural weekly magazine (based in Kraków between 1945 and 2002, then moved to Warsaw), published two short stories by Franz Kafka: *Die Verwandlung* [*The Metamorphosis*] (no. 576–80) and *In der Strafkolonie* [*In the Penal Colony*] (no. 605 and 606), both translated by Juliusz Kydryński. Coincidently, another translation of *In der Strafkoloni*, by Witold Wirpsza, was published in the October issue of *Twórczość* (no. 10). It is worth mentioning that *Die Verwandlung* was an obligatory reading for the Laboratory Theatre apprentices in Wrocław. See: Osiński, *Jerzy Grotowski. Źródła, inspiracje, konteksty*, I, 27.

[64] Editor's note: Bim-Bom was a popular student satirical theatre in Gdańsk.

our cabaret, Antoni Jahołkowski and Ewa Lubowiecka, soon moved with Jurek to Opole, accompanied by our main song, titled *Black Cat* [*Czarny Kot*], which was used in one of the productions of the Theatre of 13 Rows.

When Jurek was living in Opole, we would meet only during his visits to Kraków. Jurek would stay at his mother's place in the Wola Justowska area. I usually accompanied him on his way from the city and we would talk while walking. We talked as we usually did – quite normally. I never got to know a Prophet, or a Great Dictator – in the tales of others, surely not fictitious, he existed as such. [...] For me, Jerzy Grotowski remained the same, different than for everybody else, yet of all people, he made the greatest impact on what I do in my life.[65]

---

[65] Jerzy Huczkowski, '"Zwalisty". Moje spotkania z Jerzym Grotowskim "z tamtych lat"' [The 'Hefty One': My encounters with Jerzy Grotowski 'in those days'], *Gazeta Antykwaryczna*, 3 (1999), 40–41; repr. in Huczkowski, *Spotkałem Jerzego Gierdoycia*, pp. 197–99.

III.
Iran

IN THE BEGINNING of 1959, Grotowski, who by then held a full-time position as a director at the Old Theatre in Kraków, visited Paris. During his visit, he witnessed a ritual honouring Ahura Mazdā (Wise Lord), the Old Iranian god of Light and Virtue. It was another important religious and cultural experience for him:

> In Russia, I witnessed Orthodox ceremonies. In Central Asia, I encountered Islam and the traditional religion of the Kurds, called by Muslims 'a cult of the devil', with traces of Buddhism and Hinduism. In Western Europe, at almost every step I met new sects: from old-fashioned Lutheranism and Calvinism, to magical 'Christian gnosis'.
>
> When two years ago, in Central Asia, I was shown ruins of the ancient Zoroastrian temple, I did not expect that not too long later, and many thousands kilometers from Persia, the 'Zarathustra's cradle', [...] I would be given an opportunity to participate in the ritual of 'the last living successors of Zarathustra' in the ritual of the 'god of Virtue', Ahura Mazdā (Ohrmazd), and that the condensed exotics of the ritual moved against the foreign background would surpass the strangeness of the heritage of Islam and Hinduism observed in the vicinity of their homeland. [...] A ritual for Ahura Mazdā, an ancient Persian god, is performed in Paris – the Babylon of all faiths. Against the background of Paris with its contemporary sharp rhythm, the Neo-Mazdaism (called *mazdaznan* by its followers) gives the impression of some concentration of exotics, of something 'simply impossible', something that 'should not be'. The faithful in Paris are mainly the French, but numerous nations of Europe – among them local Poles and 'white' Russians – are represented there too.[66]

In the summer of 1959, just before taking the post of artistic director at the Theatre of 13 Rows [Teatr 13 Rzędów] in Opole, Grotowski travelled to several Middle Eastern countries: Greece, Turkey, Syria, Lebanon, and Egypt. He paid for his journey with the money he had received as the winner of the Annual Radio and Television Award. The month-long trip had two purposes: the healing effect of a hot and dry climate on his ailing kidneys was as important as his direct experience of the ancient cultures of the countries on the Eastern shore of the Mediterranean Sea.

From his correspondence with Eugenio Barba, we know that Grotowski was in Iran in August 1967. In his letter from Holstebro,

---

[66] Grotowski, 'Korespondencja z świątyni Ahura Mazdy' [Correspondence from the temple of Ahura Mazdā], *Argumenty*, 22 March 1959, p. 6.

dated 28 August, Barba writes: 'Welcome back to Old Europe. How was your stay in the land of Omar Khayyám?'[67] On 21 September, Grotowski answers: 'I returned safely from Iran and went immediately to Yugoslavia.'[68]

Besides the mention in these letters, there are no written traces of Grotowski's visit to Iran. It is highly probable that he wanted to keep this experience exclusively to himself. At that time, he used to say that talking about something important usually dissipates it. He expressed this opinion straightforwardly in his previously unpublished letter to me, written on 5 December 1966, nine months before his trip to Iran:

> I do not suppose that I was an interesting interlocutor during our last meeting. It wasn't that I was feeling bad, but something is changing in me and I increasingly perceive some devaluation of words, that is, that words are insufficient to express what is important, and, in many cases, I prefer to communicate through silence, gesture, short allusion, rather than by, say, ideas formulated through words.[69]

Many years later during one of our meetings in Vallicelle, Italy, in April 1988, he mentioned that he had been allowed – in summer 1967 – to participate in a ritual of the Kurds in the Iranian mountains.

On 23 August 1970, the Laboratory Theatre began its sixth and – as it soon turned out – final strictly theatrical tour.[70] Until 12 October, they toured the Middle East (Iran and Lebanon), giving twenty-seven performances of *The Constant Prince*; six of them at the Annual Festival of Arts in Shiraz; five in the historical palace of Emir

---

[67]   Ghiyath al-Din Abu 'l-Fath Umar ibn Ibrahim al-Khayyami (born c. 1022 [1048 according to other sources] in Nishapur, Iran), Persian poet, mathematician, astronomer, and philosopher. In Iran he was recognized as a poet only after his poetic oeuvre attracted great interest in the West, especially thanks to English translations by Edward Fitzgerald. [Consultation: Szymon Skalski].

[68]   Eugenio Barba, *Land of Ashes and Diamonds: My Apprenticeship in Poland; Followed by 26 Letters from Jerzy Grotowski to Eugenio Barba* (Aberystwyth: Black Mountain Press, 1999), p. 168.

[69]   Jerzy Grotowski, personal letter, 5 December 1966. A letter typed in Wrocław on white stationary with a new name of the institution in both top corners: on the left – in Polish (Instytut Badań Metody Aktorskiej. Teatr Laboratorium), and on the right – in French (Institut de Recherches sur le Jeu de l'Acteur. Théâtre Laboratoire), A4 format, handwritten corrections and signature made with blue ink.

[70]   Osiński, *Grotowski and His Laboratory*, p. 122.

El-Amin, near Beirut; and sixteen in Teheran.

While spectators in Europe and the US mainly associated the protagonist of the performance, Prince don Fernando, with Job and Jesus, the Iranian audience noticed a clear analogy between him and Ali, who in Iran is 'a symbol of the highest bravery, righteousness, and beauty'. He is venerated beyond the pious circles of Shia Islam. The analogy was not accidental, for 'the cult of martyrs is one of the most characteristic features of Persian religiosity [...]. It is associated with the very old local hero model – an innocent victim.'[71] In the performance, this figure was

• *Jerzy Grotowski at a press conference during the 4ᵗʰ Shiraz-Persepolis Festival of Arts, 1970*

embodied as the Constant Prince, played by Ryszard Cieślak. This possibility of the audience's far-reaching identification with the performance's protagonist was undoubtedly one of the reasons why performances of the Laboratory Theatre were so enthusiastically received. The other reason the 'experimenting Iranian artists' admired it was the impressive professional skills of Grotowski and his actors.[72]

Several years later, Ludwik Flaszen wrote about the Laboratory Theatre's summer 1970 visit to Iran and about the reception of *The Constant Prince*. His account includes information about a completely unknown episode of Grotowski's encounter with dervishes in Iran's portion of Kurdistan, and an excursion to the holy Shia city of Qom taken at the same time by Flaszen:

[71] Maria Składankowa, 'Barwy islamu' [Colours of Islam], *Kultura*, 15 (1979), 6.
[72] The impact of *The Constant Prince* and Grotowski's ideas on contemporary Iranian theatre is emphasized in Barbara Majewska, 'Tradycyjny i awangardowy teatr w Iranie' [Traditional and avant-garde theatre in Iran], *Przegląd Orientalistyczny*, 3 (1979), 277–84. Barbara Majewska transcribed data of the Persian version of *Towards a Poor Theatre* included in the early edition of the present text.

Our stay in Iran was prolonged. *The Constant Prince* received such great interest that just after Shiraz we were invited to spend several weeks in Teheran.

On days when we were not performing, our hospitable hosts proposed some excursions to the country's interior to us. Everybody was free to choose the trip's direction and destination.

Grotowski went to Kurdistan. He wanted to meet real Kurds, by whom he had been fascinated since his childhood. Karl May's novel *Durchs wilde Kurdistan* [*Through Wild Kurdistan*] was one of his favourites: the German writer of adventure/travel books was one of the authors of initiation writings for the whole of Grotowski's life. His dreams about exotic peoples and cultures – about which mysteries he was always curious – that he had dreamt of as a child and teenager were fulfilled in a perfectly literal form.

One of the prominent members of the imperial family was his guide during this real expedition to 'wild Kurdistan'. On his return, Grotowski told me, with a beaming face, that the clan chiefs had welcomed him very cordially. They recognized him as a kinsman, and treated him as a quasi-sheikh – a spiritual master – from a distant country, an unknown tribe. And they even initiated him into some rituals normally inaccessible to foreigners. Even his high rank *cicerone* had to wait for him at a distance, accompanied by the driver. He did not want to tell me what it was. He said he could not betray his hosts who had trusted him. It was supposed to be a secret between him and them – the initiated men.

As far as I was concerned, I wanted to go to Qom, the famous holy city of the Shi'ites, where the shrine of Fatimah al-Ma'sūmah, one of Islam's holiest women, is located. I went to Qom but I cannot say that I was there. After a long journey across the rocky desert we stopped at some distance to the holy city's walls. Strangers were not allowed there. We were accompanied by one of empress Farah Diba's cousins. Despite the long distance, he advised us to stay in the car and – God forbid! – not to go out to relieve ourselves. It might be interpreted as a profanation and have dangerous consequences.

I admired from a distance the medieval city walls, the mosques' blue domes, and the slender minarets above. I felt as though I was in the world of the tales of one thousand and one nights.

Some years later Qom was to become a place where the radical warriors' war of the Prophet began to smash the empire of the festival's generous host.[73]

---

[73] Ludwik Flaszen, *Grotowski & Company*, trans. by Andrzej Wojtasik with Paul Allain, ed. and introduced by Paul Allain with the editorial assistance of Monika Blige and with a tribute by Eugenio Barba (Holstebro, Malta and Wrocław: Icarus Publishing Enterprise, 2010), pp. 235–36.

Initially, Flaszen described the atmosphere that accompanied performances of *The Constant Prince* in Iran:

At Shiraz, *The Constant Prince* was performed in an old, historic pavilion – a small palace adapted for this purpose – in the beautiful garden of Del Gosha, an oasis of greenery and palms extolled by [Persian] poets – in the city of their prince, Hafez.

One evening the Empress came to see the performance. I remember bodyguards sitting on each palm, hidden in the thicket of leaves.

Substituting for Grotowski, I did the honours. An accompanying courtier ceremoniously introduced me to the Empress, a beautiful woman, slender, tall, and charming. As a student she had been a basketball player. She spoke excellent French – as did all the people of the Shah's court. I answered her questions briefly, for at that time my abilities in the language of Racine and Corneille were far from the rules of the French Academy. She was obviously impressed by *The Constant Prince*. Her words and curiosity did not seem conventional. When greeting and parting, she gave me her hand, in accordance with European *savoir-vivre*. Her entourage and the accompanying courtier made deep Oriental bows, with their hands on their chests.

The Constant Prince got a surprisingly enthusiastic reception in Iran. As some Persian friends explained to us, the audience understood it as a mystery play about their holy martyr. They associated the plot with the story of the martyrdom and apotheosis of their religious hero, Hussein ibn Ali, grandson of the Prophet Ali, an important figure of Shi'a Islam, Iran's official denomination. Thus the piece that functioned in Europe as the passion of a sacrificial victim, a Christ-like man, tormented to death by the Muslims, became here the story of a Muslim martyr… Perhaps the audience associated the scenes of the Prince's whipping and self-flagellation with the sacrificial rituals of the Shi'ites, celebrating the anniversary of Ali's death… What a paradox: it turned out that Grotowski could pass as creator of a Shi'a theatrical mystery play…

Luckily, the hosts and the spectators did not understand the text. The play as such is not specifically anti-Islamic; yet the text, though strictly cleared by the producer, included some opinions about the Prophet that surely would not be admired by zealous confessors.[74]

One evening the performance was attended by the Prime Minister of the Empire, Amir-Abbas Hoveida. As usual, Grotowski locked himself up with the actors in the theatre space to prepare psychologically for the important and tense performance. At that time I did the honours and it came to me to shake the Prime Minister's hand.

[74] Editor's note: Should be 'followers'.

Hoveida was followed by an exceptionally large group of body-guards. For safety reasons the spectators were allowed to enter the hall only after the preliminary warm-up of the actors who, with Grotowski, hid themselves in the changing room. I remember the whole flock of tall musclemen in black suits and white shirts who wanted to check even me, the host (perhaps I did not look like the host) to see if I was not hiding some lethal tool. The Prime Minister was surrounded by them so tightly that the handshake I mentioned before lasted a second and was not even followed by any conventional conversation.

Hoveida was thickset, stiff and he sort of limped. I got the impression that he was armed, hiding a pistol in his trouser-leg.

During the performance I stayed outside, as usual. The body-guards surrounding the building watched me attentively. I made some friendly gestures to them, trying to convince them not to be afraid of me. They answered with distrustful, rather gloomy smiles. When the performance was over, Hoveida, with the bodyguards encircling him tightly, left the place quickly. He did not look for the hosts to say goodbye to them.

I wondered what the Empress and her Prime Minister could possibly feel while watching a performance about a despotic court's games and the maltreatment of a lonely individual by a whimsical and capricious autocrat.

Neither Calderón de la Barca, the author of the original *El príncipe constante*, nor Juliusz Słowacki, his emphatic Polish adapter, nor Grotowski, were aware in advance of the freak of circumstances being played out with the performance of *The Constant Prince* in the context of the declining empire and the approaching Islamic revolution.

Actually, not all the invited artists behaved fairly to the hosts. It was a time when the Pahlavi monarchy was trying to reform the country and open it up to the Western world. Yet the West at that time was just experiencing an age of contestation. Some American and European theatre people tried to express their aversion to the despotic power of the Shah who was just then experimenting and deliberating about how to depart from the traditional way of Oriental despotism (organizing the World Festival Shiraz-Persepolis was one such attempt). The Western contestants, enjoying the hospitality and luxuries offered by the festival organizers, sometimes behaved with the challenging pride of freedom fighters.

It is a peculiar irony of fate that theatre people, with inborn anarchist instincts against power, order and rulers – use the financial support and protection of the mighty... And they have to do so; that's their karma.[75]

---

[75] Ibid., pp. 236–38.

It is known that this visit had a major impact on the avant-garde Iranian theatre and some of its representatives. Detailed studies of this impact and its lasting results in the theatrical practice and consciousness of Iranian artists requires urgent analysis. Such work would also be valuable to researchers of Polish theatre.

In 1970, the publishing house of the Arts Festival issued a selection of texts from *Towards a Poor Theatre* translated by Hasan Marandi. The Persian title of the book is *Besuje teatre biczic*.

In the autumn of 1976, the Laboratory Theatre was to perform again in Iran during the Arts Festival in Shiraz. This time the programme included a series of performances of *Apocalypsis cum figuris* and paratheatrical workshops. Grotowski even went to Teheran in March 1976 to set it up, yet ultimately the tour did not come to fruition. Before the festival, a group of theatre critics and artists announced a boycott protesting the terror that was taking place in Iran. The boycott was initiated by eminent American critic Eric Bentley, and joined by John Arden, David Mercer, and Kenneth Tynan, among others. Some other groups announced in the programme also did not attend the festival, without giving reasons.[76]

The last Shiraz Arts Festival took place in 1977. In 1979, under pressure from the opposition, the Shah left Iran (he died in 1980 in exile). The leader of the Muslim opposition, Ayatollah Ruhollah Khomeini, established the Council of Islamic Revolution, and, after his return to the country from his immigration to France, seized power and ordered the formation of the Provisional Revolutionary Government. On 1 April 1979, the Islamic Republic of Iran was proclaimed.

[76] Information about planned performances of the Laboratory Theatre in Iran: 'Instytut Grotowskiego jedzie do Włoch' [Grotowski's Institute is going to Italy], *Express Wieczorny*, 20–21 September 1975. Information about the boycott of the festival: 'Festiwal w Sziraz' [The festival in Shiraz], *Teatr*, 6 (1977), 24, section 'Kronika' [The chronicle].

IV.
India

1.
RADIO PLAYS
AND *SHAKUNTALĀ* BASED ON KĀLIDĀSA
IN THE THEATRE OF 13 ROWS

ON 20 JUNE 1958, as part of the Polish Radio Theatre, the Kraków Broadcasting Station aired *Shakuntalā*, a radio play based on fragments of the drama by Kālidāsa with motifs from the *Upanishads*, adapted and directed by Jerzy Grotowski with Aleksandra Mianowska. That year Grotowski received an Annual Radio and Television Award for this adaptation.[77]

On 13 October 1959, the Kraków station aired *Kredowe koło* [The chalk circle], based on Klabund's version of an old Chinese legend, which Jerzy Grotowski adapted and co-directed.[78] On 20 March 1960, another radio play adapted and directed by Grotowski was aired: *Nagarjuna*, based on old Tibetan tales translated by Marian Bielicki.

On 13 May 1960 in Opole, about eighty supporters established the Fan Club of the Theatre of 13 Rows. At the same time, with an open lecture titled 'Gra w Sziwę (przypisek do praktyki)' [The Shiva game: A footnote to practice], Grotowski inaugurated a year-long series of seminars on the Theatre of 13 Rows' artistic trajectory against wider issues of contemporary theatre. Prepared in connection with the forthcoming production of *Shakuntalā*, Grotowski's lecture was an attempt to articulate the character of the research in which he and the Theatre of 13 Rows were engaged at that time:

> Shiva, the Cosmic Dancer, who 'gives birth to everything that exists, and crushes everything that exists', who 'dances the wholeness', was a mythological patron of ancient Indian theatre. [...] In mythological tales, Shiva appears as a creator of contradictions. In old sculptures he was presented with squinted eyes, half smiling; his face bore the burden of knowing the relative nature of things. [...] If I had to define our theatrical search in one sentence, one phrase, I would refer to the myth of the Dance of Shiva; I would say, 'we are playing a Shiva game'. Our work is an attempt to absorb reality from all its sides, in its multitude of aspects, while it is remains outside, remote, and at a radical distance. In other words, it is a dance of form, a pulsation of form, a fluid, self-diffusing multitude

---

[77] 'Doroczne Nagrody Radia i Telewizji' [Annual Radio and TV Awards], *Radio i Telewizja*, 10 May 1959.

[78] Editor's note: 'Klabund' was the pseudonym adopted by Alfred Henschke.

of theatrical conventions, styles, and traditions. It is creating contradictions: an intellectual game within impulsiveness, seriousness within the grotesque, mockery in pain; it is a dance of form, which breaks all illusion in theatre, every 'life-likeness' while cherishing the insatiable ambition to include, absorb, engulf the totality, a totality of human fate, and thus the totality of 'reality in general'; and simultaneously it is keeping eyes half-closed, keeping a half-smile, keeping distance, keeping a knowledge of the relativity of things. [...] Ancient Indian theatre, just like ancient Japanese theatre, or ancient Greek theatre, was a ritual that unified within itself dance, pantomime, and recitation. A performance was not a 'presentation' of reality (building of illusion), but rather 'dancing' the reality (it was an artificial construction, some kind of 'rhythmic vision' referring to reality). Mimic dance in the liturgy of Pashupatas (a Shaivite school) was one of six main ritual acts. [...] In a mythological quotation Shiva says: 'I am without a name, without shape, and without action [...]. I am pulse, motion, and rhythm...' (*Shiva-Gita*). The essence of theatre we seek is 'pulse, motion, and rhythm.'[79]

On 13 December 1960, the premiere of Grotowski's adaptation of *Shakuntalā* took place in the Theatre of 13 Rows. It is with this production that Grotowski's collaboration with the architect Jerzy Gurawski began. In accordance with the suggestion Wyspiański included in his *Studium o Hamlecie* [The Hamlet study], both Grotowski and Gurawski sought for each work a distinctive spatial relation between the actor and the spectator, or in other words, various ways of organizing the ritual taking place between actors and spectators.[80] As Grotowski claims, both of them 'set out on an uncompromising conquest of space'.[81]

In *Shakuntalā*, they used a central stage concept: spectators were placed on two podia set opposite each other, and the main action took place on the central stage situated between the podia, while behind the spectators there were two stands for yogis-commentators. Stage architecture was made by raw structures: a semicircular bowl (its shape resembling Buddhist sanctuaries in India, called *anda*, from the Sanskrit word for 'egg') with a clearly visible seam,

[79] Grotowski added a typescript of this text to his master thesis in the faculty of directing. It is stored in the archives of the Ludwik Solski State Drama School in Kraków.
[80] Stanisław Wyspiański (1869–1907), the foremost playwright, poet, and painter of Polish Symbolism. Grotowski directed *Akropolis* based on Wyspiański in 1962 (in collaboration with Józef Szajna), and *Studium o Hamlecie* based on Shakespeare and Wyspiański in 1964.
[81] Grotowski, 'Teatr a rytuał', p. 64.

• *A poster for* Shakuntalā *based on* Kālidāsa. *Theatre of 13 Rows, Opole, 1960. Designed by children from the Fine Arts School in Opole (the class of Wincenty Maszkowski)*

• *A rehearsal for* Shakuntalā *based on* Kālidāsa: *Antoni Jahołkowski, Rena Mirecka, Jerzy Grotowski, Andrzej Bielski, Zygmunt Molik, Ewa Lubowiecka, Barbara Barska, Adam Kurczyna. In the background there are elements of the set for* Mystery-Bouffe. *Theatre of 13 Rows, Opole, 1960*

dividing the object in two halves, and a tall, phallic-shaped pole. 'The stage design, noted Flaszen in the performance programme, is two-phased: it combines dream symbolism (with a 'Freudian' architectonic form at the centre of the stage) with childish symbolism (the costumes are designed by children).'[82]

Grotowski made a lot of cuts in the text and inserted excerpts from *Kamasutra*, the ancient Indian handbook of the art of love-making; *The Manu Smrti*, a collection of ancient Indian codes of conduct; and some Hindu ritual texts. Kālidāsa's work served him as material 'for [his] own ideas and scenic inventions'.[83]

Shakuntalā was performed by a company of seven actors, although in Kālidāsa's original play there are thirty-four characters plus hermits, pupils, courtiers, and a royal entourage. In Grotowski's production, the role of 'the community' was taken by the audience. A characteristic feature of the production was an artificially stylized way of speaking, drawing on the conventions of speech in religious ceremonies. The director and the actors consciously emphasized the conflict between the delivery and the ordinary meaning of uttered words. Gestures were also stylized and artificial. There was no recorded music used in the performance. The director attached great importance to what he called at that time 'aktoro-muzyka' [actor-music] and 'aktoro-plastyka' [actor-plasticity],[84] using natural sound effects (rhythmical beats, sounds of steps, and the like), and organizing a specific 'architecture of forms, tones, sounds, languages, and chants.'[85]

Soon after the premiere, Bogdan Bąk pointed to the importance of the production in terms of the work of other Opole-based theatres and the evolution of Jerzy Grotowski as a director:

> *Shakuntalā* is an important phase in the history of the Theatre of 13 Rows [...]. The performance [...] was constructed very consistently, without the commotion so typical to Grotowski, and resulting – as I suppose – mainly from his wish to express himself fully within the context of a single work. One has to emphasize that it did not hamper the directorial invention. The spectator is again a witness of a number of surprising concepts, although much more than in previous productions subordinated to the leading idea.[86]

---

[82]   Flaszen, 'Shakuntalā. A 'How to Watch' Guide for the Audience, and Especially for Reviewers', in Flaszen, *Grotowski & Company*, p. 66.

[83]   Ibid., p. 65.

[84]   Editor's note: 'Plastyka' in Polish means both plasticity and (plastic) art.

[85]   Jerzy Lau, 'Poszukiwacze teatru środka' [Seekers of the theatre of the centre], *Argumenty*, 22 January 1961, p. 8.

[86]   Bogdan Bąk, 'Ostry erotyk' [A hot erotic piece], *Odra*, 1 (1961), 6.

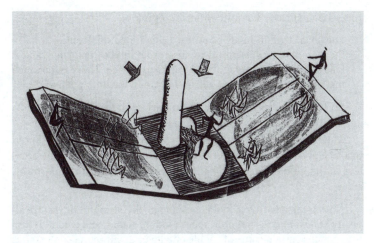

• *Jerzy Gurawski's drawing of the set design for* Shakuntalā *based on* Kālidāsa. *Theatre of 13 Rows, Opole, 1960*

• Shakuntalā *based on Kālidāsa, directed by Jerzy Grotowski: Rena Mirecka (Shakuntalā) and Zygmunt Molik (King Dushyanta). Theatre of 13 Rows, Opole, 1960*

Jerzy Lau expressed a quite different opinion:

> However, this all-in-all beautiful Indian love tale comes to us in the form of a philosophical treatise or an intellectual game, and it fails to reach other areas of theatrical experience. There is too much mathematics and conceptualism there, and too little poetry.[87]

So then, as often happens among art critics, what one accepts and praises, the other might hold against the artist.

Magda Leja, another well-known journalist of that time, pointed to a lack of coherence between declarations proclaimed by the creators of the Opole *Shakuntalā* and the very meaning of the performance:

> No matter what Grotowski says about 'the absolute of theatricality', *Shakuntalā* is not only about motion, sound, and colour. It also contains certain concepts of life and love. In our moral context, it is hardly a banal issue.[88]

However, it was Władysław Broniewski whose opinion about the production turned out to be the most important.[89] Broniewski saw *Shakuntalā* in Opole on 22 May 1961. Because of the status the poet enjoyed at that time, his judgment had some significant impact – it determined the fate of Grotowski's theatre, whose survival was tenuous as the authorities often questioned the sense of its existence:

> The Opole-based Theatre of 13 Rows is a revelation in Poland! These people – this ensemble – are a kind of apostles. Apostles of what? Of Art with a capital 'A'. They speak excellently, they are fit, and with their voices and bodies they know how to identify with the essence of the human condition; to put it in an old-fashioned way: they are good actors. I do not know what gestures were in practice in ancient India, yet those given by the Theatre of 13 Rows in the performance of *Shakuntalā* were convincing.[90]

Let us note that besides the venue of the Theatre of 13 Rows in Opole, *Shakuntalā* was performed in Kraków (8–15 January 1961, the House of Artists [Dom Plastyków]), in Łódź (21 and 22 Janu-

---

87 Lau, 'Poszukiwacze teatru środka', p. 8.
88 M[agda] L[eja], 'Cudzoziemka w Opolu' [A foreigner in Opole], *Sztandar Młodych*, 6 January 1961, p. 2.
89 Władysław Broniewski (1897–1962), one of the leading Polish left-leaning poets and a friend of the Laboratory Theatre.
90 'Władysław Broniewski o Teatrze 13 Rzędów' [Władysław Broniewski about the Theatre of 13 Rows], *Dialog*, 6 (1974), 124–25.

• Shakuntalā *based on Kālidāsa, directed by Jerzy Grotowski: Adam Kurczyna (Yogi 2), Ewa Lubowiecka (Priyamvada), Barbara Barska (Anasuya), and Rena Mirecka (Shakuntalā). Theatre of 13 Rows, Opole, 1960*

• Shakuntalā *based on Kālidāsa, directed by Jerzy Grotowski: Antoni Jahołkowski (Joker), and Zygmunt Molik (King Dushyanta). Theatre of 13 Rows, Opole, 1960*

ary 1961, Student Theatre of Satire Lemon [Studencki Teatr Satyry 'Cytryna']), in Wrocław (6 March 1961, Student Club Pałacyk), in Kędzierzyn (9 April 1961, as part of Workers' Theatrical Fete [Robotniczy Festyn Teatralny]) and in Warsaw (Spring 1962, Society for Polish-Indian Friendship). There was even un unrealized proposal to present the production in India. Reportedly, there was no money for the tour, yet perhaps the main factor was a lack of understanding and good will within the Department of Theatre Affairs at the Ministry of Culture and Art.

From today's perspective, the production of *Shakuntalā* was undoubtedly an important experience for Grotowski and his actors. In 1968, many years after the premiere, Grotowski estimated its significance in the following way:

> We noticed quite early that we could – in our own context – seek the sources of ritual play, analogous to the ones that survived in some countries. Where does it still exist? Mainly in the theatre of the East. Even a lay theatre, such as the Peking opera, has a ritual structure, and it is a ceremony of articulated signs, set by tradition, repeated invariably in each performance; it is a kind of language, ideograms of gesture and behaviour. We created a performance – *Shakuntalā* by Kālidāsa – where we explored possibilities of creating signs in European theatre. We did it not without malicious intention: we wanted to create a performance that would give an image of Oriental theatre, yet not an authentic one; rather, the kind imagined by Europeans.
>
> Thus it was an ironic depiction of representations of the East as something mysterious and enigmatic, etc. However, under the surface of this ironic provocation directed towards the spectator, there was a hidden intention to discover a system of signs suitable for our theatre, for our civilization. And we did it: the performance was indeed constructed from small gestural and vocal signs. This work later proved fruitful: our group then had to employ vocal exercises because it was impossible to create vocal signs without special preparation. When the performance was completed, it was a peculiar work, fitted with certain suggestiveness. However, I noticed that it was an ironic transposition of all possible stereotypes, all possible clichés, and that each gesture, each of the intentionally built ideograms, was in fact a 'gestural cliché', as Stanislavski called it. Even though it wasn't 'I love' spoken with the hand on the heart, it was close enough. It became clear that this was not the right path.[91]

In retrospect then, the production turned out to be an important negative experience, one often cited as an example and one directly

[91] Grotowski, 'Teatr a rytuał', p. 70.

- Shakuntalā *based on Kālidāsa, directed by Jerzy Grotowski: Rena Mirecka (Shakuntalā), Adam Kurczyna (Yogi 2), and Andrzej Bielski (Yogi 1). Theatre of 13 Rows, Opole, 1960*

- Shakuntalā *based on Kālidāsa, directed by Jerzy Grotowski: Rena Mirecka (Shakuntalā) and Zygmunt Molik (King Dushyanta). Theatre of 13 Rows, Opole, 1960*

related to the evolution of the ensemble and their attitude towards the art they practised. Grotowski himself later described that process as follows:

> At that time we debated a lot about artificiality, noting that 'art' and 'artificiality' share the same Latin etymology and that everything organic and natural is not artistic because it is not artificial. Everything that can be constructed, reduced as if to a small crystal of the sign, to a form that is simultaneously cold, crafted, and almost acrobatic – it is all artificial and thus an acceptable direction of work. However, later we abandoned this way of thinking, for the search for signs subsequently turned into the search for stereotypes.[92]

That is how the work on *Shakuntalā* prepared the way for 'the search in the domain of organic human reactions, to eventually structure them', which was evaluated by Grotowski as follows: 'I think this was what started the most fertile adventure for our group: the investigation in the domain of the actor's craft.'[93]

2.
JOURNEYS TO INDIA

EUGENIO BARBA EMPHASIZES the significance of India for Grotowski: 'Grotowski travelled a lot to the East, yet in fact he wanted to travel only to India. His other travels were actually more or less accidental.'[94]

In the periods of the 'theatre of productions' (1957–1969) and the 'theatre of participation' (1969–1978), Grotowski visited the Indian subcontinent six times: for the first time at the turn of 1969, then in July and August 1969 (until 17 August), in the summer of 1970, at the turn of 1977, between 2 and 25 February 1980 and, for the last time, between 4 and 7 July 1981.

On Saturday 18 January 1969, Grotowski told Zbigniew Raszewski about his first journey. They met in the Rycerska Restaurant in Warsaw's Old Town. Raszewski described their meeting in his diary:

---

[92] Ibid.
[93] Ibid.
[94] Barba's comments made during the launch of the author's book, *Grotowski wytycza trasy,* on 28 September 1993 in the Grotowski Centre in Wrocław. Transcribed from an audio recording and edited by Andrzej Wojtasik.

The Rycerska [Restaurant, in Warsaw's Old Town], the room on the right to the cloakroom, the second table from the entrance. Grotowski arrives at 1.30 p.m. sharp, we order dumplings. We discuss a book he published in English. It turns out that, actually, there is no [Polish] original as such. Some chapters were written in Polish, the others came from lectures given by Grotowski in Brussels in French. (Belgians shorthanded them in Flemish, and then they were translated from Flemish to English.) I ask him if he wants to publish it in Polish only to learn that Ket [Konstanty Puzyna] has already tried to persuade him to do it.[95] On Ket's recommendation, some negotiations with WAiF [Wydawnictwa Artystyczne i Filmowe publishing house] began, yet Mr [Władysław] Sternik demanded the outline of the book from Grotowski. I am encouraging Grotowski to prepare a Polish version helter-skelter and publish it whatever may happen. We also talked about *Apocalypsis cum figuris*, the new production I haven't seen yet. I am asking him if he is pleased with it. After consideration, he answers that yes he is, and that he will work on that production for about another four months. Besides, there are some other, more important issues absorbing him.

'I arrived at the conclusion', he says, 'that I should change the take-off point'.

'I do not understand'.

Grotowski is visibly prepared [for this response], yet he does not explain it to me directly, but tells me about an adventure he had some time ago.

'As you know, I was in America. One day I had to take quite a long trip to edit a documentary film on my staging of *Akropolis*.[96] I flew Air France. During the flight I looked through an atlas I found in the cabin. I reached India and I would have certainly turned that page over if I hadn't noticed on a tiny cape – perhaps unnoticed by anybody – the name Tiruvannamalai. That caption, welcoming me on the Air France plane, above a foreign territory, in fact seemed to sail to me from the abyss of time.

[95] Konstanty Puzyna (1929–1989), an renowned theatre critic, editor of *Dialog* monthly magazine, and editor of the book series 'Teorie Współczesnego Teatru' [Theories of contemporary theatre] published by the Warsaw's publishing house Wydawnictwa Artystyczne i Filmowe, where a Polish translation of *Towards a Poor Theatre* was scheduled.

[96] Jerzy Grotowski, *Akropolis*, television recording, dir. James McTaggart (BBC, 1968), first broadcast on 12 January 1969 by the New York TV station Channel 13 (educational television). This is from a black-and-white recording of the entire performance (57') shot between 27 October and 2 November in the Twickenham studio near London; the performance is preceded by a commentary in English by Peter Brook (25'). Date of editing is unknown to me. Osiński, *Grotowski and His Laboratory*, pp. 166, 168.

You must know that during the war we lived in the countryside. There were some twenty kilometers to the nearest town where we could borrow books. Yet despite the freezing cold my mother would go to the town to bring some books to read for my brother and me. Thanks to my mother I came across a once famous book, *A Search in Secret India* by [Paul] Brunton. It is a kind of journalistic report. The author travels all over India seeking great mystic traditions and encountering, almost exclusively, frauds and quackery. Finally, already quite discouraged, he meets a man called Ramana Maharshi (Ramana is his name, while Maharshi means 'a great sage'). And then he experiences revelation. Maharshi led the life of a hermit, practising contemplation, and he reached a catatonic state. Ants ate his feet, yet he did not feel it at all – this is just one example. His wisdom overwhelmed Brunton, who described in his book the practices and ideas of Maharshi and considered him a holy man. Maharshi's hermitage was in Tiruvannaamalai.

I was also shocked after I read that book, just like Brunton when he met Maharshi. I was ill, I had a fever. Actually, I was a young boy. I remember that my aunt held a grudge against my mother for giving me that book. She thought that I was too young – I was eight at that time – and that it had a bad effect on me.

Two years later, when I was ten, I read *A Search in Secret India* again and made some notes which I still have. I tried to practise what Maharshi practised. It had no influence on me other than being harmful to my health.

I returned to Brunton's book after the war. I read the writings of Maharshi in English. (There is also a Polish translation by Ms Dynowska, yet it is really poor.) My brother photographed a picture of Maharshi from Brunton's book, as well as an image of the shrine in Tiruvannamalai. I never parted with these pictures.

When I finished my work on the film, I went to a travel agency to check the prices of tickets to India. It turned out that the royalties I had received were sufficient to cover the costs of such a journey. I informed the Ministry of Culture that for professional reasons I should go to India, and they raised no objections.

So one day I found myself in Delhi. Then the issues got a bit complicated. None of the travel agencies wanted to make my pilgrimage easier. (Only later did I understand that I was going to the holy place where tourists were unwelcome; and at travel agencies I was obviously taken for a tourist.) I had to continue my journey on my own in cranky coaches, accompanied by dirty, often stinking beggars, sages, and thieves. Astonished, I sunk into the hot, sultry, bright country, where the jungle penetrates the human world, people move like panthers, and panthers look with human eyes – the real-unreal territory where I, too, experienced a strange transformation.

Then I got to Tiruvannamalai. I do not believe in reincarnation. Yet I experienced it, one can say: in a tangible way I experienced the return to a place I had already known, to a place I was obliged to return to. I visited the shrine. It is organized in such a way that it leads the visitor from rooms suggestively decorated with figurative motifs to the sanctuary that is a domain of abstraction, and the sensual character of ornaments gradually fades as one goes from one room to another. It proves a deep knowledge of the human psyche. After visiting the shrine I went to the foot of the holy mountain. Tiruvannamalai means 'the holy mount'. It is difficult to tell precisely what happened to me. Anyway, I returned home convinced that I had experienced something important and that I should change something in my life'.

That is more or less how Grotowski's story ends (I cite it here in a much-abridged version). I check the time. Grotowski talked for half an hour or so, yet very fluently, his speech was clear, sometimes flexible and vivid. Undoubtedly, he was aware how unusual and sensitive the issue was. Yet he did not try, as he used to in the past, to counterbalance that embarrassing intimacy with irony. This time he put an effort to maintain a maximum simplicity of vocabulary and tone.

I am trying to comprehend what I have just heard and I am asking cautiously:

'Do you have the impression that this adventure should have some consequences?'

'I have the impression that it was a consequence of my life and that it should now be continued.' [...]

The third part of the conversation is being established quickly. It is very exhausting, at least to me. One hour or so of constant strain on all mental powers. In fact the discussion centres around the question of whether a human being can be saved.

'If you mean: here, on the Earth, I do not believe so.'

'Here, on the Earth!' shouts Grotowski with shining eyes.

Unwittingly I am thinking about Schiller, so insistently explicating to priests that man is obliged to fight for the Kingdom of God 'here, on the Earth'.[97] Yet Schiller meant justice, while Grotowski talks about salvation; moreover, about the salvation of an individual. I do not quite understand what he means by this, although he

---

[97] Leon Schiller (1887–1954), a leading Polish theatre producer and director who founded and edited the *Pamiętnik Teatralny* quarterly journal of theatre studies. Thanks to Schiller's efforts, Zbigniew Raszewski (1925–1992), who in November 1952 published his first article in *Pamiętnik Teatralny*, was employed from January 1953 in the Theatre Section of the State Institute of Art. In 1955, after Schiller's death, Raszewski became co-editor (with Bohdan Korzeniewski) of the quarterly, a post he held until 1992.

• *Ramana Maharshi*

explains to me his intuitions – emphasizing that he values intuitive cognition more than an intellectual one – in a well-spoken way, quoting a poem by St John of the Cross (in French translation, carefully copied in his notebook), then *Widzenie* [A vision] by Mickiewicz (from memory: 'and in a strange vision / I as the light, and the eye's pupil at the same time'). When we rise from the table, I watch him with awe. I am dizzy. He – light, flexible, like an electrified cat – stands up and walks as if nothing has happened.[98]

Grotowski frequently referred to Ramana Maharshi and the mighty 'Arunachala, the holy mountain, or the Mountain of Flame', 2400 meters high, towering above a vast plain.[99] An ashram at the foot of the mountain, in the village of Tiruvannamalai, and then the slope of the mountain itself had been a home to Maharshi. In the letter from 6 February 1965, Grotowski reminded Barba that even in Opole, he had had a picture of Ramana Maharshi hung above his bed, copied by his brother Kazimierz. I can confirm it for I saw the same picture with my own eyes in Grotowski's apartment on Pasieczna Street. And over thirty years later, in October 1996, he said to Eugenio Barba that 'today he still considered Maharshi to be his spiritual master, that he had copies of Brunton's book in English, French, Italian, and Polish, and that he made everyone who worked with him read the chapter about Maharshi'.[100]

This account must be corrected: copies of pictures of Ramana Maharshi and Mount Arunachala did not come from Brunton's

---

[98] Zbigniew Raszewski, *Raptularz* [Diary], ed. by Edyta and Tomasz Kubikowscy, 2 vols (London: Puls, 2004), I, 484–88.
[99] Bonarski, 'Rozmowa z Grotowskim' [A conversation with Grotowski], *Kultura*, 13 (1975).
[100] Barba, *Land of Ashes and Diamonds*, p. 140, footnote 80.

book. The book includes some other images, yet not the pictures mentioned by Barba. The source of the pictures is the volume of Maharshi's teachings translated by Wanda Dynowska (*Nauka Szri Ramana Mahariszi*, New Delhi: Biblioteka Polsko-Indyjska, 1957) – this book, besides the copies of *A Search in Secret India* in the four languages mentioned above, was in Grotowski's reference library in Vallicelle, which was transferred to his apartment in Pontedera one year before his death.[101] It is not an exaggeration to state that Brunton's book accompanied Grotowski for his entire life.

Grotowski himself spoke publicly about the significance of Brunton's book and Ramana Maharshi in the conversation with Andrzej Bonarski cited earlier.

Let me quote an excerpt from Barba's *The Land of Ashes and Diamonds*, referring to their encounter in 1992:

> Grotowski confirmed this, and told me that he owed his 'secret vocation' for India to his mother [...]. He also spoke to me yet again of the importance of Paul Brunton's book, *A Search in Secret India* [...]. The chapters on the life of Ramana Maharishi had made a particular impression on him. [102]

The already quoted account of Raszewski is probably the only recorded testimony from the 1969 trip. Yet the fact of Grotowski's travel to India and his stay there is confirmed in his letter to Alina Obidniak, dated Wrocław, 19 February 1969: 'I returned from my several-month-long pilgrimage through various continents, and its final stage, accomplished on my own, was – can you imagine? – in India.'[103] Unfortunately, we do not know the exact dates of that trip. The *terminus a quo* can be considered 26 November 1968 (the date of the last performance of *Akropolis* in Aix-en-Provence, ending an over three-month-long tour of the Laboratory Theatre), and *terminus ante quem* – 15 December 1968.[104] It was six months after the

---

[101]   A picture of Ramana Maharshi is on the book's frontispiece, while a picture of Arunachala 'seen from the ashram' is on page XXXI. A copy of the former with an inscription by Kazimierz Grotowski on the reverse has luckily survived until today.

[102]   Barba, *Land of Ashes and Diamonds*, p. 54.

[103]   Obidniak, *Pola energii. Wspomnienia i rozmowy*, p. 260.

[104]   Osiński, *Grotowski and His Laboratory*, p. 166; Osiński, 'Występy gościnne zespołu Teatru Laboratorium i prace jego członków poza siedzibą w latach 1959–1984. Kronika działalności 1978–1984' [Guest Performances of the Laboratory Theatre company, and work of its members outside the premises, in the

first closed presentation of Grotowski's last theatrical work, *Apocalypsis cum figuris*, at the Laboratory Theatre's venue in Wrocław. He considered the period of 'theatre of productions' as finished for him, and he was in the process of summarizing it, while entering a new artistic adventure, namely 'theatre of participation' with all its paratheatrical experiments. If we keep this in mind, we will not be surprised by Barba's following words:

> When Grotowski went for the first time to India – I know it very well because it was in 1969, just after one of the seminars in Holstebro – [...] at that time we still wrote to each other. He wrote long letters to me from India, yet in none of those letters did he mention theatre. He wrote about going now into this part of Bengal because there was a gathering of Bauls, a group of half-religious beggars [...] singing and begging. And then in another letter he wrote about going to Pondicherry, to the ashram of Sri Aurobindo. All his letters were, in reality, full of references to religious traces (I would say); not theatrical ones.[105]

Eugenio Barba evidently thought of Grotowski's second visit to the Indian subcontinent, for the letter quoted by him was dated Calcutta, 10 August 1969. It is the last of twenty six letters published in Barba's book *The Land of Ashes and Diamonds*.[106] Grotowski gives an account of his experiences and impressions from the trip as follows:

> It has been a beautiful trip so far, really extraordinarily. Calcutta has just been a base; there is not much to see. But I went to the shrine of Ramakrishna which you told me about. I also met the most important Baul master (yoga through song and dance), who devotes himself to many of the same things as I do – the anatomy of the actor. It is amazing to see how certain aspects of the craft are objective. He told me that since the death of his father, who (as is the family tradition) had been his guru, he had not met anyone who was so well acquainted with these things as me. At the beginning we talked with the help of a translator, but very soon that was no longer necessary: gestures were sufficient together with a few words of English (which he hardly knows better than me) and a few of Sanskrit. I have to admit to being proud of his recognition although

---

years 1959–1984. Chronicle of Activities 1978–1984], *Pamiętnik Teatralny*, 1–4 (2000), 627–90.

105   Eugenio Barba, comments made on 28 September 1993 in the Grotowski Centre in Wrocław, during the launch of the author's book *Grotowski wytycza trasy*, transcribed from a video recording.

106   Barba, *Land of Ashes and Diamonds*, pp. 169–72.

I tell myself that I am reacting like a child. He was a true juggler of Notre Dame. But at a very high level.

I have been in the Himalayas, near Mount Everest and Annapurna, although of course not as high. I have visited a few holy places, among them the 'Częstochowa' of the Shivaists, about ten kilometres from Calcutta, and there I saw the temperature and the authenticity of people's religious reactions, and the fervour of these reactions.[107] Perhaps something of this kind can only be encountered here. I have been to Bhubaneswar and Konorak (to the Black Temple). I came back today and this evening I leave again for Bodh-Gaya, the place where Buddha meditated under that famous tree and where he became 'Buddha', Benares, Khajuraho, New Delhi and, if I manage it, Kashmir. It has been a wonderful holiday up until now. But I have some regrets because I think I have really exploited you financially too much this time. [...]

So far I have not received the transcriptions from Marianne [Ahrne] and today I have to leave the hotel in Calcutta.[108] I am leaving my address in New Delhi and they have promised to forward any letters to me. The last day of my stay in New Delhi will probably be the evening of 16 August or the morning of the 17th. I leave for Poland on the 17th (I have to be in Wrocław on the evening of the 18th).[109]

The greatest significance is usually attributed to the third visit, directly associated with Grotowski's fundamental transformation that led him to abandon the 'theatre of productions' and transition to the domain of 'active culture', also known as 'theatre of participation' or 'paratheatrical experiences'. One Polish commentator wrote:

It is worthwhile to mention that Grotowski took a long trip across India, just at the beginning of 1970 [in fact, during the summer months], which certainly caused many changes in his attitude and opinions as a stage director. India, as the country of his spiritual turning point, is very significant in understanding Grotowski's thought.[110]

---

[107] Editor's note: Grotowski refers to the Polish city known for the Pauline monastery of Jasna Góra, the shrine to the Virgin Mary, home to the famous painting of the Black Madonna. Częstochowa is the destination of annual pilgrimages of Polish Catholics.

[108] Marianne Ahrne from Sweden was Grotowski's translator (from French to English) during his public conferences in New York and seminars in Holstebro. She filmed *Ferai*, the third show of Odin Teatret, and made a film about Grotowski's work.

[109] Barba, *Land of Ashes and Diamonds*, p. 169.

[110] Ryszard Caputa [Krzysztof Pysiak], 'Jerzy Grotowski – po teatrze' [Jerzy Grotowski: After theatre], *Nowy Wyraz*, 8 (1978), 69.

Undoubtedly, this opinion exemplifies the consensus of theatrical reviewers and critics on that subject, for – in contrast to the so-called ordinary spectators – they leave behind their testimonies as texts. However, as I want to prove, such a belief is largely a myth. In my opinion, Grotowski's third visit to India was for him much more a consequence of the transformation that had already been taking place rather than a search for an opportunity to experience it. It could not have worked as a calculated or premeditated act such as 'I will go to India to change myself'. The famous 'transformation of Grotowski's personality', so widely commented on by journalists and theatre people, certainly did not last several weeks; it was rather in progress more or less since 1969, or even earlier, when Grotowski reached the peak of his theatrical success and his name was mentioned alongside the names of the greatest people of the 20th century theatre. Later, in conversation with Andrzej Bonarski in 1975, Grotowski himself described that period of his life in the following way:

> [...] That was when a man's natural inertia, fear of the unknown, the feeling that to leave the confines of a known discipline is madness and must end badly. But I knew I could not continue what I thought to be a beautiful but closed chapter of my life. Nor could I find enough strength and courage to create another. [...] So I did not have enough heart for one endeavour nor enough courage for another. What does one do in such a case? One can force oneself to continue, but one must have a very strong character, because there is something wretched in that; everything becomes a kind of lugging of heavy sacks: you can seek refuge in illness – this is not a bad solution – or become a professor or president and create some sort of extra-special theatre academy, which I thought about for a while. [...] Usually it turned out that when I knew something had to be done, I could advise others of it. I advised those whom I care about to set out and travel. Until I realized, and this has happened to me a few times in my life, that I should take my own advice.[111]

One such moment occurred during the workshop that Grotowski ran with Ryszard Cieślak at the Centre Dramatique National du Sud-Est in Aix-en-Provence between 20 June and 10 July 1970. He advised one of the participants 'to go and wander around'. Directly from France, Grotowski went to India, where he took a six-week trip across the country, and to Kurdistan.

---

[111] Osiński, *Grotowski and His Laboratory*, pp. 121–22.

On 22 February 1970, just two months after returning from a triumphant tour in England and America, Grotowski met with Polish journalists at the conference room of the Club of Artistic Unions [Klub Związków Twórczych] in Wrocław. He said:

> At this moment, numerous tours interfere with our work. The trips must be shortened. The need for focus demands it. We are returning home with great joy. [...]
>
> We live in a post-theatrical era. What follows is not a new wave of theatre but rather something else that will replace it. Too many phenomena exist by sheer habit, because it has been generally accepted that they should exist. [...] I feel that *Apocalypsis cum figuris* is a new stage for me in my research. We have crossed a certain threshold.[112]

In a request to the state-run Polska Agencja Artystyczna (PAGART) [Polish Artistic Agency], dated 17 March 1970, Jędrzej Sell, administrative director of the Laboratory Theatre's Institute of Research in the Actor's Method, asked permission for Grotowski to take a six-week trip 'at his own expense [...] to deepen his studies of Indian culture'.[113] The request was justified by the fact that '[...] during his visit in India, director Grotowski would be able to engage in conversation with Indian artists, especially with the representatives of Indian theatre who are of interest to our theatre'.[114]

We learn the meaning of the last sentence from Grotowski's correspondence to Maria Krzysztof Byrski, a thirty-three-year-old Indologist at the University of Warsaw, who had already spent several years on the Indian subcontinent. In his letter written in Wrocław on 15 April 1970 to Tadeusz Byrski, Maria Krzysztof's father, Grotowski presented the following request:

> And one more request, this time through you to Mr Byrski junior. Because I would like to spend a few weeks in the summer in India, I would be very grateful if he could give me some names of his Indian friends, not so much those professionally involved in contemporary forms of theatre, but rather those who feel closer to the old Indian tradition in general as well as to the traditions of classical or temple theatre. Perhaps he knows someone who would join me on some adventurous journey, especially across South India. I would

---

[112] Grotowski, 'W poszukiwaniu szczerości' [A quest for frankness], ed. by Zofia Raducka, *Tygodnik Demokratyczny*, 29 March 1970, p. 6. See: Jerzy Grotowski, 'W poszukiwaniu szczerości', *Tygodnik Demokratyczny*, 17 May 1970, p. 7.

[113] Editor's note: Polska Agencja Artystyczna (PAGART) organized and coordinated all foreign tours of Polish performers.

[114] Jędrzej Sell, letter to PAGART, 17 March 1970, Folder 398, 'Journeys – correspondence, 1969–1971', Grotowski Institute Archive, Wrocław.

like to set my base in Pondicherry (a French language zone) from where I could make trips to the deep South. In addition, this time I also would like to visit Kashmir. Does any Indian friend of Mr Krzysztof speak French? My English is very poor. […] Because Mr Krzysztof told me after my previous journeys that I should have made him aware of my visit in advance so that he could have given me addresses of his Indian friends, I am doing it this time, with an apology for any problems and for the indirect (yet via high offices!) form of my request.[115]

Eventually, Grotowski made his third journey across India on his own. In his recollections published in *Pamiętnik Teatralny* after Jerzy Grotowski's death, Professor Kazimierz Grotowski described this trip from his memory of his brother's stories:

Jurek […] travelled on foot, joining a pair of devout men, and accompanying them for several days. They led him from temple to temple and from monastery to monastery, where one could get a free bowl of rice and a cup of tea.[116]

When after six weeks, on 23 August 1970, Jerzy Grotowski appeared at the airport in Shiraz to meet the members of the Laboratory Theatre then beginning their last purely theatrical tour (presenting *The Constant Prince*), this time through the Middle East, Iran, and Lebanon – even his closest colleagues could not recognize him. During that short period he went through a radical transformation. For starters, he had lost forty kilograms of weight.[117]

Grotowski planned to spend his vacation between 1 and 20 July 1971 in India again, and then to go to Ceylon and Nepal.[118] However, because of an outbreak of cholera on the subcontinent, he changed his plans and applied to the Wrocław authorities for permission to go to Canada and, perhaps, Latin America 'to study Amerindian culture'.[119]

---

[115]   Osiński, *Nazywał nas bratnim teatrem. Przyjaźń artystyczna Ireny i Tadeusza Byrskich z Jerzym Grotowskim* [He used to call us a sister theatre: Artistic friendship of Irena and Tadeusz Byrski with Jerzy Grotowski] (Gdańsk: słowo/obraz terytoria, 2005), p. 210.

[116]   Kazimierz Grotowski, 'Portret rodzinny', p. 28.

[117]   Osiński, *Grotowski and His Laboratory*, p. 122.

[118]   Jerzy Grotowski, 3 May 1971, Folder 383, 'Correspondence concerning foreign trips of the management and ensemble: Ministry, PAGART, 1970–1978', Grotowski Institute Archive, Wrocław.

[119]   Jędrzej Sell, letter to Wrocław authorities, Folder 383, 'Correspondence concerning foreign trips of the management and ensemble: Ministry, PAGART, 1970–1978', Grotowski Institute Archive, Wrocław.

At the turn of 1977, Grotowski made his fourth trip to India. Together with his then seventy-nine-year old mother, Emilia Grotowska, he took part in a tour organized by the Polish Tour Agency Orbis. Kazimierz Grotowski described this trip several times, for the first time in a conversation with Teresa Błajet-Winiewczyc, published in *Notatnik Teatralny* in 1992:

> Mother had a great influence on us. She also had excellent contact with Jurek. As you probably know, many people never understood Grotowski's theatre. Obviously, mother had a special attitude towards this theatre, because it was the theatre of her son, yet she intuitively felt it and perfectly knew what was happening there and what Jurek meant. [...]
>
> They went together to India in 1976. Mother was seventy-nine years old at that time. She had long been interested in Indian philosophy; even in Nienadówka there were books about India, which she read. She maintained these interests until her old age. Thus Jurek invited mother for the trip to India for Christmas and the New Year. One day she got lost in Mumbai. She was extremely independent; she went to the city on her own, and disappeared. She forgot the name of the hotel where they stayed, yet she managed to return even though she could not speak any of the local languages. She did not know English either – she only spoke German and some French – yet she was able to find someone who figured out in which hotel she was staying and brought her there. When I went to pick them up at the airport in Warsaw, I saw mother in excellent physical shape. She was very pleased with the trip. She brought a lot of photos and, of course, a notebook. Just like my father, she always took notes.[120]

Parts of Kazimierz Grotowski's text *Portret rodzinny*, published eight years later, were based on his mother's travel diary:

> The greatest journey of her life was undoubtedly the trip with Jurek to India in 1976. She described it precisely, in detail, in her travel diary. On their way they stopped in Rome and visited St Peter's Basilica. In India: Mumbai, Madras and the surroundings, then a trip to Ceylon, visiting temples, subtropical plants and animals, exotic Indian streets. Jurek took Mila to those places in India, which impressed him most. In this area, many years before [in 1970], he had travelled on foot, joining a pair of devout men and accompanying them for several days. [...] Of course, mother could not realize that she travelled in the vicinity of the mountain southwest of Madras where some twenty years later the ashes of her son would be scattered.
>
> India fascinated our entire family. In the beginning of the 1970s, just before the war in Afghanistan, I made an almost ten-thousand-

[120] Kazimierz Grotowski, 'On poprzez teatr bada świat', p. 89.

· 75 ·

kilometre trip from Kraków through Turkey, Iran, Afghanistan, Pakistan, and India to Nepal by car. We were doing research near the Tibetan border, around the eight-thousander Shisha Pangma, in the accumulation zone of glaciers, at an altitude of five to six thousand metres. Our aim was to study global pollution. Delhi; Benares on the Ganges; the temples of Kathmandu; prayer flags and small monasteries in the Himalayas; monks; refugees from Tibet. All these images brought in my memory the descriptions in the books read by us in Nienadówka.[121]

It is also known that Grotowski was planning to return to the Indian subcontinent between 15 November and 26 December 1978 to meet and consult with the Indian participants of the Theatre of Sources project, yet ultimately the trip fell through.[122] Finally a journey with the six-person international team of the Theatre of Sources – his fifth visit to India – took place between 2 and 25 of February 1980.[123] The main organizer of the visit was Deepak Majumdar, a coordinator of Chitrabani, the Calcutta-based centre for research in communication. In an article published in a magazine issued by the centre, we read:

Grotowski stayed in West Bengal between 7 and 23 February 1980. He ran a short workshop with the Living Theatre in Khardaha [a town some fifteen kilometers from Calcutta]. Then he ran another workshop in Kenduli village, in Birbhum district (north-western part of the state of West Bengal), with eighteen participants, including several Bauls as well as members of the Living Theatre and Chitrabani. Upon his arrival, Grotowski requested a place 'the least harmed by man'. He approved the place for the planned work when he saw a forest standing at the wonderful sand dunes by the Anay River [...].

The workshop in Kendula lasted six days, starting on 16 February, and made a deep impression on the participants. It included exercises of absorbing psycho-physical energy from the elements, wrestling with oneself, collaboration, environmental awareness,

---

121 Kazimierz Grotowski, 'Portret rodzinny', pp. 28–29. See: Kazimierz Grotowski, 'Podróż w biografię. Spotkanie z Kazimierzem Grotowskim, 17 października 1999' [A journey into a biography: An encounter with Kazimierz Grotowski, 17 October 1999], transcribed and ed. by Maria Hepel, *Notatnik Teatralny*, 22–23 (2001), 8–25; Kazimierz Grotowski and Andrzej Michał Kobos, 'Wędrowałem za fizyką', 276–77.

122 Folder 383: 'Correspondence concerning foreign trips of the management and ensemble: Ministry, PAGART, 1970–1978', Grotowski Institute Archive, Wrocław.

123 Five months earlier, in October 1979, Grotowski's envoy, American theatre scholar Steve Weinstein, went to Calcutta.

• *Jerzy Grotowski in Tamilnadu, India, 1976*

• *Jerzy Grotowski in Tamilnadu, India, 1976*

silence, techniques of spiritual communication of Bauls, bio-mechanics of the inner theatre, and 'encounters' in which 'one neither refuses, nor imposes oneself'. The workshop had a moving beginning that took place on the road to Kendula, near Bolpar. It happened on the day of the historical solar eclipse. When the moment of eclipse came, we felt a peculiar closeness with the people around although we were not really getting close to each other. The scenery became a medium. We experienced a theatrical ode to the Sun.[124]

This is what we know about the work of Grotowski's ensemble in West Bengal in February 1980. We also know that he invited six participants of the workshop in Kendula to join the international team of the Theatre of Sources: Baul Gaur Khep, Dibyendu Ganguli, Deepak Majumdar, Prabir Guha, Ramakrishna Dhar, and Abani Biswas. The last three were members of the Living Theatre in Khardaha. Two of them, Ramakrishna Dhar and Abani Biswas, soon went to Poland to take part in the Theatre of Sources. The entire month of May 1980 (the first week in Warsaw and then, from 7 May until the end of the month in Wrocław) was a preparatory period. Then, between 30 May to 31 August, in both field bases of the Actor's Institute of the Laboratory Theatre, Brzezinka and Ostrowina near Oleśnica, there was a 'workshop seminar' involving invited guests. The final period (8–31 August) was restricted to only the closest collaborators of Grotowski.

It seems significant that, during his visit to the Indian subcontinent, Grotowski never visited the famous Kathakali school in Cheruthuruthy, Kerala, or the school established by Rabindranath Tagore in Shantiniketan, Bengal. Thus, in the late 1960s and 1970s, it wasn't theatre and theatrical performances that interested him the most. However, it is still justifiable to point out various kinds of parallels between Grotowski's artistic stance and the one encountered in some classical Oriental theatres.

---

[124] Quoted after 'Wyprawy terenowe Teatru Źródeł' [Field trips of the Theatre of Sources], ed. by Robert Różycki, *Notatnik Teatralny*, 4 (1992), 156. See: Deepak Majumdar, 'Report: Chitrabani and Theatre. Grotowski in West Bengal. In Poland with Grotowski', *Chitrabani* (1981), 5–11. On Bauls, see: Sri Anirvan, Lizelle Reymond, *To Live Within: Teachings of a Baul* (London: Penguin Books: 1973), Polish translation: Śri Anirwan, Lizelle Reymond, *Żyć w sobie – nauki baula*, trans. by Magda Złotowska (Warsaw: Pusty Obłok, 1994). Magda Złotowska, a collaborator of Grotowski in the periods of Paratheatre and Theatre of Sources, and a translator of some of his texts, told me that it was an important book to him.

Grotowski's final, sixth visit to India took place between 4 and 17 July 1981. Together with Marianne Ahrne, he spent time in Bombay and Calcutta. In the middle of their stay, they were joined by Chiquita Gregory. After Grotowski's departure, Ahrne and Gregory stayed in India some time longer, as they were planning to make a film.[125]

3.
THE LEGEND OF THE IMPACT
OF INDIAN THEATRE ON GROTOWSKI

THERE IS A LEGEND that classical Oriental theatre, primarily Indian theatre and specifically Kathakali, had a significant impact on the theatrical practices of Grotowski and his Laboratory. Some early opinions of Grotowski himself, as well as references in *Towards a Poor Theatre* might contribute to such a belief. For example, in 1958, during an interview with a journalist from *Współczesność*,[126] Grotowski mentioned Oriental theatre as one of seven elements of 'his tradition', justifying it in the following way: '[…] Oriental theatre, especially classical Chinese and Indian theatre, [means] a synthesis of gesture and the metaphorical use of props, [and] a radical dependence on convention in the use of theatrical space […]'.[127]

However, we must note that when Grotowski mentioned Kathakali among the elements of theatrical tradition important to him, he knew it only from books in Russian, for at that time there were no Polish texts of any value on that subject. It was only after Barba's visit to the Indian Academy of Arts in September in 1963 (Kerala Kala Mandalam in Cheruthuruthy) that Grotowski was able to get an eyewitness report on Kathakali.[128] Barba best describes

---

[125] Eugenio Barba, email to the author, 19 February 2011. I would like to thank Marianne Ahrne and Eugenio Barba for this information.

[126] *Współczesność* was a monthly, then bi-monthly, magazine on art and literature published in Warsaw between 1956 and 1971.

[127] 'Z Jerzym Grotowskim o teatrze', p. 8. Osiński, *Grotowski i jego Laboratorium*, p. 285 [not available in English].

[128] Eugenio Barba, 'Indyjski teatr kathakali' ['The Kathakali Theatre'], trans. by Witold Kalinowski, *Dialog*, 12 (1979), 107–15; 'Nasze zderzenie z kathakali' [Our clash with Kathakali], *Dialog*, 12 (1979), 116–26; Krzysztof Renik, *Kathakali. Sztuka indyjskiego teatru* [Kathakali: The art of Indian theatre] (Warsaw: Wydawnictwo Akademickie Dialog, 1994); Renik, *Śladem Bharaty* [Following Bharata] (Warsaw: Wydawnictwo Akademickie Dialog, 2001), pp. 146–65.

that situation himself:

> For the first year and a half [from January 1962 to June 1963] we rarely spoke of Asian theatre. I had seen a few performances in Singapore, Hong Kong, Shanghai and Calcutta when I was a sailor. I remember almost nothing; they had left no traces in my memory. Grotowski had been to China in August 1962 for three weeks and had come back with many impressions and a great deal of information. He had noticed that in the Beijing opera the actors begin an action by starting out in the opposite direction to where they want to end up. If they want to move to the left, they take a step towards the right and then go to their objective on the left. This observation became an effective working tool that we baptized 'the Chinese principle', and under the same name it also entered into the terminology and the practice of Odin Teatret. Grotowski had also been struck by a meeting he had had in Shanghai with a Dr. Ling [Dr Lin Junqing], a voice specialist. Dr. Ling had shown him how to check whether the larynx was open or closed when an actor was speaking. This form of control was incorporated into the vocal training, and was meticulously described by me on page 142 of *In Search of Lost Theatre*.
>
> The situation changed somewhat after my trip to India from July to December 1963. I had travelled there by car, crossing Europe, Turkey, Iran and Pakistan. Amongst the various forms of Indian theatre that I saw, Kathakali from Kerala had made the greatest impression on me. I studied it for three weeks, noting down the physical exercises, those for developing the mobility of the eyes and of the facial muscles, and the gaits. I reported on all this on my return to Opole and for a short period some of the exercises were added to the training.[120]

And in another place he wrote:

> What I saw in Kerala is engraved for ever in my memory. The children were admitted to the school at the age of nine or ten. They started at dawn. Still numb from sleep, they began on their own to repeat again and again the laborious *kathakali* postures and steps. They were friendly and curious. They became my companions.
>
> Even more than the beauty of the performances, it was my own incapacity to understand that surprised me. Why was I, a European spectator, so bewitched by these actors when I could neither understand the story they were telling, nor the meaning of their message, nor their language or the conventions. What was it that made me follow every gesture, every step, dance or deaf-mute dialogue of these actors? Was it their technique that kept me spellbound during an entire night, seated on the ground amongst a crowd who slept or continually got up to stretch their legs, or to eat or drink?

[129]   Barba, *Land of Ashes and Diamonds*, p. 53.

These questions constituted the true influence on me of *kathakali*. For years and years they have remained alive, and have then reappeared in other contexts, leading me towards an attempt at an answer that I have called Theatre Anthropology.

In mid-December I returned to my mother's home in Rome only to discover that the Italian government had, for the fourth time, renewed my scholarship to Poland. I sent a telegram to Grotowski and set off immediately to Opole. [...] In my room or in the station restaurant Grotowski brought me up to date with everything that had happened during my absence. [...] I described my trip to him and the performances I had seen, and I told him about *kathakali* and the religious ceremonies I had attended in Iran, Pakistan and India. I had started to write down my observations on *kathakali* and had adapted some 'exercises' for the training of the Teatr-Laboratorium's actors. I had taken a series of photographs of the *kathakali* children. They were doubtless far more suggestive and eloquent than my descriptions could ever be.[130]

The next two paragraphs of *The Land of Ashes and Diamonds* confirm and develop what I have already stated in brief about what Grotowski and Barba knew about classical forms of Asian theatre before Barba's visit to the Kerala Kala Mandalam centre, the first modern artistic educational institution funded by Kerala poet Vallathol Narayana Menon in 1930, in the period of rapid decline of interest in traditional performances:

Grotowski and I often referred to Asian theatre, but most of our knowledge came from articles or books. The constellation from which we used to take our bearings was made up of archetypes, rituals, trance, shamanism, certain schools of Hindu and Buddhist philosophy and the tradition of the *Wielka Reforma*, the Great Reform, that is the experiences of the innovators of European theatre during the first thirty years of the twentieth century.

Grotowski was not very familiar with the different forms of classical Asian theatre. It was certain aspects of Indian philosophy that were crucial to his vision of the world, permeating his existential attitude and his theatre practice. This was traceable in the smallest detail of the dramaturgy or technical composition. I spoke at length to Grotowski about this conviction of mine in Pontedera in 1992, teasing him about the imaginatively elaborate relationships with Asian theatre that critics and scholars had attributed to him. In my view he was only interested in one thing: India, or rather Hinduism. [...]

---

[130]   Ibid., pp. 76–77.

This influence from Hinduism was present in Grotowski from his very first steps in theatre.[131]

Grotowski himself affirmed the legend about his connections with Oriental theatre, or at least – as far as I know – he never publicly corrected those opinions. He had an opportunity to do so in *The Grotowski Sourcebook*, which was published before his death and, according to the declarations of both editors, prepared in detailed consultation with Grotowski.[132]

Grotowski's texts have been published in India and Japan since the mid-1960s. Publishing houses in these countries have shown great interest in Grotowski. Those who sought contact with him were, in the first place, theatre people, especially directors and actors. The common convictions of his deep interest in Oriental theatre and his knowledge of this issue were certainly of some influence. As a clear example let me quote a statement of Suresh Awasthi, the Secretary General of the National Academy of Music, Dance and Drama (Sangeet Natak Akademi) in New Delhi. Dr Awasthi puts the issue of Grotowski's connections with classical Indian theatre in the context of the twentieth-century reception of Oriental theatre in the West:

> Most interesting in our theatre today is its close relations between the East and the West. Although these traditions are so different, in recent decades they became close to each other. Mutual impacts and exchanges of experience became an everyday practice. When Western theatre found itself at the dead end of naturalism, it had to seek new means of expression, and during this quest it established contacts with the theatre of the East. Sometimes it seems to me that experiments in Western and Eastern drama and theatre are inspired by these mutual contacts and exchanges.
>
> To illustrate it, I would like to bring in some historical facts. When in 1914 Alexander Tairov, an eminent Russian director, quit naturalism, he set to work on Kālidāsa's *Shakuntalā*, hoping that the Sanskrit theatre of poetry and imagination would show new directions for his ensemble. Also Meyerhold included work on Sanskrit drama in the actor's training. Nowadays, as we know, Grotowski is fascinated with Kathakali theatre and he introduced elements of yoga into actor's training. The French 'prophet of theatre', Artaud, after seeing a theatrical performance from Bali, claimed in the 1930s

[131]   Ibid., pp. 53–54.
[132]   See: *The Grotowski Sourcebook*, especially Donald Richie, 'Asian Theatre and Grotowski', pp. 142–49; I. Wayan Lendra, 'Bali and Grotowski: Some parallels in the training process', pp. 310–25.

[…] that Eastern theatre is a pure theatre while Western theatre is a domain of literature. Seeking a synthesis of these two traditions gave the most magnificent result in the theatrical achievements of Bertolt Brecht and his theory of 'epic theatre'. In fact, more of Brecht's ideas are close to Eastern tradition, especially Indian.[133]

Without engaging in any polemic with its author, I will leave this statement as an expression of a certain attitude.

In *The Land of Ashes and Diamonds*, while mentioning some discussions with Grotowski from 1962 and 1963, Barba explicitly claims: 'Hinduism was our privileged point of encounter. Ramana Maharshi (not to be confused with the guru of Transcendental Meditation) had played an important part in the life of Grotowski, and Ramakrishna in mine.'[134]

In the 1990s, Grotowski publicly confessed that he thought in Hindu categories. Even in the early 1960s – for example while working on *Shakuntalā* in Opole – a comparison of his own work with Indian culture was not strange to him. On 6 February 1965, soon after moving the Laboratory Theatre to Wrocław, Grotowski described the new situation in a letter to Eugenio Barba:

> I have spent the last few weeks thinking back and comparing the past with what needs to be done and built. The transfer of the ashram [Sanskrit term meaning a hermitage, an isolated retreat, which Grotowski sometimes used for his theatre], even without any changes, will in itself produce a different ashram. To continue in the same metaphor: the Opole period is Maharishi in Arunach-

---

[133] 'O teatrze w Indiach, rozmawiał Maria Krzysztof Byrski' [About theatre in India, [Suresh Awasthi] in conversation with Maria Krzysztof Byrski], *Teatr*, 7 (1971), 22. There is comprehensive literature on relations between Oriental and Western theatre in many languages – see, primarily, Leonard Cabell Pronko, *Theater East and West: Perspectives Toward a Total Theater* (Berkeley, Los Angeles and London: University of California Press, 1974); *Teatro Oriente/Occidente*, ed. by Antonella Ottai (Roma: Bulzoni Editore, 1986); Nicola Savarese, *Eurasian Theatre: Drama and Performance Between East and West from Classical Antiquity to the Present*, trans. from Italian by Richard Fowler, updated version revised and ed. by Vicki Ann Cremona (Holstebro, Malta and Wrocław: Icarus Publishing Enterprise, 2010); Elena V. Shakhmatova, *Iskaniya evropeiskoi rezhissury i traditsii Vostoka* [Quest of the European stage direction and the traditions of the East] (Moscow: Editorial URSS, 1997); Svetlana A[ndreevna] Serova, *Teatralnaya kultura serebryannogo veka v Rossii i khudozhestvennye traditsii Vostoka (Kitai, Yaponiya, Indiya)* [Theatrical culture of the Silver Age in Russia and the artistic traditions of the East: China, Japan, India] (Moscow: Institut vostokovedeniya RAN [Institute of Oriental Studies of the Russian Academy of Sciences], 1999).

[134] Barba, *Land of Ashes and Diamonds*, p. 48.

ala's hermitage; Wrocław, on the other hand, will be Aurobindo's ashram in Pondichery (a heritage-institute that lives amid the din of a big city). But perhaps the comparison with an ashram is no longer possible.[135]

It is also significant that during the period when Grotowski was working on the Mountain Project with a team of young collaborators (and with Jacek Zmysłowski as an artistic director), he wished to visit Arunachala. The direct experience of that mountain, the image of which accompanied him since his childhood and was somehow imprinted in his mind, was closely yet subtly connected with a work-process that was so important to him. In this way, as always, art became synonymous with life for Grotowski; he made no distinction between them. As he wrote in April 1988: 'that way which became my life'.[136]

Grotowski probably saw another Kathakali performance at the BITEF 212 Festival in Belgrade. Yet it did not meet his expectations in the domain of the actor's technique. In his letter to Maurice Béjart, dated 17 October 1967, he stated explicitly:

> I received your postcard from Japan, and I think you found new associations and new stimuli there; the phenomenon of Noh theatre has always been extremely attractive to me as well. From my own recent exotic experiences, let me mention my visit to Persia [summer 1967] and also that I had a chance to see Indian Kathakali theatre. Aesthetically, it was a very beautiful show, yet technically speaking, the acting in the Peking opera was on an incomparably higher level.[137]

This is an important confession, for its meaning breaks a stereotypical opinion that Grotowski was almost an uncritical admirer of classical Indian theatre. Rather, it turns out that his opinion was much more complicated. Grotowski did not blindly adore Indian theatre and anything that was Indian. In fact, among classical [Asian] theatres he had an opportunity to see, he valued Japanese Noh and Peking opera decisively higher.

[135] Ibid., p. 140.
[136] From Grotowski's inscription, dated Pontedera, 28 April 1988, in the copy of a brochure titled *Centro di Lavoro di Jerzy Grotowski – Workcenter of Jerzy Grotowski* that he gave to me. See: Zbigniew Osiński, *Jerzy Grotowski. Źródła, inspiracje, konteksty*, II, 5 [photocopy].
[137] Jerzy Grotowski, letter to Maurice Béjart, 17 October 1967, Folder 445, 'Occasional greetings, courtesy correspondence, 1965–1969', Grotowski Institute Archive, Wrocław, Poland.

Also, the quite common conviction that Grotowski's productions were distinctly influenced by the aesthetics of one of the classical Oriental theatres proves to be inaccurate. What was really important to him was the actor's technique and, primarily, the actor's attitude towards his work understood as a profession and a vocation at the same time.

The belief in a deep connection between Grotowski's theatrical practice and classical Indian theatre was – and, apparently, still is – so firmly established that still in the late 1980s Stanisław Tokarski would argue with me when I associated Grotowski's ideas with Jiddu Krishnamurti (1895–1986) and Sri Ramana Maharshi (1879–1950) rather than with the practices of Rabindranath Tagore in the school theatre of Shantiniketan. In his book *Orient i kontrkultury* [The Orient and counter-cultures] Tokarski justifies his opinions in the following way:

> If we carefully analyze the relation between Grotowski's artistic work and his self-realization practices, passing over the voices of critics who claim that its core was inspired by Krishnamurti or Maharshi, we will see that the two mentioned Eastern sages had little knowledge of theatre, while Tagore was a leader of a theatre collective that was an object of fascination for Osterwa – a pioneer of the theatre-collective movement in Poland placed in the same tradition as Grotowski.[138] It seems logical, then, to associate the attempts at reviving archaic myth as a means to recover the lost centre in contemporary culture with Grotowski's practices involving rites of uniting with a tree. Both techniques have connections with the ashram – the first one is the idea of Eliade, who was deeply impressed by the works of Tagore, while the other was known to every disciple of Tagore. For they took their natural science classes and poetry classes, sitting on trees.[139]

Tokarski's speculation seems logical indeed. It is a fact that Osterwa read an article by Michał Friedländer about the Shantiniketan school.[140] It was probably the only source of information

[138] Juliusz Osterwa (1885–1947), one of the most eminent Polish actors and directors. In 1919, together with Mieczysław Limanowski (1876–1948), he established the first Polish theatre laboratory, Reduta, active until 1939. In the early 1960s Grotowski adopted the Reduta emblem for the Laboratory Theatre.
[139] Stanisław Tokarski, *Orient i kontrkultury* [The Orient and countercultures] (Warsaw: Wiedza Powszechna, 1984), pp. 128–29. See: Tokarski, *Jogini i wspólnoty. Nowoczesna recepcja hinduizmu* [Yogis and communities: Contemporary reception of Hinduism] (Wrocław, Warsaw, Kraków, Gdańsk and Łódź: Zakład Narodowy im. Ossolińskich, 1987), p. 194.
[140] Michał Friedländer, 'Szkoła Rabindranatha Tagorego w Szantiniketan' [The

on that subject available in Polish before the Second World War. One could say that it was natural that the Tagore school interested Osterwa, who could discover there deeper analogies between the Shantiniketan school and his own attempts to form a man by means of theatre arts. In a letter written during the [Nazi] occupation to Eugeniusz Świerczewski (1894–1944), one of his close collaborators, a secretary of Reduta and a lecturer of theatre history at the Reduta Institute, Osterwa included detailed instructions on how to prepare to write the true story of Reduta. Osterwa noted that 'there would be no harm in also learning about the school of Rabindranath Tagore, which bears some resemblance to the Pythagorean school, although it is "contemporary" to us'.[141]

That is where the trace ends. The rest can be only the result of various speculations and hypotheses. However, it seems quite improbable that Osterwa, and Grotowski as his follower, were seeking in Tagore's work knowledge of how to shape their own theatres.

In Grotowski's case, another problem is that he never visited the famous 'forest school' in Shantiniketan, and never referred to it or to its founder. After all, unlike Osterwa, Grotowski spent some time in the vicinity of Shantiniketan and, undoubtedly, if he had felt a need to visit it, he would have done so.

4.

THE BAULS, THEATRE OF SOURCES, AND SOME LATER TRACES

IT IS KNOWN that during his first stay on the Indian subcontinent, Grotowski met a female guru from Auroville – the famous Mother, Mirra Richard (1878–1973). In Bengal, he was interested mainly in Bauls, who usually lived alone, without an ashram around them. We actually know nothing about Grotowski's first encounter with them. Yet traces of his collaboration with Bauls turned out to be lasting.

During his journey to India with the Theatre of Sources team, Grotowski met Abani Biswas, who began his artistic career as

School of Rabindranath Tagore in Shantiniketan], *Ruch Pedagogiczny*, 3 (1926), 80–82.

[141] Juliusz Osterwa, letter to Eugeniusz Świerczewski, [Kraków?], c. 13 May 1941), in *Listy Juliusza Osterwy* [Letters to Juliusz Osterwa], with an introduction by Jerzy Zawieyski (Warsaw: Państwowy Instytut Wydawniczy, 1968), p. 252.

a teenage boy involved in political theatre in Calcutta. Biswas took part in the workshops, and in 1980 Grotowski invited him to Poland to work with the international team based in Brzezinka and Oleśnica near Wrocław. Biswas participated in various Theatre of Sources events including one in Kolonia, a village near Szczytno in September 1981.[142] He remained in Poland during martial law (1981–1983) and returned to India in 1983. Currently, he is director of Milón Méla, an Indian theatre, which during the last ten years has often visited Poland. Milón Méla operates as a part of Theatre House, an international centre for research and teaching in the performing arts, founded in 1990 and situated in a natural environment just a few kilometres from Visva-Bharati University of Rabindranath Tagore in Shantiniketan. When asked about the character and significance of his work with Grotowski, Biswas answered:

> Grotowski wanted to create the Theatre of Sources at the time [...]. He gathered people from all over the world: Haitians practising Vodou, actors of Japanese Noh theatre, Bauls from West Bengal, and so on. We learned from each other. The most important was 'silence and observation', quite strange in theatre, yet still so absorbing, so contagious that when I returned to India in 1983 after four years in Poland, I did not want to do anything else. I began to seek appropriate people in all Indian provinces. And I found them: in Bihar, in Bengal, in Kerala. And in 1990, in Bengal, we established the Theatre House. Grotowski's rule of 'silence and observation' is also employed in our Centre. Various people seeking initiation come to us. They learn techniques of dancing, acting, and singing. The objective of the workshops led by masters of particular domains is an attempt to find contact with the source of individual creative potential hidden in every human being.[143]

In another interview, Biswas adds:

> Grotowski explained to me how important our own Indian tradition was to us. He opened my eyes to the Indian past. Thanks to Grotowski I also understood the importance of silence. When I came to Poland for the first time, he sent me to the forest so that I could find there, in silence, concentration before leading my workshop.

[142] Tadeusz Szyłłejko, 'Mazurski ślad. Po śmierci Jerzego Grotowskiego, wielkiego Mistrza teatru XX wieku' [The Masurian trace: After the death of Jerzy Grotowski, the great Master of twentieth-century theatre], *Gazeta Warmii i Mazur* [local (Olsztyn) supplement of *Gazeta Wyborcza*], 18 January 1999.
[143] Rina Burzyk-Krempeć, 'Z tysiąca i jednej nocy' [From one thousand and one nights], *Gazeta Olsztyńska*, 19–21 June 1998.

In India, we have a special theatrical centre, also located in the forest. We spend there six months of the year meditating, observing nature, and training. Then for six months we give shows all over the world. [...]

We collaborate with masters in many fields of Indian tradition. We want our theatre to impact people's lives, to be a part of their everyday life. That is why we organize theatrical workshops, shows, parades, exhibitions, and lectures. We conduct research on the history of Indian theatre. The main centre of our activity is located in West Bengal, yet we have branches in Italy, France, Austria, and Switzerland. And more and more often we visit Poland.[144]

About the performance prepared by his group, Biswas stated:

Our show combines various forms: dance, singing, martial arts, and religious ritual. Part of the script is based on the tales of Indian storytellers called 'patua'. My group consists of Chhau dancers, holy Bauls and masters of the martial art of kalarippayattu[145]. The Chhau dancers perform an ancient tribal dance. They wear masks symbolizing demons, gods, and goddesses. In ancient times, the dancers were famous warriors. Bauls are our holy men, playing religious music on such instruments as ektara, kol, dotara, and dupki. Bauls do not have to play in temples. Each place where they play and where people gather around them becomes a temple. The third element of the performance is a presentation of the oldest Indian martial art. The intention of it is not to kill an opponent but to disarm him.[146]

[144]   'Kol, dotara i dupki. Rozmowa z Abanim Biswasem, reżyserem indyjskiego teatru Milón Méla, wywiad przeprowadził Stanisław Łupak' [Kol, dotara and dupki: Abani Biswas, a director at the Indian theatre Milón Méla, interviewed by Stanisław Łupak], *Gazeta Morska*, local (Gdańsk) supplement of *Gazeta Wyborcza*, 11 July 2000. See: Anna Czekanowska, *Kultury muzyczne Azji* [Musical Cultures of Asia] (Kraków: Polskie Wydawnictwo Muzyczne, 1981), 154–56: 'Kultura muzyczna Indii. Instrumenty' [Musical culture of India: Instruments]; Czekanowska, *Kultury tradycyjne wobec współczesności. Muzyka, poezja, taniec* [Traditional cultures and the present: Music, poetry, dance] (Warsaw: Trio, Collegium Civitas, 2008).
[145]   Also known as kalaripayatt. Tokarski, *Sztuki walki. Ruchowe formy ekspresji filozofii Wschodu* [Martial arts: Motional forms of expression of the philosophies of the East] (Szczecin: Glob, 1989); Ziółkowski, 'Tafla lustra. Myśli o sztukach walki i teatrze' [Mirror surface: Reflections on martial arts and theatre], *Didaskalia. Gazeta Teatralna*, 36 (2000), 82–86.
[146]   'Kol, dotara i dupki'.

5.
RAMANA MAHARSHI AS DEPICTED
BY GROTOWSKI

JUST AFTER GROTOWSKI'S death, Jairo Cuesta told his own version
of the remembered tale of an apple tree in Nienadówka, and its
secret relation to the '*yurodivy*' from Mount Arunachala.[147] Cuesta,
a Columbian of Amerindian descent, was one of Grotowski's closest
collaborators from the period of the Theatre of Sources, and then of
Objective Drama. Their first meeting, which resulted in Grotowski's
proposal 'to start collaborating', took place in 1976, perhaps in the
spring, in Paris. According to Cuesta, it happened as follows:

> During my first conversation with Grotowski, he told me to look
> into the past. He tried to awake in me a connection with life. It
> was not about gathering some truths, nor solving my problems with
> identity, but about discovering life, or, more precisely, about enter-
> ing into contact with it.
>
> I told him about my dances around Piedra de Enrerrios, about
> my 'ritual' dances in ice-cold waters east of Antioch, and about
> other activities related to water in the swimming pool in the house
> where I spent my childhood. These stories turned out to be similar
> to stories from his childhood.
>
> In turn, he told me how he had lived among peasants in a cer-
> tain Polish village. There was an apple tree of a peculiar shape
> there. He told me that the tree had attracted him. He would climb
> it possessed with almost irrational temptation to behave as a priest
> of that apple tree; he would act as if conducting masses in front of
> the tree, he told me. [...]
>
> When Grotowski was still young, his mother gave him a book
> that became very important to him: *A Search in Secret India* by
> Brunton. In his book, Brunton describes his voyages through India
> following the traces of the tales he would hear at train stations, or
> in small towns – tales about colourful figures living in complete
> solitude, or about masters of some monasteries.
>
> Brunton tells in his book about a man who lived on the slopes of
> Mount Arunachala. To describe that man, Grotowski used a Russian
> word, '*yurodivy*'; it could be translated as 'a holy madman'.
>
> Grotowski repeated the words of the man from the mountain:
> 'If you work upon the question 'Who am I?', that question will send
> you to some other important place and your limited "I" will disap-
> pear, and you will find "something different", "something real".'

---

[147] Grotowski, 'Teatr Źródeł', pp. 103–04.

The '*yurodivy*' was visited by other '*yurodivye*', and reading the book about so many holy madmen calmed Grotowski down, for it turned out that he was not the only one who conducted strange rituals for trees.[148] His desire to meet some holy madmen increased and he sought opportunities for such encounters for many years, yet always in his own way. Only in 1977 did the Laboratory Theatre and private foundations give him a chance to organize a project he named 'Theatre of Sources', in which 'theatre' was understood as a stage or a place for events. It was also a chance to meet '*yurodivye*' or their disciples openly and publicly.[149]

Grotowski dedicated his last lecture as a professor at the Collège de France (delivered on 26 January 1998) to Ramana Maharshi. He said, among other things: 'It is not a doctrine, but rather instructs people what to do on the inner path to verticality.'[150] And then:

> Eventually, everything is reduced to a pragmatic aspect. It is not ideas that decide; it is practice that decides. In culture, in fine arts; in publicly discussed topics, as well as in issues of inner life (I prefer to speak about verticality) – these are all practical issues. Words can change, doctrines can be expressed in another way – it does not matter; what matters in all domains is: how to do. I spoke here about a certain personal adventure, yet it is the same in all domains: not ideas but doing decides. What I told you is a certain personal myth, and by no means an 'objective position'.[151]

It must be noted that, of nine of Grotowski's lectures at the Collège de France, only *two* – the final one, concerning Ramana Maharshi, and the inaugural one in Théâtre des Bouffes du Nord on 24 March 1997 – were followed by discussion with the audience,

---

[148] Plural for *yurodivy*.

[149] Jairo Cuesta, 'W drodze z Grotowskim' [On the road with Grotowski], trans. from Spanish to Polish by Katarzyna Kacprzak, *Pamiętnik Teatralny*, 1–2 (2001), 233, 235–36.

[150] Excerpts from Jerzy Grotowski's lecture transcribed from audiotapes issued by Collège de France (Cours du 26 janvier 1998) and trans. from French by Zbigniew Osiński. See: Osiński, 'Tradycja i pamięć w wykładach Grotowskiego w Collège de France' [Tradition and memory in Grotowski's lectures at Collège de France], in Osiński, *Jerzy Grotowski. Źródła, inspiracje, konteksty*, II, 382.

[151] Ibid., p. 382. See: Agnieszka Kumor, 'Grotowski w Collège de France' [Grotowski at Collège de France], *Teatr*, 1–3 (2000), 77–9; Osiński, 'Utopia praktykowana. Na przykładzie wypowiedzi Grotowskiego: "Święto" i "Przedsięwzięcie Góra. Project: the Mountain of Flame"' [The practised utopia, exemplified by Grotowski's statements 'Holiday' and 'Project: the Mountain of Flame'], in Osiński, *Grotowski wytycza trasy*, pp. 235–78.

which lasted only a few minutes.[152] In a moving article written after Grotowski's death, Ludwik Flaszen referred to the Collège de
France lectures, giving them the following conclusion:

> A strange assistant professor at Kraków's drama school, carrying
> a worn-out, black briefcase – the man that I met forty years ago with
> the news that we could take over a little theatre in the small town
> of Opole – arrived at the professorship of the Parisian Collège de
> France. And before he began his inaugural lecture, he burrowed for
> a long time in an old black briefcase, seemingly the same one that
> he used to carry around in the Kraków of his youth.
>
> That peculiar man – who used to deliver odd (as for that time)
> lectures on yoga and Hindu philosophy in the Student Club Pod
> Jaszczurami, and who for a long time was considered a mediocre
> director and a swindler by our local theatrical 'Olympus' (with some
> exceptions!) – lived an artistic life that marked significant dates in
> the history of theatre. His death will also become a meaningful date.
>
> His ashes – as a young boy in the village of Nienadówka near
> Rzeszów he read a book about sages of India – are to be scattered
> on Mount Arunachala, near the abode of Ramana Maharishi, a sage
> to whom he was faithful for his entire life.[153]

Grotowski's relation with Ramana Maharshi allows us to grasp
his entire attitude towards life: to see the general in the particular,
and, the other way around, to see the particular in the general. For
Grotowski, cultural barriers did not, in fact, exist.

---

[152] Osiński, 'Grotowski w Collège de France. Lekcja pierwsza, 24 marca 1997'
[Grotowski in Collège de France. The First Lesson, 24 March 1997], in Osiński,
Jerzy Grotowski. Źródła, inspiracje, konteksty, I, 227–44.
[153] Flaszen, 'Po śmierci Jerzego Grotowskiego. Świat żegna proroka' [After
Jerzy Grotowski's death: The world bids the prophet farewell], *Gazeta Wybor-
cza*, 18 January 1999, p. 12.

v.

China

1.
SUMMER 1962:
SOJOURN IN THE PEOPLE'S REPUBLIC OF CHINA
AND ITS SIGNIFICANCE

GROTOWSKI VISITED THE People's Republic of China between 15 August and 15 September 1962 as a delegate of the Team for Theatre Issues [Zespół do Spraw Teatru] of the Ministry of Culture and Art. Jerzy Falkowski[154] reported on the character of that visit as follows: 'In China, the director of the Opole experimental stage is going to establish close artistic contacts with representatives of contemporary Chinese theatre [...] and he is going to study the style, form, and tradition of that theatre.'[155]

Grotowski was probably quite well prepared on the subject before his journey to the People's Republic of China, because during his studies in acting, and later, in directing, Chinese groups performed in Poland almost every year, also showing classical Chinese operas.

He went there on his own request, as an official delegate – an assignment that he applied for with no real competition, since his professional colleagues (actors, directors, stage designers, artistic directors) were at that time mainly interested in voyages to Western Europe and to the US. Grotowski once told me that his visit to China took place because there was a vacancy within the official exchange between Polish and Chinese ministries of culture.

He flew Polish Airlines from Warsaw to Beijing on 11 August 1962.[156] According to Barba, 'Grotowski had been to China in August 1962 for three weeks and had come back with many impressions and a great deal of information.'[157] Jerzy Falkowski, relying on

---

154 Jerzy Falkowski (1930–1971), an activist of the Revolutionary Union of Youth [Rewolucyjny Związek Młodzieży] from the October '56 period; theatre critic, publicist, friend of Jerzy Grotowski and the ensemble of the Laboratory Theatre in Opole.

155 J[erzy] F[alkowski], 'Opolski eksperyment na światowym forum' [The Opole experiment on the world forum], *Trybuna Opolska*, 2 August 1962, p. 3.

156 It was the day of his twenty-ninth birthday. In my books *Grotowski i jego Laboratorium*, p. 105, and *Teatr '13 Rzędów' i Teatr Laboratorium '13 Rzędów' Opole 1959–1964. Kronika – bibliografia* [The Theatre of 13 Rows and the Laboratory Theatre of 13 Rows, Opole 1959–1964. Chronicle – bibliography] (Opole: Wydawnictwo Uniwersytetu Opolskiego 1997), p. 97, I gave the wrong date of his departure: 15 August 1962.

157 Barba, *Land of Ashes and Diamonds*, p. 53.

information certainly from Grotowski himself, claims that the visit took an entire month.[158] A recently found photograph, taken at the performance of *Forefathers' Eve*, based on Adam Mickiewicz and staged by the Laboratory Theatre in Opole, has the following hand-written dedication on its reverse: 'Beijing, 10 September [19]62. For the director Sun Weishi, in remembrance of the concrete craft-oriented conversation. Jerzy Grotowski. Opole, Rynek 4, Theatre Laboratory of 13 Rows.'[159] This inscription seems to settle the discrepancy in favour of Falkowski. In any case, the first rehearsal with Grotowski took place in Opole on 19 September, as indicated in a diary of Rena Mirecka, an actress of the Laboratory Theatre, who on that day wrote: 'Beginning of the season 1962/1963. The first plastique exercises.' It is worth recalling an earlier letter written by Grotowski to the members of the Theatre Laboratory of 13 Rows. Before his trips, first to the 8th World Festival of Students and Youth in Helsinki (between 29 July and 6 August 1962),[160] and, then, to the People's Republic of China, he left the following disposition, dated 21 July:

> In case of some breakdown and resulting delay of my return (after 16 September), I transfer the duties of artistic director to colleague Flaszen, and studio work management to colleague Mirecka.
>
> In case colleague Flaszen is absent, I transfer the duties of artistic director to colleague Mirecka.
>
> While awaiting my return, the ensemble is obliged to practise intensive studio-training (minimum 6 hours daily, including Sundays, except for holidays): plastiques (Mirecka), rhythm (Cynkutis), enunciation (Molik), etudes (Barba).
>
> Besides that, colleague Barba or colleague Mirecka are obliged to organize a rehearsal (1–2) to run the lines for *Akropolis*.
>
> After 16 September, colleague Komorowska is obliged to begin collaboration with colleague Czajkowska (gradually taking over her function).
>
> I would like to draw [your] attention to the neatness and cleanliness, etc. of theatre spaces.[161]

---

[158] J[erzy] F[alkowski], 'Opolski eksperyment na światowym forum', p. 3.

[159] In May 2005 Zygmunt Molik donated the photograph to the Archive of the Grotowski Centre in Wrocław. I was informed about it by Bruno Chojak, who passed me a photocopy of the photograph. I do not know why Grotowski brought the photograph back to Opole.

[160] Osiński, *Grotowski and His Laboratory*, p. 65.

[161] Rena Mirecka, 'Z notatników, 1959–1964' [From the Notebooks, 1959–1964], sel. and ed. by Zbigniew Osiński, in *Podróż. Rena Mirecka – aktorka Teatru Laboratorium* [The journey. Rena Mirecka: An actress of the Labora-

• *Jerzy Grotowski in Hangzhou, China, 1962*

• *Jerzy Grotowski and the instructors of the Shanghai School of Traditional Peking Opera, 1962*

It is known that Grotowski visited drama schools and theatres in Beijing and Shanghai at that time. Thanks to his 'Chinese Diary' we know the precise dates of his stay in China.

In Wrocław, there is also a copy of a book he brought from China, titled *Chuan ju dan jiao biao yan yi shu*,[162] which could be translated as 'The art of performing female "dan" roles in Sichuan opera', with an introduction by Mei Lanfang, 'My artistic experiences'. The book was edited by Yang Youhe, and published in 1960 by the Chinese Institute of Theatrology in Beijing. The copy includes handwritten notes by Grotowski, mostly beneath photographs of actors; they are without exception technical remarks.

I should point out that Grotowski went to China during the period of advanced rehearsals for *Akropolis*, based on the play by Stanisław Wyspiański. However it would be useless to seek direct connections between this production and what he experienced in the People's Republic of China. That impact was much deeper and subtler: it was about the approach of the director and the actor to their work. There is no doubt that none of Grotowski's previous productions was prepared with such precision and with such mastery in carving each detail with the actor's body and voice as *Akropolis*. In my opinion, it was due to a lesson he learned during his encounters with Chinese actors and their teachers, that he then applied to his own work in the final phase of rehearsals for *Akropolis*. The conclusions drawn from that lesson were permanent, even though the theatrical aesthetics were fundamentally different. It is possible that Grotowski had already aspired to similar precision, and among Chinese actors he found confirmation. He found it in craft, which was always a decisive argument to him.

Over thirty years later, Grotowski told me that – in accordance with the procedure applied to official trips – he gave a detailed report of his visit to China, in which, among other things, he pointed out symptoms of what would soon take place on a large scale as the Cultural Revolution. I searched for that report in the Ministry of

---

tory Theatre], ed. by Zbigniew Jędrychowski, Zbigniew Osiński, and Grzegorz Ziółkowski (Wrocław: Ośrodek Badań Twórczości Jerzego Grotowskiego i Poszukiwań Teatralno-Kulturowych, 2005), p. 45. Editor's note: The term 'colleague' used before the last name is a formal way of communicating, somewhat similar to 'Mr', but more egalitarian and politically correct in communist Poland (in Polish, 'mister' (*pan*) means 'master').

[162] Yang Yoyhe, ed., *Chuan ju dan jiao biao yan yi shu*, with an introduction by Mei Lanfang (Beijing: Zhongguo xi ju chu ban she, 1960). A copy is available in the Grotowski Institute Archive and Reading Room in Wrocław.

Culture and Art archives, and in the Central Archives of Modern Records, where old documents of the International Relations Office of the Ministry of Culture and Art were deposited. No results.

Fortunately, Maciej Prus, who at that time resigned from his engagement at Kraków's Stary Teatr to begin collaboration with the Theatre Laboratory of 13 Rows, remembers this period very well. During an interview with Agnieszka Wójtowicz in February 1997, he said:

> When I came to the first rehearsals of *Akropolis*, Grotowski had just returned from his trip to China. […] I came to take a position at the theatre just before the summer vacation. I stayed in Ryszard Cieślak's attic. (We had known each other from the [drama] school, although I studied in the Acting Department and he in Puppetry. Rysiek was just about to go to a rehearsal for *Akropolis* and he had no idea about one scene. 'What else can be done in a [concentration] camp?' I remembered my distant cousin who had been in a camp; she could not stand it anymore, she gave up and decided to 'throw herself on the wires' [high-voltage wire fence]. Fortunately, the camp was liberated the very same day. I told him: 'throw yourself on the wires.' There was no such episode in the performance yet. I suggested to Rysiek a behaviour in a camp. I remember what *Akropolis* was to look like in the beginning: characters locked in a concentration camp – symbols of the twentieth century, created by artists; surely there was supposed to be Chaplin's tramp among them, perhaps Gelsomina too. Then it all evolved, thus the Bible, [ancient] Greece, and the camp. I returned to work after the vacation and it turned out that they fired Ewa Lubowiecka, and I took over her role. I played the Maid, Clio, and Helen, replacing Ewa. In *Akropolis*, I actually entered a ready production. […] I had to enter the role immediately. It was Ewa who took part in rehearsals. I just entered the production instead of her. For that matter, Grotowski, already during my first rehearsal, created a theory, in which he referenced his journey to China. He told us about the incredible skills of Chinese actors who at the age of sixty or seventy could perform sixteen-year-old girls. I do not remember the name of that most famous Chinese actor whom Grotowski had a chance to see in China, though I even have his picture somewhere at home.[163] I was sitting next to Rysiek and I had the feeling

[163] The picture mentioned by Maciej Prus is a photograph of Mei Lanfang. Grotowski visited China one year after Lanfang's death. He probably saw pictures of and books about Lanfang; he could watch documentaries and features that included Lanfang, and certainly heard stories about Lanfang told by the Chinese, yet he could not see Lanfang on stage. Maciej Prus told me in one of our telephone conversations of 12 and 18 January 2005 that during the sum-

that the [Grotowski's] speech was directed to me. And it turned out that I was given the role after Ewa Lubowiecka. I replaced her instantly. I cannot remember if my rehearsals lasted one week or one-and-a-half. I came to Opole in September, the premiere was on 10 October 1962, and I performed; thus my conclusion that I had to instantly enter the finished production.[164]

The above quotation needs some commentary. Maciej Prus, born in 1937, graduated from Kraków's State Drama School in 1961. In the 1961/1962 season, he was employed at Kraków's Stary Teatr, managed by Władysław Krzemiński. On 30 May 1962, he signed a contract with the Theatre Laboratory of 13 Rows in Opole for the next season. Just after his return to Opole, Grotowski spoke about his experiences in China at the ensemble meeting. In one issue of *Kwartalnik Opolski* [Opole quarterly magazine], there is a note about the meeting with Grotowski organized on 28 September 1962 by the Small Forms Theatre [Teatrzyk Małych Form] of the Regional Community Centre to discuss classical Chinese theatre. Further in the interview, Maciej Prus comments on the relation between some actor exercises in the Laboratory Theatre, primarily vocal (exploring the so-called resonators) and acrobatic, and exercises observed by Grotowski in China. While discussing the issue, Prus adds his unambiguous critical comment:

The Chinese train their voices and resonators from childhood. It is an integral part of their tradition and culture. And we, aged twenty-something, educated in an entirely different culture, suddenly had to command all resonators. The most tragic one was the so-called occipital resonator, which was to give an extremely thin voice, simply a squeak. In the end we all went voiceless. The exercises gave no results; we could not command the resonator, but only tried to do it with our throats and lost our voices. Grotowski did not start with a theory [method]; he had only an intuition of

---

mer holidays of 1962, his friend, actor Maciej Robakiewicz, had given him a photograph of Mei Lanfang, of whom Grotowski told the ensemble in Opole immediately after his arrival from China, at the first *Akropolis* rehearsal after the holidays. Even today Prus is puzzled by this coincidence.

[164] 'I dystans do tego świata nie pozwalał mi tam zostać' [And my distance to this world would not let me stay there], Maciej Prus interviewed by Agnieszka Wójtowicz, *Pamiętnik Teatralny*, 1–2 (2001), 164–65; repr. in Wójtowicz, *Od 'Orfeusza' do 'Studium o Hamlecie'. Teatr 13 Rzędów w Opolu (1959–1964)* [From *Orpheus* to *The Hamlet Study*. The Theatre of 13 Rows in Opole (1959–1964)] (Wrocław: Wydawnictwo Uniwersytetu Wrocławskiego, 2004), pp. 240–41.

something, a need to go beyond a certain threshold. He was run-
ning there blind. What I am talking about is acquiring the tools
an actor should have. His moves were often predatory. Sometimes
I felt that cruelty, and I will never forget the time when we started
really intense gymnastic training. The theatre rented a gym [on
Sempołowska street in Opole]. And although we had no skills instead of warm-ups we would begin with a somersault. And there
was no 'but', there was only 'must'. [...] Grotowski was always
present during opening exercises, supervising us. There was no
way that someone would not want to – or could not – participate
in them. It was out of the question. And we were obediently doing
those somersaults.[165]

During that time, Grotowski himself often talked about the
significance of Chinese inspirations. He did so during two public
meetings I attended on 16 December 1962 in the Student Club
Od Nowa in Poznań and on 15 March 1963 in Opole, when he met
with the editorial board of the *Pamiętnik Teatralny* magazine. He
said then:

We hold two-to-four-hour training sessions every day. There are the
following kinds of exercises: 1) vocal/breathing [exercises], based
mainly on the exercises of Chinese actors. We learn to use five
resonators. We also include here enunciation exercises: actors have
to learn how to close their larynx. 2) Plastiques, based primarily
on Delsarte: centripetal and centrifugal movements. 3) Rhythmical
exercises, simultaneously a lesson in concentration. The rhythmical [exercises] also include aural/auditory composition, involving
an arrangement of movements as notes or aural values. They were
used by Stanislavski. 4) Gymnastic-acrobatic [exercises], inspired
by the training of Chinese actors. 5) Interpretative etudes. It is
a kind of tinkering with one's own body, very rarely practised in
theatre by actors.[166]

Thus, the impact manifested itself mostly in vocal-breathing
and gymnastic-acrobatic exercises. In a conversation with Jerzy
Falkowski (published in Odra, June 1964), when asked what was important in theatre and what would remain in it, Grotowski, answers:

What will remain is an actor. And what an actor can do. I mean actors who know their craft [...]. A performance must be musical, but
it is the actor's acting that must be musical. Great acting is always to

---

165   Prus, 'I dystans do tego świata nie pozwalał mi tam zostać', p. 167.
166   Osiński, 'Zapiski ze spotkań 1962–1963' [Notes from meetings 1962–1963],
Notatnik Teatralny, 20–21 (2000), 110–11.

some degree music and to some degree dance. That is why I see in an actor-master one of the most essential assets of theatre. This postulate may seem utopian against the background of prevalent theatrical practices, for there are very few actor-craftsmen. Not because of a lack of talent, but because of a terrifying lack of... diligence. Let me repeat a truth old enough to sound like a truism: a pianist cannot play concerts if he does not practise fingering exercises everyday; a dancer who does not train daily will not be able to last through a longer performance. Yet, an actor feels eligible to play on stage without a daily several-hour-long training of the voice, enunciation, plasticity of gesture and movement, physical exercises, and etudes, i.e. composition exercises. 'We have rehearsals and performances', theatre people answer. Thus one must exercise outside of rehearsals and performances. 'But when? It would exceed an eight-hour working day!' I would like to see a good pianist following the requirements of an eight-hour working day...

After all, every great and self-respecting actor does this kind of training every day (for example, among the most prominent Polish actors, Jacek Woszczerowicz, not to mention actors in classical Oriental theatre, whose daily diligence and resulting achievements are beyond all of our comprehension).[167]

Here is another of Grotowski's comments from the same conversation:

In our theatre, we attach great importance to actors' training and to the study of the laws of the craft. Besides rehearsals and performances, the actors train every day for two to three hours (doing the exercises I already mentioned). It resembles scientific research a bit. We attempt to discover some objective laws that govern human expression. We find preliminary material in already elaborated systems of acting, such as the methods of Stanislavski, Meyerhold, and Dullin, in the specific systems of training in classical Chinese and Japanese theatres, and in dance drama in India, as well as in the explorations of great European mimes (e.g. Marceau), of practitioners and theorists, of expressiveness, and in psychological studies focused on the mechanism of human reactions (Jung and Pavlov). It can be said without exaggeration that each 'laboratory' premiere is realized through the hard, almost backbreaking labour of the eight-member team of actors.[168]

Also in later texts, such as 'Głos' [Voice] (1969), Grotowski refers to the observations he made during his stay in China:

[167] 'Teatr – godzina niepokoju', p. 57.
[168] Ibid., p. 58.

[…] in Shanghai, I had an opportunity to encounter the scholarly research of Dr Ling. Dr Ling was a professor in the Medical Academy and simultaneously a professor of Peking opera. He was a descendant of a family of classical opera actors, and he himself worked as an actor in his youth, which was the reason for his interest in practical work on voice. Thanks to him, I understood for the first time what a larynx was.[169]

In one of our conversations in Vallicelle, near Pontedera, Grotowski once told me that he had not met Dr Ling personally, only his collaborators and students. Perhaps it is not very important after all. Undoubtedly, however, it is important that 'the Chinese principle' in acting and in working on voice as practised by Dr Ling inspired Grotowski, and through him also Barba, and that it turned out to be useful in their work with actors.

Three months after returning from China, and over two months after the first performances of *Akropolis* in Opole, on 29 December 1962, Grotowski sent the following greetings to Beijing:

With the New Year, I am sending into your hands, Comrade Tung, my best wishes and regards for Comrade Lyu-Yi, Comrade Secretary of the Association of Dramatists, for you personally and for all Comrades whom I had the pleasure to meet during my journey across your beautiful Chinese Land. I think about your country and your unmatched classical theatre with great affection. Gr[otowski].[170]

The quoted text – especially its conclusion – contains more than merely customary pleasantries. Over five years later Grotowski used almost an identical phrasing in the already quoted letter to Béjart. Otherwise, the achievements of Grotowski and his ensemble in the period of 'theatre of productions' validate the hypothesis formulated in 1949 by the noted Polish Sinologist Witold Jabłoński:

The impact of Chinese theatre [and its significance for the West] can come about in a way different than adaptation: by means of the laboratory analysis of particular actors' techniques – not by imitating them, but by transposing them into appropriate situations.[171]

---

[169] Grotowski, 'Głos', in Grotowski, *Teksty z lat 1965–1969*, p. 122.

[170] Jerzy Grotowski, Pekin Tung [Beijing, Tung], 29 December 1962, Folder 444, 'Holiday greetings, etc.', Grotowski Institute Archive (Wrocław), one-page letter typed on white paper, signed at the bottom, with a handwritten insertion at the top (between the date and the body of the text).

[171] Witold Jabłoński, 'Teatr chiński' [Chinese theatre], *Problemy*, 9 (1949), 616.

Grotowski repeatedly referred to his Chinese experiences in his Collège de France lectures. I talk about it in detail in the subchapter on the connections between Grotowski and Mei Lanfang. In it I also discuss Grotowski's opinions on Mei Lanfang, presented in his lectures as well as in 'The Chinese Diary'. Here I will only bring up what Grotowski meant by 'classical Oriental theatre', as he discussed it during his lecture on 2 June 1997 in the Odéon-Théâtre de l'Europe. This issue was one of the key topics of the entire series of lectures:

> We use the term 'classical Oriental theatre'. That is true. Yet we also speak about 'Peking opera'. Then the question immediately arises: is it theatre or opera? Evidently, definitions are extremely relative in different cultures, in various human experiences, in every part of the world. Today, this problem is more understandable, yet twenty or thirty years ago it was extremely complicated. It was really difficult for people to understand it.
>
> Take, for example, the concept of 'classical theatre'. What does it mean, for instance, in France? Classical theatre in France is probably the Comédie-Française, while classical theatre in India or in China means very ancient forms, transmitted from generation to generation and reconstructed, revised, and cultivated by each new generation. It is something extremely complex and, one can say, artificial.
>
> And what is, for example, classical theatre in African cultures? We can say that, indeed, there is such a form in African culture. [...] In Haiti one can say that it is an ethnodrama, or a certain form of a ritual possessing some encoded elements, and its reality is very distant from our theatrical reality.
>
> Thus in the very act of reflecting on the question of what 'classical theatre' is, it can be seen that the boundaries between theatre and ritual become blurred. Even more: let's take an example of Peking opera. Is it opera or theatre? And what is theatre? It is very difficult to answer this question. [...] The point is that one should not limit a genre. A genre, if it is alive, takes various forms. [...] In the greatest theatrical forms, in the greatest productions (masterpieces), the boundaries between particular genres always shift. Always. Take for example *The Tragedy of Carmen* directed by Peter Brook. It was a very alive production. Yet was it an opera or dramatic theatre?[172]

---

[172] The French text was transcribed from an audiotape and translated into Polish by Leszek Demkowicz; the translation was verified by Zbigniew Osiński with the consent of the translator.

The subject of Grotowski's impact on contemporary Chinese theatre, especially on Gao Xingjian, was comprehensively discussed by Izabella Łabędzka in one chapter of her book, *Teatr niepokorny* [Rebellious theatre], published in 2003.[173] She considers Grotowski to be a theatrical artist 'exceptionally close to the Chinese avant-garde', and argues her point as follows:

[...] The perception of Western theatre by the contemporary Chinese avant-garde is fragmentary and selective; it expresses itself in such terms as 'theatricality', 'acting with distance', 'montage', 'total theatre'. The reception of Grotowski's theatre in China in 1980s is a good example of this phenomenon. Taking into consideration the frequency of references to his *Towards a Poor Theatre* in that period, one can even risk a perverse statement that he is a spiritual patron of the Chinese avant-garde. However, he and his work are mainly associated with the idea of poor theatre, with the rejection of complicated theatrical machinery and sophisticated sets, and with the actor located in the main focus and standing face to face with the spectator, and with the directness of their mutual contact.

Grotowski, Meyerhold, Brecht, and Artaud are theatrical artists exceptionally close to the Chinese avant-garde because of 'Oriental motifs' present in their practice, or at least in their theory – and, as a result, they are recognized as artistically 'akin'. [...] All of the reformers of European theatre mentioned above – although their works were interpreted in a biased way – influenced contemporary Chinese theatre as positive catalysts of change. They became a kind of mirror in which the Chinese avant-garde saw itself in a fuller and better way; they pointed out the importance of Far-Eastern theatrical tradition. That peculiar encounter of the East and the West resulted in the emergence of a new and original theatre stretched between avant-garde and tradition, formally and intellectually progressive [...], and at the same time not uprooted from its native ground, from China's past and present; simultaneously global and local, universal and specifically Chinese.[174]

---

[173] Izabella Łabędzka, 'Grotowski i chińskie koncepcje teatru ubogiego' [Grotowski and Chinese concepts of poor theatre], in Łabędzka, *Teatr niepokorny* [Rebellious theatre], series 'Literaturoznawstwo porównawcze' [Comparative literary studies] (Poznań: Wydawnictwo Naukowe UAM, 2003), no. 3, 80–98.

[174] Ibid., pp. 8–9.

2.

MEI LANFANG, THE LEGEND
OF PEKING OPERA

THE LEGENDARY CHINESE actor, Mei Lanfang, was gifted with many talents.[175] He was an eminent pedagogue and theatre activist, an esteemed painter and a writer of texts for Peking opera. However, his world-wide fame and recognition came from his performances of female roles in Peking opera – commonly considered a synthesis of the entire theatrical tradition of China, a symbol of national Chinese theatre, as well as the most popular form of traditional theatre in China.

Particular historical significance is given to Mei Lanfang's American tour in 1930 and his performances in Moscow and Leningrad in spring 1935. Meetings and public presentations of the skills of 'the king of Chinese actors' in the capital of the USSR were immortalized in photographs taken together with Constantin Stanislavski, Vladimir Nemirovich-Danchenko, Vsevolod Meyerhold, Sergei Eisenstein, Erwin Piscator, and Alexander Tairov, and in important articles written by Meyerhold,[176]

---

[175] *Enciclopedia dello spettacolo* [Encyclopedia of Performing Arts], s.v. 'Mei Lan-Fang', 11 vols (Rome: Fondata da Silvio d'Amico, Casa Editrice le Maschere, 1960), VII, p. 366; I[rina] V[ladimirovna] G[aina], *Teatralnaya Entsiklopediya* [Theatrical Encyclopedia], s.v. 'Mei Lan-fan (23 X 1894 – 8 VIII 1961) (Mei Lanfang (b. 23 October 1894, d. 8 August 1961)' (Moscow: Izdatelstvo Sovetskaya Entsiklopediya, 1964), III, 1022–23; Dana Kalvodová, *Čínské divadlo* [Chinese Theatre] (Prague: Panorama, 1992), pp. 193–99, 277–78; Savarese, *Eurasian Theatre*, pp. 453–62; *Mei Lanfang. Mistrz opery pekińskiej* [Mei Lanfang: A Master of Peking Opera], ed. by Ewa Guderian-Czaplińska, Grzegorz Ziółkowski (Wrocław: Ośrodek Badań Twórczości Jerzego Grotowskiego i Poszukiwań Teatralno-Kulturowych, 2005).

[176] Vsevolod Meyerhold, 'O gastrolyakh Mei Lan-fana. Vystuplenie v VOKS-ie 14 aprelya 1935 goda' [On Mei Lanfang's tour. The speech in the VOKS on 14 April, 1935], in *Tvorcheskie nasledie V[sevoloda] E[milyevicha] Meierkholda* [Creative legacy of V[sevolod] E[milevich] Meyerhold] (Moscow: Vserossiiskoe Teatralnoe Obshchestvo, 1978), pp. 95–97, 120–21; 'O występach gościnnych Mei Lanfanga w Moskwie. Wystąpienie w WOKS-ie 14 kwietnia 1935 roku', in *Mei Lanfang. Mistrz opery pekińskiej*, Polish translation by Katarzyna Osińska, pp. 167–71; Shakhmatova, 'Traditsii vostochnogo teatra v estetike i teatralnoi praktike Vs. Meierkholda' [Traditions of Eastern theatre in the aesthetics and theatre practice of Vs[evolod] Meyerhold], in Shakhmatova, *Iskaniya evropeiskoi rezhissury i traditsii Vostoka*, pp. 91–109; Serova, 'Meierkhold i khudozhestvennye traditsii Kitaya i Yaponii' [Meyerhold and artistic traditions of China and Japan], in Serova, *Teatralnaya kultura serebryannogo veka v Rossii i khudozhestvennye traditsii Vostoka*, pp. 83–158.

Eisenstein,[177] and Brecht.[178] Together with Edward Gordon Craig, Mei Lanfang saw the famous production of *Princess Turandot*, directed by Yevgeny Vakhtangov and performed in the Vakhtangov Theatre (the premiere took place on 27 February 1922, in the MAT Third Studio).

Soon after Mei Lanfang's tour, the book *Mei Lan-fan i kitaisky teatr* [Mei Lanfang and Chinese Theatre] was published in Russia.[179] It was a testimony of admiration and highest respect from Russian cultural circles for the artist. Although Mei Lanfang visited the USSR two more times, in 1952 and 1957, it was his first tour that turned out to be the most important.[180]

Mei Lanfang came to Poland once, travelling by train from Moscow to Western Europe. His less than three-day stay in Warsaw – from 21 to 23 April 1935, which overlapped with Easter – was unknown to Polish historians of theatre for sixty-two years. It seems odd because his visit was well noted by the press. Many journals, including the most widely read *Ilustrowany Kurier Codzienny*, the popular *I.K.C.*, published more or less detailed notes; there were even some more comprehensive articles (also in the local press) and three interviews. The number of interviews and articles may be greater, for the Polish press of that period amounted to hundreds

---

[177] Sergei Mikhailovich Eisenstein, 'Mei Lan-fan' [Mei Lanfang], *Komsomolskaya Pravda*, 11 March 1935; Eisenstein, 'Charodeyu grushevogo sada' ['To the Magician of the Pear Orchard'], in *Mei Lan-fan i kitaisky teatr. K gastrolyam v SSSR* [Mei Lanfang and Chinese theatre: Towards the USSR tour] (Moscow and Leningrad: Izdanie Vsesoyuznogo Obshchestva Kulturnoi Svyazi, 1935), pp. 17–26; a later version of the text, revised and extended by the author in 1939, in Eisenstein, *Iizbrannye proizvedeniya v shesti tomakh* [Selected works in six volumes], 6 vols (Moscow: Iskusstvo, 1964–1971), V; Polish translations: 'Czarodziejowi z sadu grusz', trans. by Tadeusz Szczepański, *Dialog*, 10 (1979), 108–16; 'Czarodziejowi z Sadu Grusz', trans. from English by Ewa Guderian-Czaplińska, in *Mei Lanfang. Mistrz opery pekińskiej*, pp. 151–65.

[178] Bertolt Brecht, letter to Helene Weigel, 'I saw a Chinese actor Mei Lanfang with his ensemble. He plays roles of young girls and he is really great', in Roman Szydłowski, *Brecht. Opowieść biograficzna* [Brecht: A biographical tale] (Warsaw: Ludowa Spółdzielnia Wydawnicza, 1986), p. 258. Influenced by the performance of Mei Lanfang in Moscow, Bertolt Brecht wrote his 1936 text 'Bemerkungen über die chinesische Schauspielkunst' [Remarks on Chinese Art of Acting], in Brecht, *Schriften zum Theater* [Writings on Theatre] (Berlin and Frankfurt 1957), pp. 77–89, used later in his essay 'Verfremdungseffekt in der chinesischen Schauspielkunst' [Distancing/alienation effect in the Chinese art of acting], completed probably in 1937.

[179] *Mei Lan-fan i kitaisky teatr*, p. 37.

[180] I[rina] V[ladimirovna] G[aina], 'Mei Lan-fan (23 X 1894 – 8 VIII 1961)', p. 1023.

• *Constantin Stanislavski and Mei Lanfang, Moscow, 1935*

• *Mei Lanfang and Vsevolod Meyerhold, Moscow, 1935*

of titles (including many ephemeral ones) and one cannot be completely sure if one has uncovered all of the sources.

Mei Lanfang was born on 22 October 1894. He lost his parents early, yet he was commanded to become an actor in accordance with family tradition. His paternal uncle, Mei Yutian, a well-known theatrical musician, took responsibility for the boy's education. At the age of eight, Mei Lanfang began to learn acting, and at eleven he performed on stage for the first time. He received his earliest training from one of his relatives who gathered several boys at his place to introduce them to the technique of acting. Mei Lanfang proved to be such a talented and diligent pupil that, when he completed his education, he could almost instantly begin to play in theatrical productions. However, to expand his skills he entered the famous school for actors of classical theatre, Xiliancheng [later called Fuliancheng], known for extremely strict discipline.[181] In his memoirs, published in 1961 in Beijing and titled *Wutai shenghuo sishi nian* [Forty years on the stage], Mei Lanfang tells how at seventeen he started his systematic observations of the aerobatics of pigeons in order to train his eyes, 'the most alive part of a face'. As a child he was physically weak, and sometimes his eyes would extensively tear up. Yet he knew well that an expressive glance is absolutely essential for an actor to create a really alive character.

At fourteen, he had an acting debut in the full sense of the word, and he joined the famous Peking opera company, Xiliancheng. In 1913, 1914 and 1916, he went to Shanghai for guest performances that were very successful and made him a star.[182] When he was nineteen years old, he received his nickname, 'the king of actors', and by 1924 he was considered the most popular actor in China.

His popularity in America during his tour in the first months of 1930 can be proven by the enthusiastic opinions of eminent representatives of the local artistic milieux, press and radio reviews, honorary doctorates granted by universities in Chicago and Washington, and an invitation to the White House. An exceptionally big part of the audience at his performances consisted of representatives of the diplomatic world. The tour included San Francisco, Los Angeles, Hollywood, San Diego, Chicago, New York, Seattle, and Washington, where Mei Lanfang was greeted by city

---

[181]   Editor's note: Fuliancheng, originally named Xiliancheng School, was founded in Beijing in 1903.

[182]   Kalvodová, *Čínské divadlo*, pp. 193–99, 277–78; Jacques Pimpaneau, *Promenade au Jardin des Poiriers. L'opéra chinois classique* [A walk in the pear orchard: The classic Chinese opera] (Paris: Musée Kwok On, 1983), pp. 135–36.

• *Mei Lanfang at the Main Station in Warsaw, 1935*

mayors and appeared in photographs with great movie stars, such as Mary Pickford, David Belasco, Charlie Chaplin, and Douglas Fairbanks. I must add, however, that already prior to the American tour, noted representatives of modern dance, Ruth Saint-Denis and Ted Shawn, as well as the well-known English writer William Somerset Maugham, had expressed their highest admiration for Mei Lanfang. These facts were noticed by the Polish press of the time.[183]

The visit to Soviet Russia mentioned above was also triumphant. The Welcoming Committee established for the purpose of Mei Lanfang's visit by the Union of Soviet Societies for Friendship and Cultural Relations with Foreign Countries (VOKS) included, among others: Stanislavski, Nemirovich-Danchenko, Meyerhold, Tairov, Eisenstein, and Sergei Tretyakov.[184] Mei Lanfang was welcomed at the Moscow railway station by the People's Commissar for Foreign Affairs Maxim Litvinov – the Soviet representative to the

[183] 'Najsłynniejszy aktor chiński' [The most famous Chinese actor], *IKC*, 15 March 1930, p. 3.
[184] 'Sostav komiteta po priemu Mei Lan-fana pri Vsesoyuznom Obshchestve Kulturnoi Svyazi s Zagranitsei' [Members of the welcoming committe in the Union of Soviet Societies for Friendship and Cultural Relations with Foreign Countries], in *Mei Lan-fan i kitaisky teatr*, p. 4.

League of Nations and member of the Central Committee of the All-Union Communist Party (Bolsheviks) – and his performances were attended several times by Joseph Vissarionovich Stalin. On 30 March 1935, Mei Lanfang visited Constantin Stanislavski, who was already seriously ill and rarely left his apartment at Leontievsky Pereulok, and after that meeting the Chinese artist saw the rehearsal of *The Barber of Seville*, led by Stanislavski.[185]

On 14 April, in the VOKS office in Moscow, Mei Lanfang spoke about the principles of traditional Chinese theatre and demonstrated some vocal and physical exercises. He was welcomed and introduced by Vsevolod Meyerhold, and the audience – besides Russian actors, directors, and critics – included Edward Gordon Craig, Erwin Piscator, and Bertolt Brecht. It was then that Brecht observed the alienation effect characteristic of Chinese acting, soon to become famous as the V-effect – the *Verfremdungseffekt*.[186]

Mei Lanfang died in Beijing on 8 August 1961 'as a result of heart disease that developed rapidly before his death', Chinese officials reported.[187] The public opinion and media unanimously stated that the deceased was 'the greatest contemporary Chinese actor'. The Polish monthly magazine *Chiny* [China] published an obituary written by an anonymous author, signed Z.S., who summed up the merits of Lanfang in the following way:

> He developed and enriched [...] Peking opera; he introduced new elements to singing and movement – the fundamentals of Peking opera. His performing abilities and the vitality of his mesmerizing voice were almost limitless and inexhaustible. The long history of Peking opera knows no other example of an actor over sixty years old who would perform the characters of young girls so wonderfully, so convincingly and so charmingly. He was an unparalleled master of this skill.

185 Irina Vinogradsky, *Zhizn i tvorchestvo K.S. Stanislavskogo, letopis*, IV: *1927–1938* [Life and works of C[onstantin] S[ergeyevich] Stanislavski: The chronicle] (Moscow: Vserossiiskoe Teatralnoe Obshchestvo, 1976), p. 401.

186 Barba, 'Priëm Ostranneja, Verfremdung, Hana', trans. by Liliana La Cava Erikson, *Sipario*, 406 (1980), 68–70. The article first appeared in Danish, in a magazine edited by Barba and published by Odin Teatret in Holstebro: *Teatrets Teori og Teknikk*, 15 (1971), 46–47. The same issue of *Teatrets Teorii* also includes an article by Barba on page 44, titled 'Mei Lan-fan' [Mei Lanfang], and was signed with only the author's initials. In the 1970/1971 academic year Barba lectured on Oriental theatre at the Theatre Faculty of the Århus University; the lectures provided the basis for both texts.

187 (Z.S.), 'Wielki aktor i obywatel' [A great actor and citizen], *Chiny*, 10 (1961), 8.

Mei Lanfang had a great influence on Chinese theatre. He was the first one who dared to modernize classical opera by striving for full stage sets, for the gradual contemporization of language in classical plays, and even for their new adaptations. Moreover, inspired by the theatrical doctrine of Stanislavski, [...] he paid attention, especially as a pedagogue, to the psychological deepening of a role. Thus it is safe to say that he established a new school of acting in China.[188]

The Second International Theatre Festival held in May and June 1955 in Paris (in 1957 it was renamed Théâtre des Nations) was marked by the first presentation of Peking opera in Western Europe.[189] It was the moment when Peking opera conquered cultural Europe.[190] After the Paris performances, a twenty-minute documentary film was made, L'un soir l'Opéra de Pekin [An Evening of Peking opera].[191] Jerzy Grotowski used excerpts from this film during his second lecture at the Collège de France, in the Odéon – Théâtre de l'Europe in Paris, on 2 June 1997. He said then:

> The film we are going to watch in a moment presents the Peking opera ensemble's visit to Paris in 1955. Twenty years earlier, in 1935, Peking opera visited Europe, yet performed only in Moscow.[192] The ensemble was accompanied then by the famous master Mei Lanfang. Later came the political era of General de Gaulle and the General decided to establish relations with China, and that is why Peking opera was invited. The Chinese accepted the invitation, yet

---

188   Ibid.

189   Pierre Abraham, 'Pékin à Paris' [Beijing in Paris], *Europe*, 116–17 (1955), 131–34.

190   André Travert, 'Caractères originaux et évolution actuelle du théâtre pékinois' [Original characteristics and current developments in Beijing theatre], in *Les théâtres d'Asie. Conférences du Théâtre des Nations (1958–1959). Journées d'études de Royaumont (28 mai – 1er juin 1959)* [Theatres of Asia. Lectures at the Théâtres of Nations (1958–1959)], collected by Jean Jacquot, 2nd edn (Paris: Éditions du Centre National de la Recherché Scientifique, 1968], pp. 99–126 (1st edn was published in 1961); Liang Pai-tchin, 'Le théâtre dialogue chinois en contact avec l'Occident' [Chinese theatre dialogue in contact with the West], pp. 127–30; Arno Paul, 'Brecht e l'arte teatrale cinese' [Brecht and the art of Chinese theatre], trans. from English by Valentine Ajmone Marsan, in *Teatro Oriente/Occidente*, pp. 335–43.

191   Dir. Marc Maugrette and Victoria Mercanton, with commentary by Clode Roy (produced by Procinex 1955). A copy of the film in the collection of the Grotowski Institute was provided by Mario Biagini. See: Osiński, 'Mei Lanfang, legenda opery pekińskiej. Polska recepcja i konteksty' [Mei Lanfang, the legend of Peking opera: Polish reception and contexts], in *Mei Lanfang. Mistrz opery pekińskiej*, p. 116, footnote 52.

192   The group of Mei Lanfang also performed in Leningrad.

• *Pages from Grotowski's 'Chinese Diary', 1962*

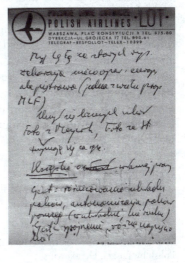

they wanted very much to make something breathtaking for 'the barbarians from the West'. That is why they invited actors from different groups, the best actors, to give the best performance; then they selected many fragments full of acrobatics to entertain the barbarians from the West, who could watch well-done acrobatic stunts. On the other hand, I had been to China and I know that watching long – sometimes even several-hour-long – dramatic fragments, which are made up of a distinctive alphabet, was absolutely incomprehensible even for the modern-day Chinese.[193]

Jerzy Grotowski was in China only a year after the end of the Great Leap Forward, as it was called. Its main goal was to increase steel production, and consequently, to quickly industrialize China – all achieved by means of mass mobilization and revolutionary enthusiasm. However, rather than industrialization, the effect of the Great Leap was the destruction of agriculture, which caused great famine. Between 1959 and 1961, about sixty million people died of hunger and cold.[194]

To avoid repetition, I am going to focus here only on Grotowski's direct references to Mei Lanfang, so frequent in his 'Chinese Diary'. [195] Thanks to his notes we know the precise schedule of his visit to China: the first week, from 17 to 24 of August, he spent in Beijing; on 24 August at noon he left for Nanjing (he stayed there for three days, from 25 to 28 August); then he went for five days to Shanghai (28 August to 2 September); and then for two days to Hangzhou; on 4 September at 6.30 p.m. he returned to Shanghai and at 11.30 p.m. he took a train to Beijing where he arrived on 6 September at 6.00 a.m. and stayed until 9 September.

In 'The Chinese Diary', we find various transliterations of Mei Lanfang's name: 'Myi Lan Fan', 'Myj Lę Fą', 'Myj Lą Fą'. It may

---

[193]   The French text was transcribed from an audiotape; it was translated into Polish by Leszek Demkowicz.

[194]   W. Scott Morton and Charlton M. Lewis, *China: Its History and Culture*, 4th edn (New York: McGraw-Hill, 2004), pp. 214–15; Monika Szmyt, *Współczesna sztuka chińska. Tradycja klasyczna, socrealizm, estetyka zachodnia* [Contemporary Chinese art: Classical tradition, socialist realism, Western aesthetics] (Kraków: Zakład Wydawniczy Nomos, 2007).

[195]   'The Chinese Diary' consists of 143 pages with notes in back and blue ballpoint pen (without pagination) in a pocket notebook of LOT Polish Airlines, format 10 x 14.7 cm; white paper, now yellowed and stained by humidity. It belonged to Jerzy Grotowski's private collection of documents. Professor Kazimierz Grotowski, who received the collection in autumn 1982, kept it for twenty-five years before he donated it to the Manuscipt Section of the Ossolineum in Wrocław in summer 2007.

prove that Grotowski had not heard about him before his journey to China, and certainly he did not know the correct spelling of his name. Here are some of his notes:

17 August 1962, page 5: 'Exhibition dedicated to Myi Lan Fan'.

18 August, pages 10–11, Chinese characters and Polish transliteration: 'Myj Lę Fą', 'Opera Pekińska' [Peking opera].

21 August, page 79: 'In Mus[eum] of Rev[olution] entire hist[ory] of China, stretching to the distant past. G[uide]: it is about Marxist chronology. [...]
Could the reform of Myj Lę Fą be a return to the past? In any case, it was seen that way. And maybe only in trad[itional] Pe[king] op[era] an orchestra was an evil. What a stage in the Palace (old!).'

22 August, page 83: 'Exhibition of Myj Lę Fą in the King[s'] Palace. Stage furnishings: beautifully embroidered background, 2 entrances, cut-out curtains. The orchestra on the right?'

Page 85: 'Exhibition on Myj Lę Fą, old draw[ings]. Stage sets quite oper[atic] [and] Europ[ean], yet storied (one of many prop[osals] of MLF). [...] Photo[graph] with Meyerh[old]. Photo[graph] with St[anislavski] – they hold each others' hands. Books on his own work.'

27 August, page 104. Nanjing: 'Eye exercise. Myj Lę Fą would fasten bells to pigeons and follow them with his eyes.'

It seems that Mei Lanfang, who had died one year before, was nevertheless constantly present for Grotowski during his visit to China. It explains why Grotowski brought Mei Lanfang's photographs to Opole and told the Laboratory actors about him.

In her June 1967 article 'Zrcadlo pravého poznáni' [Mirror of true cognition], published in *Divadlo*, a brilliantly edited magazine, Dana Kalvodová points out some parallels between acting in classical Chinese theatre and the theatre of Grotowski.[196]

In time, Grotowski's experiments turned out to be inspiring for the Chinese. Gao Xingjian, the winner of the Nobel Prize in Literature in 2000, confirms this fact explicitly. Izabella Łabędzka also points out his interests in the artistic ideas of Tadeusz Kantor and in the acting of Ryszard Cieślak.[197]

In 1963, two years after the publication of the original Chinese edition, the Iskusstvo publishing house issued a Russian transla-

---

[196] Dana Kalvodová, 'Zrcadlo pravého poznáni' [Mirror of true cognition], *Divadlo*, June 1967, pp. 24–30.
[197] Łabędzka, *Teatr niepokorny*, pp. 10, 95.

tion of Mei Lanfang's book, *Sorok let na stsene* [Forty years on the stage].[198] The publication includes a portrait of the author and numerous illustrations (photographs and drawings). The book is not available in Polish libraries. The only copy known to me was a part of Ludwik Flaszen's private book collection in Paris. This fact seems suggestive to me for two reasons: first – in the period when the import of Russian books to Poland, especially to large public libraries, was relatively easy and inexpensive, that title attracted no librarians; second – the only Polish man who bought the book was one of Grotowski's closest collaborators. Perhaps it was just a coincidence, but maybe not.

[198]   Mei Lanfang, *Sorok let na stsene*, trans. from Chinese by E. Rozhdestvensky, V. Taskin (Moscow: Iskusstvo, 1963).

VI.
Japan

1.
NOH THEATRE

THE FIRST PERFORMANCES of Noh theatre in Western Europe took place in summer 1954 in Teatro Verde dell'Isola di San Giorgio in Venice, where the Tokyo National Theatre presented, among others, the play *Aoi no Ue*, with Yoshiyuki Kanze as a *shite*.[199] In 1957, the same company, invited by Jean-Louis Barrault, took part in the opening season of the Théâtre de Nations in Paris, giving several shows in the Théâtre Odéon.[200]

In Poland, the first official Noh performances took place in 1980, twenty-six years after Venice, twenty-three after Paris.[201]

Before 1980, Polish encounters with Noh had been unofficial and marginal. Yet Grotowski was exposed to Zeami already in 1962. Between 22 March and 8 April 1962, the Opole-based Theatre Laboratory of 13 Rows visited Kraków with three productions shown in Krzysztofory and in Teatr 38: *Forefathers' Eve*, based on Mickiewicz; *Kordian*, based on Słowacki; and *The Idiot*, based on Dostoyevsky – the first two directed by Grotowski, and the third by Waldemar Krygier. One performance of *Forefathers' Eve* was attended by two Swiss journalists from *Journal de Genève*, a newspaper well-known in Europe: the editor-in-chief Olivier Reverdin, and writer, playwright, and translator Walter Weideli.

---

[199] 'Mostra del Trentennio del Festival (1934–1964). Catalogo ufficiale' [Shows of the thirty years of the Festival (1934–1964): The official catalogue], ed. by Giovanni Poli (Venice: La Biennale di Venezia. XXIII Festival Internazionale del Teatro di Prosa, 1964), p. 21; 'Giappone: cambiamenti e interferenze nella vita dello spettacolo dal 1853 al 1970. Le anse del fiume Sumida' [Japan: Changes and interference in the life of performance arts from 1853 to 1970. The loops of the Sumida River], ed. by Nicola Savarese, *Sipario*, 406 (1980).

[200] Jean-Louis Barrault, *Japonia* [Japan], in *Wspomnienia dla jutra* [Memoirs for tomorrow], trans. by Ewa Krasnowolska (Warsaw: Czytelnik, 1977), pp. 383–95: Viola Reclies, 'W Teatrze Narodów' [In the Theatre of Nations], *Teatr i Film*, 7 (1957), 24–25 (Korespondencja własna) [From our correspondent].

[201] The first press news known to me concerning two performances of Noh theatre planned in Warsaw as part of a European tour of a Japanese ensemble were published in March 1967. See: (woy), 'Teatr Nō wystąpi w Warszawie' [Noh theatre will perform in Warsaw], *Express Wieczorny*, 21 February 1967; 'Od mikroestrady – do wielkich teatrów. Japońską rewię zobaczymy w Polsce. Rozmowa z kierownictwem artystycznym PAGART-u' [From micro-stage to great theatres. We will see a Japanese revue in Poland. A conversation with the artistic director of PAGART], Jacek Dobierski interviewed by Maria Chudzyńska, *Kurier Szczeciński*, 3–4 March 1967.

On 26 April 1962, Weideli published an article titled 'Essayer le pour, essayer le contre' [Try for, try against]. Its comprehensive fragments were published in Polish translation as 'Próbować pro, próbować kontra' in the April 1963 issue of *Materiały – Dyskusje*. Grotowski always considered this text to be one of the most important publications on the early activities of the Laboratory Theatre.

Several letters following the Kraków's meeting survived. One of them was written to Grotowski by Walter Weideli on 19 April 1962. It begins as follows:

Dear Sir,
As promised, and with great pleasure, Mr Reverdin and I are sending you a book by Zeami, the founder and theoretician of Noh theatre, whom we discussed with you. The book will reach you the same way as registered mail. We are convinced that it may be useful in your efforts to revive theatre.[202]

The book mentioned in the letter is *'La tradition secrète du nō' suivi de 'Une journée de nō'* ['The Secret Tradition of Noh' followed by 'A Day of Noh'], translated and annotated by Renée Sieffert, a world-famous French Japanologist, and published in 1960 by Gallimard.[203] In his reply, dated 18 May 1962, Grotowski thanked Weideli for the book, and for his text about the Theatre of 13 Rows: 'Je vous remercie cordialement pour le livre sur le théâtre Nō et pour votre chaleureuse description de notre théâtre'.[204] On 6 July he informed Weideli about his planned journeys to Finland and China and his intended return to Poland at the end of September: 'A la fin

---

[202] In original: 'Cher Monsieur. Comme nous vous l'avions promis, nous faisons un plaisir, M. Reverdin et moi-même, de vos adresser ce livre de Zeami, le créateur et le théoricien du théâtre Nō dont nous vous avions parlé. Ce livre vous est adressé par même courrier et recommandé. Nous sommes persuadés qu'il vous sera utile dans vos efforts en vue d'un renouvellement du théâtre', one-page letter, typed on white paper, A4 format, with a printed inscription reading *'Journal de Genève*, 5–7 rue Général-Dufour. Rédaction' in the top left corner, and a handwritten signature, Grotowski Institute Archive, Wrocław.

[203] Zeami, *'La tradition secrète du nō' suivi de 'Une journée de nō'*, trans. and ed. by Renée Sieffert (Paris: Gallimard/Unesco, 1960).

[204] [I cordially thank you for the book on Noh theatre and for your warm description of our theatre.], a one-page letter, typed on white paper, A4 format, with a stamp reading 'Kierownik Artystyczny i Dyrektor Teatru 13 Rzędów Jerzy Grotowski' [Artistic Director and Manager of the Theatre of 13 Rows Jerzy Grotowski] in the bottom right corner and a handwritten signature, Grotowski Institute Archive, Wrocław.

de juillet j'irai en Finlande et ensuite en Chine d'où je rentrerai à la fin de septembre.'[205]

In Poland, one must acknowledge Jadwiga Rodowicz's role in spreading knowledge about Noh theatre. She is known as a 'Japanologist by profession; an actress of the Centre for Theatre Practices 'Gardzienice', a disciple of Noh master Kanze Tetsunojo by passion, and a diplomat by choice',[206] yet it is not a commonly known fact that she was also a member of the artistic team of the Laboratory Theatre, or that her personal contact with Grotowski at the beginning of her path was of crucial importance to her.[207] In one of her books, Rodowicz states:

> [...] Noh theatre has more than one point of convergence with Grotowski's work... In autumn 1972, as a student in the first year of Japanese studies, I encountered Grotowski's texts 'Jak żyć by można' ['How One Could Live'], 'Takim, jakim się jest, cały' [As one is, whole], and 'Święto' ['Holiday: The Day that is Holy'] in a reading room of the University of Warsaw.[208] If I had not done it, I would not have sought in theatre something very important,

---

[205] [At the end of July I will go to Finland and then to China, from where I will return at the end of September.], a one-page letter, typed on white paper, A4 format, with a stamp reading 'Teatr Laboratorium "13 Rzędów", Opole, Rynek 4' in the top left corner, a stamp stating 'Kierownik Artystyczny i Dyrektor Teatru 13 Rzędów Jerzy Grotowski' [Artistic Director and Manager of the Theatre of 13 Rows Jerzy Grotowski], and a handwritten signature, Grotowski Institute Archive, Wrocław. See: Osiński, *Grotowski and His Laboratory*, pp. 65–66; Osiński, 'Mei Lanfang, legenda opery pekińskiej. Polska recepcja i konteksty', in *Mei Lanfang. Mistrz opery pekińskiej*, pp. 125–35.

[206] Beata Kubiak Ho-Chi, *Estetyka i sztuka japońska. Wybrane zagadnienia* [Japanese aesthetics and art: Selected topics] (Kraków: Universitas, 2009), p. 230.

[207] Osiński, *Polskie kontakty teatralne z Orientem w XX wieku*, II, 117–18; 'Po występach teatru japońskiego. Rola na całe życie' [After performances of a Japanese theatre: A role for the entire life], Hideo Kanze interviewed by Roman Pawłowski, *Gazeta Stołeczna*, local [Warsaw] supplement of *Gazeta Wyborcza*, 13 July 1994, p. 6.

[208] Those texts were first published in the Wrocław-based monthly magazine *Odra* between April and June 1972: 'Jak żyć by można', *Odra*, 4 (1972), 33–38; 'Takim, jakim się jest, cały', *Odra*, 5 (1972), 51–56; 'Święto', *Odra*, 6 (1972), 47–51. In English: 'How One Could Live', an abridged version of an open press conference with Jerzy Grotowski held in the autumn of 1971 in Teatr Ateneum, Warsaw, *Le Theatre en Pologne/The Theatre in Poland*, 4–5 (1975), 33–34; 'Holiday: The Day That Is Holy', trans. by Bolesław Taborski, *TDR: The Drama Review*, vol. 17, no. 2 (1973), 113–19; 'Such as One Is: Whole', ibid., pp. 119–35; 'Holiday – the day that is holy' was also published by the Laboratory Theatre as an offprint, repr. in a reworked version, 'Holiday [Święto]: The Day That Is Holy', in *The Grotowski Sourcebook*, pp. 215–24.

which resides outside its limits, and I would not have suspected the existence of a spiritual dimension so concretely located in the physical dimension of acting. In a strange way, thanks to Grotowski, I found Zeami. It was over thirty years ago.[209]

During my two visits to the Workcenter of Jerzy Grotowski in Vallicelle, Italy, in 1988 and 1996, Grotowski told me that the objective of his work in Italy was to test whether it was possible to create an equivalent of Noh theatre within the context of Western culture. While undertaking this task, he was aware that Noh theatre needed several hundred years to form and develop. He thought nevertheless that such a possibility must be examined even if the chance of succeeding was close to zero.

In 1980, three Noh actors of the Zeami Theatre from Tokyo, Hideo Kanze, his younger brother Shizuo Kanze, and Shizuo's son, Akeo Kanze, came to Poland to perform at the Second International Theatrical Meetings. Despite the very limited cast, without full orchestra and chorus, the artists gave a performance in the Studio Theatre, presenting *Hagoromo* [*The Feather Mantle*], a play attributed to Zeami.

Hideo Kanze also conducted workshops for students at the Aleksander Zelwerowicz Theatre School. He taught them the role of the hunter chasing a fox from the classical Noh play *Sesshōseki*. According to Andrzej Ziębiński's account:

> The exercises, which resembled our choreography rehearsal (yet in this case the 'choreography' had been fixed by six-hundred years of tradition), allowed the participants to encounter in practice a Noh actor's technique and method of work (torso position, walk, breathing, gesture, handling a fan, directions of gaze, etc., as well as their inner content). The 'workshop' was repeated for another group of participants in Stara Prochownia.[210]

On 28 and 29 April, Kanze and his group gave three presentations in the Studio Theatre.

This first Polish encounter with Noh ended with a seminar with Hideo Kanze, organized by the Akademia Ruchu Theatrical Centre and the editorial board of *Dialog* on 30 April 1980 in Stara Prochownia [a performance venue in Warsaw]. Among the participants were:

---

[209] Jadwiga M. Rodowicz, *Boski dwumian. Przenikanie rzeczywistości w teatrze nō* [The divine binomial: Interprenetration of realites in Noh theatre (Wrocław: Instytut im. Jerzego Grotowskiego, 2009), p. 227; Rodowicz, *Aktor doskonały*, p. 6.

[210] Andrzej Ziębiński, 'Nō w Warszawie' [Noh in Warsaw], *Teatr*, 22 (1980), 4–5.

• *Hideo Kanze during a performance of Noh theatre, Warsaw, 1980*

Andrzej Borkowski, Wojciech Krukowski, Henryk Lipszyc (also a translator of the debate), Elżbieta Matynia, Zbigniew Olkiewicz, Konstanty Puzyna, Jadwiga Rodowicz, and Hanna Tomaszewska. The text of the debate, titled 'Aktor w teatrze nō' [The actor in Noh theatre], was published in the November (1980) issue of *Dialog*.[211] The same issue also included an article by Jadwiga Rodowicz, 'Nō: uwagi o technice ciała i głosu' [Noh: Comments on body and voice technique], and a text by Hisao Kanze, 'Żyjąc w nō' [Living in Noh], consisting of fragments of his posthumously published book, *Koko-ro-kara kokoro-ni tsutauru hana* [A flower transmitted from heart to heart] (Tokyo: 1979).[212] Hisao Kanze was a great Noh actor and Hideo Kanze's brother.

Hideo Kanze also visited the Centre for Theatre Practices Gardzienice: '[t]ogether with members of the Gardzienice group, he visited villages, listened to tales and songs of their inhabitants, and in the group's rehearsal room, he demonstrated some actors' training techniques used in Noh for generations'.[213]

---

[211] 'Aktor w tearze nō', *Dialog*, 11 (1980), 115–23. See: Rodowicz, 'Teatr nō' [Noh Theatre], *Radar*, 3 (1980), 8–10.
[212] Rodowicz, 'Nō: uwagi o technice ciała i głosu', *Dialog*, 11 (1980), 124–31; Hisao Kanze 'Żyjąc w nō', *Dialog*, 11 (1980), 132–37.
[213] Lipszyc, 'Obecność teatru japońskiego w powojennej Polsce' [The presence of Japanese theatre in post-war Poland], in *Moi bitelsi. Wybór dramatów japońskich* [My Beatles; A selection of Japanese plays] (Warsaw: Wydawnictwo Akademickie Dialog, 1998), p. 203. See: Rodowicz, 'Nō, czyli umiejętność'

Eight years later, on 8 November 1988, in the Stanisław Ig- nacy Witkiewicz 'Studio' Arts Centre, the Tessenkai group per- formed for the second time in Poland. The event was accompanied by two lectures on Noh. Led by Hideo Kanze, the ensemble pre- sented actors' techniques (*kata*) and excerpts from three Noh plays: *Izutsu* and *Tōru* by Zeami, and *Dōjōji*, attributed to Nobumitsu Kanze.

On 10 and 11 July 1994, on the Teatr Wielki stage in Warsaw, Japanese National Theatre (Kokuritsu Gekijō) from Tokyo present- ed, in a single production of *Shunkan* (a Noh play), three traditional Japanese conventions – Kabuki, Noh and Bunraku. The piece was directed by Hideo Kanze. In the finale of the performance, charac- ters of all three conventions appeared simultaneously side by side: the main *shite* actor wearing a mask; *tachiyaku*, a Kabuki actor per- forming a male role, with the makeup typical for Kabuki theatre; and *ningyō*, a Bunraku puppet with its animators. It would be hard to overestimate the significance of that performance, as various re- viewers and writers agree.[214]

In an interesting interview with Hideo Kanze, Roman Pawłow- ski, a journalist of *Gazeta Wyborcza*, asked the Japanese actor about his relationship with Jerzy Grotowski:

Roman Pawłowski: In Italy, you met Jerzy Grotowski. What was the role of that meeting in your career?

Hideo Kanze: An important one. Grotowski told me that he in- tended to aim his theatre towards the East. He wanted to show

---

[Noh; or, a skill], *Didaskalia. Gazeta Teatralna*, 45 (2001), 42–45; repr. in Rodo- wicz, *Boski dwumian*, pp. 203–25.

[214] Rodowicz, 'Nō, kabuki, bunraku' [Noh, Kabuki, Bunraku], *Życie Warsza- wy*, 8 July 1994, p. 4; Dorota Wyżyńska, 'Kabuki, nō i bunraku' [Kabuki, Noh, and Bunraku], *Gazeta Stołeczna*, local [Warsaw] supplement of *Gazeta Wybor- cza*, 9–10 July 1994, p. 6; Pawłowski, 'Do trzech razy sztuka. Japoński Teatr Narodowy w Warszawie' [Third time is a charm: Japanese National Theatre in Warsaw], *Gazeta Wyborcza*, 12 July 1994, p. 10; Kanze and Pawłowski, 'Po występach teatru japońskiego. Rola na całe życie'; Kowalczyk, 'Japończycy w Warszawie. Teatr pełen dostojeństwa' [The Japanese in Warsaw: A dignified theatre], *Rzeczpospolita*, 13 July 1994, p. 4; Hanna Baltyn, 'Magia konwencji. Występ japońskiego teatru ściągnął tłumy' [Magic of convention: The perfor- mance of Japanese theatre attracted crowds], *Życie Warszawy*, 15 July 1994, p. 4; Jacek Sieradzki, 'Czego możemy pozazdrościć Japończykom? Trzy w jednym' [What can we envy the Japanese? Three-in-one], *Polityka*, 23 July 1994, p. 15; Bożena Winnicka, 'Japońska lekcja' [A Japanese lesson], *Wiadomości Kultu- ralne*, 24 July 1994, p. 15.

on stage not only people but also nature, the relation between nature and man; he wanted to cover the entire world with his theatre. That is how I understood it. Then I participated in a seminar organized in Warsaw by Grotowski, and in Gdańsk we worked together with ten young actors on techniques of voice and dance.

Roman Pawłowski: How do you remember Grotowski?

Hideo Kanze: I liked him, for he looked like an honest, careful and subtle man. Yet his spirit was very strong. I liked that very much.[215]

In his beautiful essay written in 1980, 'No, albo o znakach' [Noh, or about signs], Jan Kott points out how the encounters with Noh inspired some of the most eminent European theatre artists of the twentieth century, and how these encounters solidified in his personal experience:

> There may be many different inspirations from this art of Noh. Modern theatre's fascination with Noh – the oldest of all existing theatres, six centuries of almost uninterrupted tradition, frozen but at the same time self-renewing – is concentrated on its dramatic ceremonial and psychomachia, its system of signs, and the psychodrama that is played out between *waki* and *shite*. In a moment of rare perspicacity, Grotowski admitted that the only ritual a theatre can present and fulfill that would not prove to be fake or apish is the ritualization of theatre as such; the only sacrifice that can save the theatre is that of its actors. Their whole bodies – heads, hands, legs, abdominal muscles, midriffs, throats which can modulate or trap the voice – are a medium that transmits signs. Brook kept asking his actors to look for truth in rediscovered gestures, that is, in signs existing as a language independent of a personal idiom. [...][216]
>
> During my first stay in Japan, Noh fascinated me with its perfection in estrangement. During my second stay, when I slowly and patiently learned the system of signs, I began to discover its similarities to ancient and medieval theatre. During my third stay Noh theatre became even closer to me. I discovered in it a community of shared experience of the same history. [...] During my last stay in Japan not only did I learn Noh signs of the same, identi-

[215] Kanze and Pawłowski, 'Po występach teatru japońskiego. Rola na całe życie'.
[216] Jan Kott, *The Theater of Essence* (Evaston: Northwestern University Press, 1986), p. 115.

cal, unchangeable story but also signs of mankind present in that drama.[217]

Inspirations are one of the most difficult issues to understand and to explain.

2.
THE JAPANESE ON GROTOWSKI

TITLED *JIKKEN-ENGEKI-RON. MOTAZARU engeki mezashite* [Treatise on experimental theatre: Towards a poor theatre] Grotowski's book was published in Japan in summer 1971 by the Tokyo-based editing house Teatoro Esha. The translation, based on the first English printing, was made by Oshima Tsutomu. Besides an introduction by Peter Brook, the Japanese edition included a commentary by director and theatre scholar Toshimitsu Tetsuo, and a bibliography.

Between 17 and 20 April 1972, Grotowski led a seminar for the Theatre de Nations in Paris. On the final day, in the Théâtre Récamier he held a public debate with the participants of the seminar.[218] One of them was Tadashi Suzuki, a famous Japanese director and founder of Waseda-shōgekijō [Small Theatre at the Waseda University] in Tokyo, who later wrote about his impressions from this meeting with Grotowski:

> I saw him for the first time in Theatre Espace Pierre Cardin in Paris. At the same time a somewhat 'hippy' American group was there. Grotowski – topless – was playing with those young people. For me it seemed quite foolish, yet he evidently enjoyed it. When I asked him later (in August 1973) about it, he put it off lightly: 'Oh, it was just a joke.' We tend to evaluate a work in direct reference to the artist who created it. However, as it is known, the impressions can be different, often deceptive, and have nothing in common with the actual person.[219]

The above anecdote is worth quoting at least because of the consequences of that meeting, as well as because of the final reflection.

---

[217]   Kott, 'No, albo o znakach', in Kott, *Pisma wybrane* [Selected writings], III: *Fotel recenzenta* [The reviewer's armchair], pp. 319, 321.

[218]   Claude Godard, 'Rencontre avec Grotowski' [Meeting with Grotowski], *Le Monde*, 22 April 1972.

[219]   hl [Henryk Lipszyc], 'Japończyk o Grotowskim' [A Japanese on Grotowski], *Dialog*, 11 (1974), 167.

Between 13 and 15 August 1973 – during his world tour across the US, New Zealand, and Australia – Grotowski was in Tokyo. Accompanied by Tadashi Suzuki, he visited the Shibuya district at night and attended a Noh theatre rehearsal. In October 1973, the theatrical monthly magazine *Shingeki* published an interview with Grotowski as well as Suzuki's account of their meeting. I am quoting below some of the most characteristic fragments of this text:

Grotowski arrives in Japan with a sleeping bag in his rucksack, his only luggage. He walks around the city at night, observes, listens. He does it without prejudice, he does not accept ready-made formulas; he listens with true curiosity. He believes nothing he cannot affirm. Observing him, I thought to myself: 'This guy can really get himself moving, he knows how to be where something happens.' It was the most interesting impression to me. Indeed I felt more intimacy and kinship being with him than while accompanied by Senda Koreya or Uno Jūkichi (both are main figures of the *shingeki* movement of Japanese theatre). Grotowski often spoke about overcoming cultural barriers. I can only guess that Polish specifics could help breed such ideas. He was brought up in the country historically and geographically located at the junction of various cultures and influences. Being in contact with the cultures of other European nations, Grotowski could assume that people notice their differences also through language, which is the foundation of culture. How things are perceived, a worldview, ways of looking at matters turn out to be similar and common – especially if a body is the instrument. Grotowski studied in the Soviet Union, he travelled to China and India. On the other hand, he also worked at the Royal Shakespeare Company, so he could become convinced of the possibility of mutual understanding despite language barriers; or rather, that where there is something to be understood, people can always understand each other. […]

He is preoccupied by the question of whether a human being can communicate with another by means of theatrical work. Thus he claims that communication between humans can be of two kinds. First, there is communication resulting from external similarity, from the fact of sharing the same culture. This kind of communication is offered, for example, by the knowledge of Esperanto. However, this kind of unity is dead, it is the unity in death. The other way of communication is the one by human spontaneity, through sensitivity of human body. He probably meant the second kind of communication when he said that he would like to carry on his experiments in Japan. […] In Japan, Grotowski seeks stimuli and impulses for his own work, and he does it persistently and uncompromisingly. That is probably why he seldom takes into account how his opinion would be received. […]

During our conversation we were both also wondering why it felt so good to talk. Grotowski, laughing, explained it by the fact that we have similar attitudes towards life. And perhaps, I would add, attitudes towards the nation. I asked him: 'What is Poland for you?' He answered with a light smile: 'Poland is a mother to me. But not a father. I look for the father'. [...]

I guess that Grotowski's future fate is that he will become an eternal wanderer without a homeland, or that he will bury himself somewhere in Poland, become insane, and as a madman – ideologically and emotionally – he will become isolated from the world. Taking into consideration his character, his psychological structure, I see no other alternative. On the other hand, in his character I see a guarantee that he will never rest satisfied with his accomplishments, enjoying the praises in France or somewhere else.[220]

The final sentences of the text are especially stirring. One must also admit that Suzuki's reflections, regardless of the accuracy of his diagnosis, are very perceptive.

In October 1975, *Shingeki* magazine published an article by Akihiko Senda, a well-known theatre critic, titled 'Gurotofusuki. No na hana to hebi no ichiya' [Grotowski: A night among wild flowers and snakes]. The author presents his personal experiences during his training at the University of Research of the Theatre of Nations, which took place in Wrocław between 14 June and 7 July 1975 under Grotowski's guidance. One year later the same text was published in Senda's book of reports, essays, and theatrical reviews on Japanese and foreign avant-garde.[221]

3.
SYMPOSIUM 'THE ART OF THE BEGINNER' IN 1978: WARSAW AND GRZEGORZEWICE NEAR WARSAW

ON MONDAY, 5 June, Grotowski gave a talk lasting more than three hours at the international symposium 'The Art of the Beginner', held in the Old Orangery building of the Royal Baths Park in War-

---

[220] Ibid., pp. 168–71.
[221] Akihiko Senda, *Hirakareta gekijō* [Open theatre] (Tokyo: Shobunsha, 1976), pp. 249–62. Information about this book and about the Japanese translation of Grotowski's *Towards a Poor Theatre* was provided by Henryk Lipszyc.

saw.[222] He declared that, from a spectator's perspective, Oriental theatre remained most fascinating to him. He illustrated his statement by giving an example of father and son performing every other day in the same production of a classical Peking opera: on the surface, for each of them everything was the same, equal precision of performance could be seen; however, the audience was enthusiastic when the father appeared on stage, while the son evoked cold reactions. The difference, unnoticeable to someone foreign to the [Chinese] culture, was that on the body of the son one could see sweat, a mark of fatigue, thus excluding true mastery for people raised in that culture. I should point out here that Grotowski took a similar attitude towards real mastery in the actor's craft, for example in the following statement made in 1966: 'As a matter of fact, undisciplined spontaneity results in a kind of biological chaos, shapeless and accidental reactions. [...] It is "heavy", while true spontaneity is "light" and unforced.'[223]

'The Art of the Beginner' symposium was followed by a training workshop of the same name led under Grotowski's guidance between 4 and 7 June 1978 in Warsaw and in Grzegorzewice near Warsaw.[224] Among the participants were: the already mentioned Japanese actor Hideo Kanze, master of classical Noh theatre, and Krishnan Nambudiri, an actor-dancer of Indian Kathakali theatre.

During the meeting in the Old Orangery, Grotowski quoted and commented on a fragment of Hermann Hesse's *Journey to the East*. The following quotation is an English translation of the *ad hoc* Polish version made by Grotowski at that time:

> I realized that I have joined the journey to the East, which resembled or seemed a defined simple pilgrimage, yet in reality, in its more essential meaning, this journey, this expedition to the East, was not only mine and not only now. This procession was always constantly in motion, it moved always and ceaselessly towards the East, towards home, enlightenment, through centuries and through roads, through light and through fascination, and every participant,

---

[222] Grotowski, 'The Art of the Beginner', p. 7–11.

[223] Jerzy Grotowski and Janusz Budzyński, 'Teatr Laboratorium "13 Rzędów". Jerzy Grotowski o sztuce aktora, rozmawiał Janusz Budzyński' [The Laboratory Theatre of 13 Rows: Jerzy Grotowski discussing the actor's craft with Janusz Burzyński], *Itd*, 10 July 1966; repr. in Grotowski, *Teksty 1965–1969*, p. 35.

[224] Coincidentally the birthplace of Feliks Jasieński-Manggha, a famous art critic, patron of artists, and collector of works of arts (especially Japanese), active during the Young Poland period. Editor's note: The Young Poland [Młoda Polska] period in literature and art lasted from 1891 to 1918.

every group, whether a whole or only a part of the great pilgrimage, was a piece of that great stream of human beings, that perennial river of human spirit seeking home.[225]

One of the important projects prepared at the Laboratory Theatre and officially announced by Grotowski at that time was titled Journey to the East [Podróż na Wschód], in reference to the title of Hesse's book:

> From the core group that did not have theatrical, but instead (from the beginning) paratheatrical experiences, from which *Vigils* and *The Mountain Project* transpired – from the highly specialized cultural experiments this team had led – a new project will be born [...] totally based on active participation of all present. We refer to it as *Journey to the East* [...]. It is planned for the autumn of 1981. An important feature is that both the co-participants and the project leaders will be *en route* (literally). The vigor of play, of movement, and of crossing distance constitutes its distinctiveness and its perspective.
>
> [...] So when I talk about action *en route* in connection with *Journey to the East*, I do not mean the acting out of certain occurrences in symbolic space and arbitrary time, but rather actions performed literally *en route*, in the course of literally being on the road, and in the whole singular literalness of human behaviour.[226]

Journey to the East was to be a culmination of the entire path of the younger members of the Laboratory Theatre, with Jacek Zmysłowski in the lead. Circumstances in Poland resulting from martial law, and within the group as well (Jacek Zmysłowski's serious illness and death at the beginning of 1982), made it impossible to realize the project.[227] Ultimately, Journey to the East remained

---

[225] According to a tape recording of the meeting. Grotowski, 'The Art of the Beginner', p. 11. Let me quote the same fragment of Hesse's book translated by Hilda Rosner for comparison: 'I realized that I had joined a pilgrimage to the East, seemingly a definite and single pilgrimage – but in reality, in its broadest sense, this expedition to the East was not only mine and now; this procession of believers and disciples had always and incessantly been moving towards the East, towards the Home of Light. Throughout the centuries it had been on the way, towards light and wonder, and each member, each group, indeed our whole host and its great pilgrimage, was only a wave in the eternal stream of human beings, of the eternal strivings of the human spirit towards the East, towards Home.' Hermann Hesse, *Journey to the East* (New York: Picador, 2003), pp. 12–13.

[226] Grotowski, 'The Laboratory Theatre: 20 Years After', p. 35.

[227] Osiński, 'Występy gościnne Teatru Laboratorium 1959–1984. Kronika działalności 1978–1984' [Guest Performances of the Laboratory Theatre 1959–1984. Chronicle of Activities 1978–1984], *Pamiętnik Teatralny*, 1–4 (2000), 673.

an idea, a longing, and a task to be completed. Yet that task was to be taking place outside the ensemble, individually, primarily as a personal experience and as an individual response to the old challenge.

We owe the most complete description of the meeting in the Old Orangery and the events in Grzegorzewice to Anna Czekanowska, a professor at the University of Warsaw, world-famous ethno-musicologist and author of two important books: *Kultury muzyczne Azji* [Musical cultures of Asia] (1981) and *Kultury tradycyjne wobec współczesności. Muzyka, poezja, taniec* [Traditional cultures versus modern times: Music, poetry, dance] (2008). Her article 'Teatr – muzyka – człowiek' [Theatre – music – man], published in the bi-weekly magazine *Ruch Muzyczny*, begins with two quotations: the first one she took from 'a tale danced in the Hawaiian Archipelago', and the second 'from Jerzy Grotowski's report'. I have to cite the second quotation, for Czekanowska depends on it in her analysis: 'There is a place in the Karakum Desert, near the historical city of Merv, where the river sinks into the desert. In this place an oasis formed.'[228] What then follows are Czekanowska's reflections, which I quote below with some abbreviations:

> The initiative of the symposium's organizers was directly connected with Jerzy Grotowski's research undertaken several years before on Theatre of Sources, and on ethno-sources in particular. Grotowski named this new venture 'Journey to the East', or rather 'to the sunrise' [the word 'wschód' means both 'East' and 'sunrise' in Polish]. Grotowski proposed the rejection of the conventions not only of craft, but even of civilization. Consequently it was supposed to lead to the 'un-inhibiting' of human beings and to their liberation from mechanisms governed by the great strategists of modern world civilizations. The future should tell to what extent this undertaking was to become real and to what extent the 'Art of the Beginner' symposium was helpful in this respect. What came from the presented guidelines was that one has to seek the answer to that question within oneself, in the work on oneself, and in solitude. Certainly, the presented proposals cannot suit everyone. Not everyone will agree to accept the fate of a river sinking into a desert, even if an oasis might form there. Not everyone will agree to remain lonely on a narrow path, which only one man can follow. Not everyone – that is, not every member of the contemporary Euro-American civilization – will believe that these sacrifices will give him new strength because getting a new life force – *mana* – is an obvious thing for

---

[228] Anna Czekanowska, 'Teatr – muzyka – człowiek' [Theatre – music – man], *Ruch Muzyczny*, 20 (1978), 15.

representatives of many old cultures. That's enough about the aims of the symposium.

What were its participants like? A multinational, multiracial, intercontinental assembly. Jerzy Grotowski's ensemble, people of theatre, of art, of science, many accidental fellow believers, or just interested friends, as well as adversaries. It is hard to provide numbers and names, as we usually do in reports, because discretion was one of the foundational rules of the event. It was accepted as a convention that no one would introduce anyone to anyone; there were no nametags, although a list of participants was available upon request. Thus what seems to be more appropriate is a more general description of the individuals encountered there.

There is no doubt that the participants had very strong, ambitious personalities. There were presidents of great academies, artistic directors of experimental theatres, organizers of big festivals, eminent scholars, well-connected people, successful people, and also some individuals so critical of their own work that for many years they would keep it away from the public. In most cases there were people seeking a new path. It is not easy to imagine a group of individuals more diverse and more difficult to manage. Thus there were many struggles, ambitions, frictions, and conflicts. Did the participants end up sufficiently satisfied? If they did not, it was perhaps because Grotowski did not initiate them enough into the secrets of his method, and basically did not reveal to them his art of controlling the team – in fact, a team similar to the one they were themselves – of avant-gardists and rebels. He proposed that the participants – following the example of Constantin Stanislavski – start with work on themselves; he spoke about the necessity of merging with the environment and surroundings, about a river sinking into a desert, and about an oasis growing green there.

What fruits will this programme bring? At present, the crop of the 'Art of the Beginner' symposium includes many not-really-well-thought-out statements, many misunderstandings, material for reflection, and an invitation to revise one's own opinions, and one's own partially realized attitude towards the world and people.

Why do I pay so much attention to ethno-sources? The answer is simple. It is hard to imagine a 'journey to the sunrise' without reference to the thinking and the arts of other cultures. Only Oriental or Asian? No, not exclusively: just other ones, those not yet crushed by the steamroller of contemporary civilization, those essentially different and, thus, more durable. For Europeans, the art and philosophy of the East – known, as early as in the Middle Ages, as Morgenland – have for a long time had a different dimension, a different time, a dissimilar process. Those specialized in temporal logic define these cultural phenomena using mathematical formu-

Japan

las. Representatives of less formalized disciplines use such terms as cycle, circle, spiral; sociologists speak about the static character of the structure. It is difficult to interpret in other ways a culture based on a belief in perennial laws, holy numbers, and a permanent view on social relations. It would be best to refer to some statements and ideas from representatives of these cultures. There is no other way to explain the divine order of five concepts and their interrelations – the emperor, his deeds, executors of his will, their artifacts, and the people. Without deep faith, it is difficult to accept the power of rebirth and reincarnation; it is hard to succumb to self-annihilation, subjecting oneself to a higher purpose.

Vadaku Krishnan, a dancer Grotowski invited from the famous school in Kerala, presented to us a danced tale about the birth of a god. Adrienne [Kaeppler] from Hawaii told us a danced parable about flowers, birds, fishes, and a lonely man. This story was once dedicated to one of the rulers of Hawaii. There are many similar motifs in Japanese Noh theatre and in Balinese stories about Panji the hero.

Unfortunately much too late, just before his departure, did we have a chance to talk to professor Louis Mars from Haiti. We met accidentally in a small group of ethnomusicologists. 'It is extremely important', he said to us, 'it is very good that you are here. Without music there is no drama, no dramatized religion, no connection between people, no calming, no life.' Is it just because music is one of the factors of human actions and deeds? Is it because together with gestures music is a part of sonorous activities? There may be other reasons. Not always, but in many cases, music plays a superior role. Professor Mars is a leading expert on Haitian ethnodrama, or one of the forms of religious performances once disseminated in Latin America by the Yoruba tribes and very popular in the Bahia region of Brazil, known there as Candomble. For this reason, he is perfectly aware of the function of music in the transformation of conscious activities into unconscious ones, including dreaming and hypnosis. Representatives of other cultures feel it more intensely than skeptical Euro-Americans. Indeed, one has to be at least an heir of African culture to fully understand the role of rhythms performed collectively, the role of drums supporting, accelerating and enriching the rhythm. Only an African can appreciate how diversely, how dramatically, how painfully, or how joyfully one can feel and comprehend the rhythm of a drum, its talk, especially in the case of a 'talking' drum with anthropomorphic or zoomorphic shapes. Drums often represent deities; their voice is a voice of god, their rhythm is a rhythm of god. Thus they bring fear and awe, but also a joy of meeting and connection. So the East – 'ex Oriente lux' – is not only the geographical east and Asia – it also includes other continents.

Music makes it easier for us to get closer to others, to get to know others, and to identify with them. That is why it plays the main role in nuptial songs, which resemble bird calls. One who listens to the nuptial songs of Bedouins in a desert can hear only sequences of falling intervals, masterfully shifting by a semitone, a quartertone, and sometimes even smaller value. Yet if one tries to participate in these musical competitions, one becomes a witness of the process of communication between people. At the moment when a sound of basic intonation ideally 'distorted' by the partners releases an acoustic phenomenon known as the emergence of differential tones, the performers feel a particular vibration, which is interpreted as a manifestation of connection between them, an evidence of cohesion. This feeling of an ideal bond between partners is often associated with the feeling of contact with the universe.

It is regrettable that there were almost no musical instruments in Grzegorzewice. One day, in the morning, one could hear a Japanese flute, *ryūteki*, and a bell, used by Filipino Ricardo [Trimillos] to attract a swan. On the last day, a flute could be heard from a garden, and Indian drums were perfectly imitated; yet there were no *veena* and *tambura* – basic string instruments of India. It is a pity, because without these instruments it is difficult to understand both the art of the continuous drone, and the craft of seeking and identifying sounds and their relation to the foundation – *universum*. Thus there was no introduction to the basic foundations of Indian thought.

So then, in accordance with Professor Mars' definition, music lets us crystallize certain opinions; through its practice, we find material that allows us to order and specify concepts; music becomes a means of meditation and investigation. This happens in highly developed cultures of sophisticated philosophical reflection, while in primitive cultures music is a direct instrumental factor of religious practices. Without music there is no ethnodrama, just like without ethnosources there is no way to understand the basic functions of music. [...]

Many theories of the origins of music, so far considered quite naive, can gain a new meaning today. 'Music originated from songs of birds, their mating calls', 'in the beginning was the word', 'rhythm', 'work' – here are the theories of the origin of music conceived by Jean-Jacques Rousseau, Jules Combarieu, Herbert Spencer, and Carl Bücher. Thinkers of the past knew ethnosources to a limited degree, yet they were guided by intuition, maybe folklore and family environment, at that time not yet destroyed and not so significantly transformed. Our critical view today allows us to appreciate many old hypotheses and suggestions.[229]

---

[229]   Ibid., pp. 15–16.

4.

IN RELATION TO THE JAPANESE TRANSLATION
OF 'PERFORMER'

IN 1992, FOUR years after the first publication in Italy – simultaneously in English, French, and Italian – the programme text from the
final period of Jerzy Grotowski's life was published in Japan, translated by Tokimasa Sekiguchi, an eminent professor of Polish studies,
translator, and lecturer of Polish culture at the Foreign Languages
University in Tokyo. Professor Shōzō Yoshigami (1928–1996), a legend of Polish studies in Japan, published the text in the 1992 edition of the annual *Polonica*, of which he was the editor-in-chief. The
circumstances of this publication were presented many years later
in a letter written to me by Henryk Lipszyc, then the ambassador of
the Republic of Poland in Tokyo, a scholar of Japanese studies and
an expert in theatre:

> The annual magazine *Polonica* had been published since 1990 at the
> initiative and expenditure of the late professor Yoshigami.[230] Two is-
> sues, of 1991 and 1992, were almost exclusively dedicated to Polish
> theatre. The first one mostly to [Tadeusz] Kantor, yet there were also
> many other interesting materials, including recollections of Kujō
> Kyōko (widow of Terayama) about the visit of the Tenjō Sajiki group
> to Poland, impressions of Ōta Shōgo on his performances in Po-
> land, [an article] by Suzuki Tadashi on the visit and performances of
> Waseda-shōgekijō, and impressions and report of Ms Ogiwara, who
> accompanied Kanze Hideo during his performances in Warsaw in
> 1980 and 1988. The issue also includes interesting historical mate-
> rial about subjects close to your heart (reception), namely an article
> by Yoshigami on Sada Yacco and Kawakami Otojirō (actually part
> of a bigger series about Japanese actors and people of the Polish
> stage continued in later issues). There is also Tokimasa Sekiguchi's
> translation of *Water Hen* [*Kurka Wodna*] (a play by Stanisław Ignacy
> Witkiewicz), Gombrowicz's *Diary*, translations of the newest Polish
> poetry, reflections of Risako Uchida (a wife of the editor-in-chief) on
> her contacts with Polish children and youth literature (she was its
> greatest propagator and translator), etc., etc.
>
> Issue no. 3, published in 1992, included an almost sixty-page
> collection of various texts on Grotowski, including your article
> 'Od Dramatu Obiektywnego do Sztuk Rytualnych' [From Objec-
> tive Drama to Ritual Arts], translated by Yoshigami,[231] preceded

---

230 Editor's note: Shōzō Yoshigami died in 1996.
231 Osiński, 'Gurotofusuki no hiraita michi: obujekutibu dorama kara richuaru

by Grotowski's 'Performer', translated by Sekiguchi.[232] (Incidentally, I participated in persuading Grot[owski] to agree to publish the text in Japanese. He demanded my personal guarantee that the translation will be flawless and I gave it to him. I think I still have our letters about this issue. I remember that he complained about some serious ailments at that time; perhaps he was recovering after a heart attack?). Besides, the magazine includes Brook's 'Art as a Vehicle', also translated by Sekiguchi,[233] an article by Toshimitsu Tetsuo, 'Towards a Poor Theatre',[234] dealing with Kanze Hideo's sentimental memoirs of his visits to Poland, titled 'The Encounter with Grotowski',[235] as well as an extensive photographic documentation of the activities of the Laboratory Theatre before the Theatre of Sources period.

The issue also includes excerpts from Maciej Karpiński's notes on staging [Dostoyevsky's] *The Idiot*, directed by Wajda; a piece by Yomota Inuhiko titled 'Imitating Kantor'; essays; reviews of performances by Polish groups and artists; and regular entries, like translations of poetry (Różewicz, Herbert, Leśmian), a continuation of Gombrowicz's *Diary*, etc. Each issue ends with a detailed chronicle of Polish cultural events for the previous year. It is a pity that after Yoshigami's much regretted death the magazine ceased to exist.[236]

Thanks to Henryk Lipszyc, two important letters have been preserved: Grotowski's undated letter to Lipszyc, and Lipszyc's response dated Tokyo, 18 October 1992. They provide details about the Japanese translation of 'Performer', as well as Grotowski's planned (but never realized) visit to Japan following an invitation by Tadashi Suzuki. The following is a generous selection from Grotowski's letter:

Dear Henryk, your letter and the information about the new developments in your life delighted me. Please forgive the brevity of my letter but I am in a post-heart attack condition and can't afford more. I am answering successively to your questions and proposals:

ātsu made' ['Grotowski Blazes the Trails: From Objective Drama to Ritual Arts'], trans. by Shōzō Yoshigami, *Polonica*, 3 (1992), 37–57.

[232] Grotowski, 'Performer', trans. by Tokimasa Sekiguchi, *Polonica*, 3 (1992), 12–21.

[233] Peter Brook, 'Gurotofusuki, nakadachi toshite no geijutsu' [Grotowski, Art as a Vehicle], trans. by Tokimasa Sekiguchi, *Polonica*, 3 (1992), 22–26.

[234] Toshimitsu Tetsuo, 'Motazaru engeki mezashite' [Towards a Poor Theatre], *Polonica*, 3 (1992), 28–36.

[235] Hideo Kanze, 'Gurotofusuki to no deai' [The encounter with Grotowski], *Polonica*, 3 (1992), 60–61.

[236] Email from Henryk Lipszyc, dated 13 June 2006, the author's collection. See: Osiński, *Polskie kontakty teatralne z Orientem w XX wieku*, I, 234–35.

1. I can agree on the publication of 'Performer' in Japanese provided only that the translation will be literally word for word, especially in its metaphysical parts. What I am afraid of the most is that a translator thinks he translates with comprehension. He should not translate the way he understands but only literally, word by word. Thus you would have to make a new translation based on these indications. Only on condition that you give me your word of honour that it will be done this way, I agree on printing.

2. I do not have, and I won't have for a long time, enough strength to be interviewed by T[adashi] Suzuki. In this case health reasons are decisive. [...]

3. No pictures are taken during my current work in Pontedera, thus there are no such pictures. As far as photographs from the Laboratory Theatre period are concerned, they can be obtained exclusively from Osiński; here I do not have these photographs. Certainly I have nothing against your idea to include them in the book. So that's concerning your proposals. [...] I congratulate you on your post as an ambassador, although I do not envy you for sometimes it must be a nightmare.[237]

And here are fragments from Henryk Lipszyc's reply:

Dear Jerzy, I read your letter with great joy. It evoked memories and reflections and mobilizes me to think. I was saddened only by the news about your health problems. [...]

Thank you for your explanations concerning the issue of translating 'Performer'. I passed your intentions to the publisher and to the translator. I took the translation under my personal supervision and now I can guarantee, at my own liability, that you will be satisfied with it. The translator [...] (Mr Sekiguchi, a professor of the Polish language and culture in the Tokyo University of Foreign Languages) did not 'talk big' and translated (not 'interpreted') with due humility. [...] After saying that, on behalf of the *Polonica* annual, I repeat the request for your permission to publish the Japanese translation of 'Performer' in this journal.[238]

Several years later, on the occasion of reviewing Tokyo's 1997 premiere of Witold Gombrowicz's *Yvonne, Princess of Burgundy* [*Iwona, księżniczka Burgunda*], Tokimasa Sekiguchi briefly summarized the reception of Polish theatre in Japan, stating that 'Jerzy Grotowski is known to the older generations of theatre people, and rather as a "theorist"'.[239]

---

[237] Computer printout, two pages.
[238] Computer printout, one page.
[239] Tokimasa Sekiguchi, '"Iwona" w Tokio' [*Yvonne* [*Princess of Burgundy*] in Tokyo], *Pamiętnik Teatralny*, 1–4 (2004), 646.

And that's perhaps fair, taking into consideration that Grotowski visited Japan just once for only three days. He did not present any of his productions in Japan, thus he is primarily known there for his texts.

Finally, I would like to mention Grotowski's continuous interest in Zen Buddhism. As early as his first years in Opole, he had in his reference library French translations of two books on this subject: *Le Bouddhisme zen* [*Zen Buddhism*] by Alan W. Watts,[240] a copy given to him by Eugenio Barba, with a humorous inscription: 'Per Opole ad Satori. Directori teatralis laboratorii ab E. Barba', and *Essais sur le Bouddhisme zen* [*Essays in Zen Buddhism*] by Daisetz Teitaro Suzuki.[241] However, this subject demands a separate discussion. Here I can only hint at it.

---

[240]   Alan W. Watts, *Le Bouddhisme zen*, trans. by P. Berlit (Paris: Payot, 1960).
[241]   Daisetz Teitaro Suzuki, *Essais sur le Bouddhisme zen* [*Essays in Zen Buddhism*], trans. by Jean Herbert (Paris: Éditions Albin Michel, 1958).

VII.

Contexts
and
consequences

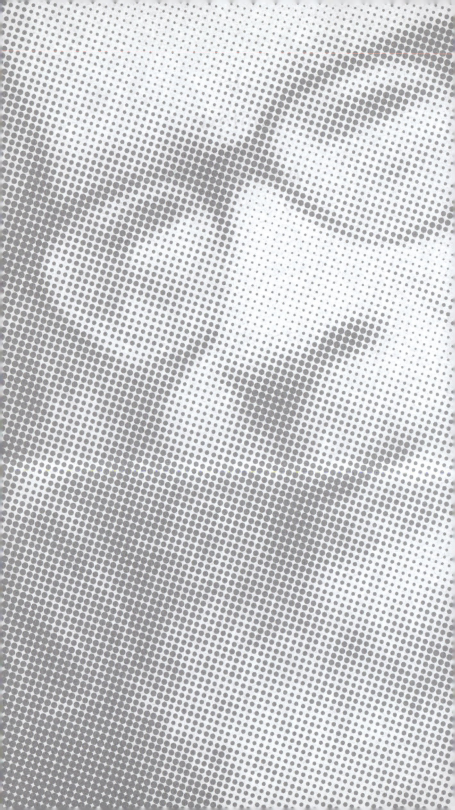

1.
EUGENIO BARBA
AND
PETER BROOK

IN HIS BOOK *Performative Circumstances from the Avant Garde to Ramila*, published in 1983 in India, Richard Schechner quotes the acknowledgements Eugenio Barba wrote on 29 September 1963 in the visitors' book at the famous Kathakali school in Cheruthuruthy, Kerala Kalamandalam, at the end of his visit. Let me quote Barba's note, omitting only its opening and closing customary pleasantries:

> I had not the occasion last night at the performance to thank you [the Secretary of Kerala Kala Mandalam] for all the kind help you have given me during my stay here. To you, and to the Superintendent, and to all boys who were so willing to be of service, I would like to express my gratitude and sincerest thanks.
>
> My visit in Kalamandalam has greatly helped me in my studies, and the research material I have collected will surely be of the greatest assistance to those people working at the Theatre Laboratorium in Poland.[242]

In winter 1994, *TDR: The Drama Review* published Barba's article, 'The Steps on the River Bank', in which he quotes his own words written over thirty years before; he also reflects on the meaning and results of his visit to India.[243]

I remember very well a frosty morning near Christmas 1963 when I accompanied Grotowski at the railway station in Opole to greet Eugenio Barba, who was returning from his journey to India. From then on, Asian theatre became a domain of creative exploration and inspiration for Barba and his Odin Teatret, which he founded in Oslo in early autumn 1964 before moving it to Holstebro, Denmark, in 1966. It is also hard to overestimate the meaning of Asian theatre, or, as he calls it, the 'Eurasian theatre and actor' for the International School of Theatre Anthropology

---

[242] Barba, *Theatre: Solitude, Craft, Revolt*, ed. by Lluís Masgrau, trans. by Judy Barba (Aberystwyth: Black Mountain Press, 1999), pp. 261–62. See: Richard Schechner, *Performative Circumstances from the Avant Garde to Ramila* (Calcutta: Seagull Books, 1983), p. 147.

[243] Barba, 'The Steps on the River Bank', *TDR: The Drama Review*, 4 (1994), 107.

'ISTA', established by Barba in 1979, and managed by him since then.[244]

When Grotowski began travelling to India, he was interested in something entirely different than working on another production. Initially he was unwilling or unable to name that 'new thing'. Only later did he find satisfying terms, often expressed through metaphors and images. However, from the beginning, the art of theatre was for him a vehicle, if not as 'material substance' (for initially he had no adequate tools), certainly as a longing and aspiration, which gradually became more precisely expressed and more self-conscious. That is what Peter Brook called it during a meeting in Florence in March 1987, the first public conference on the Workcenter of Jerzy Grotowski (Centro di lavoro di Jerzy Grotowski) in Pontedera, Italy.[245] Brook spoke about a vehicle as early as after his first meeting with the Laboratory Theatre in May 1966, when he watched *The Constant Prince* in Paris. In the article published in autumn 1966, in *Flourish* (the press organ of the Royal Shakespeare Company Club), he put it in the following way:

> [...] acting is [for this handful of people] an art of absolute dedication, monastic and total. [...] With a proviso. This dedication to acting does not make acting an end in itself. On the contrary. For Grotowski acting is a vehicle. How can I put it? The theatre is not an escape, a refuge. A way of life is a way to life. Does that sound like a religious slogan? It should do. And that is about all there was to it. No more, no less.[246]

Peter Brook's text was published as a preface to *Towards a Poor Theatre*, which the renowned Italian critic and theatre scholar Antonio Attisani called 'probably the most influential theatre book of the twentieth century'.[247]

---

[244] Barba, *Beyond the Floating Islands*, with a postscript by Ferdinando Taviani, trans. by Judy Barba, with Richard Fowler and others (New York: PAJ Publications, 1986); Barba, *The Paper Canoe: A Guide to Theatre Anthropology*, trans. by Richard Fowler (London and New York: Routledge, 1995).

[245] Peter Brook, 'Grotowski, Art as a Vehicle', in *Grotowski Sourcebook*, pp. 381–84: repr. in Brook, *With Grotowski: Theatre is Just a Form*, ed. by Georges Banu and Grzegorz Ziółkowski with Paul Allain (Wrocław: Grotowski Institute, 2009), pp. 31–35.

[246] Brook, 'Grotowski', in Grotowski, *Towards a Poor Theatre*, pp. 11–13.

[247] Antonio Attisani, *Un teatro apocrifo. Il potenziale dell'arte teatrale nel Workcenter of Jerzy Grotowski and Thomas Richards* [An apocryphal theatre: The potential of theatre art in the Workcenter of Jerzy Grotowski and Thomas Richards] (Milano: Edizioni Medusa, 2006), p. 11.

Twenty-one years after the first publication of the article 'With Je-rzy Grotowski', Brook developed the notion of art as vehicle. His 1987 text, 'Grotowski, Art as Vehicle', ends with the following paragraph:

[...] I would like to ask my friend, our friend Grotowski, to make more clear to us how and to what degree his work on dramatic art is inseparable from having around him people whose real need is for a personal inner evolution. I would like him to throw some light on this. As far as I am concerned, I am convinced that his activity in the realm of 'art as vehicle' is not only of great value, but that no one else can imitate his way, or do it for him. For this reason, I would draw one simple conclusion: Let him speak for himself.[248]

Grotowski's reply came in two texts: 'Performer'[249] and 'From the Theatre Company to Art as Vehicle'.[250]

Approaching the end of the book, I would like to refer again to what Eugenio Barba said in Wrocław on 28 September 1993:

I remember that when we were in Opole, much of our nightly dis-cussions at Restauracja Dworcowa [the railway station restaurant] was about different branches of Hinduism. The 'six major points of view', as they call it in Hinduism – and each of them is right, according to Hinduism, only the point of departure is different, but the goal at the end is the same: liberation from the bondage of illusion. [...] [From Grotowski's texts] never come an indication [...] of a deep knowledge about Asian technique, but at the same time the Asian world is extremely present in his way of thinking. [...] Grotowski is probably the only artist for whom contact with Asia had so profound an influence on his theatrical work, although not because he was interested in Asian theatre but because he was interested in Hinduism, and in the characteristic feature of Hin-duism: how the whole rhythm of life is based on oppositions or contrapositions, that all this dance of energies we are, the dance of Shiva, which is both destructive – through his feet – and creative – through his hands and arms.

But all this was exactly what he called, after Polish critic Tadeusz Kudliński, 'a dialectic of derision and apotheosis'. It was another expression of his need of confronting himself with the wisdom of Hinduism. He was able to understand the essence of this spiritual

---

[248]   Brook, 'Grotowski, Art as a Vehicle', p. 382; repr. in Brook, *With Grotow-ski*, p. 35.

[249]   Grotowski, 'Performer' in *Grotowski Sourcebook*, pp. 376–80.

[250]   Grotowski, 'From the Theatre Company to Art as Vehicle', in Thomas Richards, *At Work with Grotowski on Physical Actions* (London and New York: Routledge, 1995), pp. 113–35.

• *Kazuo Ohno, Sanjukta Panigrahi, Eugenio Barba, and Jerzy Grotowski. Odin Teatret, Holstebro, 1994*

system, and, intuitively, to transform it into technical indications for his actors, although in the beginning he could not find words for it. All the terminology of Grotowski [during the Opole years] was very 'fluid', and then he found very often in other people the right formulation [...]. But essentially what was interesting was that this deep interest in Hinduism functioned as a very concrete 'motor' at that period of his life when he worked in theatre, when he worked with actors, when he worked with spectators – thanks to which he was able to transform his knowledge into very precise professional indications. It was not a technique of the Asian actor but rather some kind of spiritual fascination – and this is the only case I know in European theatre history that a sort of spiritual fascination is transformed into the elements of a craft.[251]

In India, Barba was primarily interested in actor training and technique, and only then did he ask himself if something could be distilled from it for the needs of the European actor and how it could be done. Throughout his artistic trajectory, one can find practical answers to these questions. It is a fascinating topic, but a discussion of it would be outside of the scope of this book.

[251] Recorded on audiotape, Grotowski Institute Archive, Wrocław.

What was the Orient for Jerzy Grotowski? It was never an escape; quite the contrary, it was an experience of existence as a whole, its essence, yet always through specificity and technique.[252] Also, it was never only about words and concepts. This inclination towards experiencing wholeness, towards the archetype of the centre, simultaneously meant the overcoming of the limitations of Eurocentrism and anthropocentrism. Thus encountering the Orient was a call and a challenge, and at the same time it meant discovering, unfolding, revealing (in the literal meaning of these words). As Carl Gustav Jung observed, this process may lead to the '*revelatio* of hidden contents, [...] opening of the depths of the human soul', thus what is accomplished here belongs to the psychological mode in the first place, and not 'only a result of the "playing smart" of the human *ratio*'.[253]

The material presented here is incomplete and fragmentary, yet it sufficiently paints a picture of Jerzy Grotowski as a man seeking adventure and at the same time carrying out cultural research. Supplementing this material with that of Orientalists would facilitate comparative studies. There is no doubt that comprehensive study on the subject – 'Grotowski, the Laboratory Theatre, and cultures of the Orient' – requires collaboration between theatre scholars and Orientalists.

However, even this incomplete material makes it possible to question at least some popular opinions and convictions. For example, it is not true that Grotowski's interest in the cultures of the Orient began with his work on *Shakuntalā* in 1960, as it is commonly thought. Actually, he had been fascinated with the Orient since childhood and this fascination was by no means limited to theatre. As far as geographic range is concerned, against quite common beliefs, Grotowski did not limit himself to India; he got to know many other countries and cultures, and 'to get to know' in his case primarily meant 'to experience'.

Finally, one must state that, in this respect, Grotowski's journey to the East was also a unique phenomenon in the entire history of Polish

---

[252] Grotowski, 'Wschód – Zachód' [The East – the West], trans. from French by Ludwik Flaszen, *Didaskalia. Gazeta Teatralna*, 27 (1998), 6–10. The text is based on a lecture given at Istituto dello Spettacolo (University of Rome) as part of a seminar on the East and the West, 24 September 1984. First edition in Italian: Grotowski, 'Oriente/Occidente', in *Teatro Oriente/Occidente*, pp. 7–19.

[253] Carl Gustav Jung, *O istocie psychiczności. Listy 1906–1961* [On the Nature of the Psyche. Letters 1906–1961], sel., trans. and ed. by Robert Reszke (Warsaw: Wrota, 1996), pp. 95, 97–98.

theatre. It is true that among Polish theatrical artists Grotowski was not the only one interested in Oriental theatres and, more broadly, in the cultures of the East.[254] However, his relation was particularly intimate, probably because of his high competence in this field and his unique sensitivity. The task of this text was to give evidence of that relation, or at least to somehow indicate and provisionally clarify it.

Bibliographical Note:

On 24 September 1984, during the opening of the international congress on relations between the theatrical cultures of the East and the West, 'Teatro Oriente/Occidente', at the Centro Teatro Ateneo at the University of Rome,[255] Grotowski delivered a talk in French, titled *'Orient/Occident'*, noted in the conference programme under the Italian title 'I malintesi fra le due culture. L'est nell'occhio dell'ovest e l'ovest nell'occhio dell'est' [Misunderstandings between two cultures: The East in the eyes of the West, and the West in the eyes of the East].[256] A Polish translation of the text, by Ludwik Flaszen, was published in 1998, twelve years after the first edition.[257]

---

[254] Konrad Swinarski, after his return from India, where he spent several weeks in autumn 1973 as a delegate of the Ministry of Culture and Art, said: 'I saw a lot of theatres. Western European and American theatres usually have no moral background. The most fascinating for me was a Hindu religious ritual theatre in Kerala. It is one of the few schools where the acting profession is trained from the age of four. A few months ago I was involved in preparations for a show, which began at 2 a.m. and lasted until the next day's evening. The performance presented a rite connected with some kind of contemplation. This theatre made a big impression on me.' In: 'Co mnie fascynuje?' [What fascinates me?], Konrad Swinarski interviewed by Lidia Nowicka, *Kurier Polski*, 10–11 August 1974, p. 4. On the temple theatre in Kerala: Byrski, 'Teatr najantyczniejszy' [The most ancient theatre], *Pamiętnik Teatralny*, 1–2 (1969), 11–47.

[255] The congress was held from 2 to 28 September.

[256] There is a multiplicated 20-page typescript of this speech in French (Roma: Istituto del Teatro e dello Spettacolo, 1984). Two years later it was translated to Italian by Luisa Tinti and published as 'Oriente/Occidente', in *Teatro Oriente/Occidente*, pp. 7–19. English translation: 'Around Theatre: The Orient – The Occident', trans. by Mauren Schaffer Price, in *Asian Theatre Journal* vol. 6, no. 1 (1989), 1–11. First French edition: 'Orient/Occident', in *Confluences. Le dialogue des cultures dans les spectacles contemporains. Essais en l'honneur d'Anne Ubersfeld* [Confluences: The Dialogue of Cultures in Contemporary Spectacles. Essays in Honour of Anne Ubersfeld], ed. by Patrice Pavis (Saint-Cyr l'Ecole: Prépublications du petit bricoleur de Bois-Robert, 1990), pp. 231–43.

[257] Grotowski, 'Around Theatre: The Orient – The Occident'.

2.
LUDWIK FLASZEN
ABOUT GROTOWSKI'S ORIENTALIZING

ON 14 JANUARY 2010, the eleventh anniversary of Grotowski's death, *Gazeta Wyborcza* published an extensive conversation between Tadeusz Sobolewski and Ludwik Flaszen. We can learn from it how radically differently both founders of the Laboratory Theatre experienced the East:

Tadeusz Sobolewski: Are you attracted by the East? You spent the war years there.

Ludwik Flaszen: Yes, I spent the war in the Soviet Union. First in the Mari Autonomous Republic, East of Moscow, in the woods, where I worked as a young lumberjack, a child-lumberjack indeed. Together with my parents I was brought there from Lviv in a freight carriage in June 1940, after a night search [of our home by NKVD]. However, it was not a gulag but the so-called 'spets-poselok', with a status between resettlement and a labour camp, where people lived with families and one was allowed to move without permit within a two-kilometre radius.

We lived in barracks, in the forest, in a tight space, many families together, in one room. Wooden beds, bedbugs, flocks of cockroaches, outside mosquitoes in summer, frost in winter, minus twenty degrees centigrade on average. In winter wolves were coming close to the settlement, in summer vipers in the forest, but also plenty of mushrooms, blueberries, raspberries. My great experience of wild nature. Although under the watchful eye of a NKVD guard with a dog. One night we were awakened by an extraordinary brightness in the sky, aurora borealis. A cosmic theatre for a little Siberian exile. Horror – and wonder.

Liberated in autumn 1941 thanks to the Sikorski-Mayski Agreement,[258] we went south – first on a ship down the Volga, then across the Caspian Sea, to Uzbekistan. The Orient, camels, donkeys, bazaars, women wearing yashmaks, men in tubeteikas, in colourful robes, each of them with decorated khanjars at their belts. We lived like medieval people – in shanties made of unburned clay. Scorpions, lots of frogs, like in a doomed Biblical Egypt. Vipers in the garden, where one relieved oneself squatting.

---

[258] Re-establishment of diplomatic relations between the Soviet Union and Poland, signed on 30 July 1941. It resulted in the invalidation of previous pacts of the USSR with Nazi Germany and the release of thousands of Polish POWs imprisoned in Soviet camps.

This was probably why I was a little skeptical about Grot[owski]'s orientalization, his wanderings in the capacity of a privileged student of Moscow's GITIS, and later, to India, as a well-known artist. For him those were spiritual journeys to other civilizations in search of the truth. I lived there. Famine, dysentery, people dying on the streets. My father was dying, my mother was dying, I was also close to death. We lived under constant threat, under the watch of NKVD, feeling that there was no escape from that world.

We survived – it was a miracle – all three of us: father, mother, and I.[259]

Quite peculiar is this posthumous dialogue with Grotowski, carried on by the co-founder of the Laboratory Theatre, a companion on his artistic path and its invaluable commentator.

---

[259] 'Trzewik Montaigne'a. Z Ludwikiem Flaszenem, współtwórcą Teatru Laboratorium i współpracownikiem Jerzego Grotowskiego, rozmawia Tadeusz Sobolewski' [Montaigne's shoe. Ludwik Flaszen, a co-founder of the Laboratory Theatre and Jerzy Grotowski's collaborator, interviewed by Tadeusz Sobolewski], *Gazeta Wyborcza*, 14 January 2010, pp. 14–17; See: Flaszen, *Teatr skazany na magię* [A theatre condemned to magic], ed. by Henryk Chłystowski (Kraków and Wrocław: Wydawnictwo Literackie, 1983); Flaszen, *Grotowski & Company*.

A Final Note

CONCLUDING THIS BOOK, I would like to make two points.

First, for me as an author who tried to gather and interpret all possible evidence related to Jerzy Grotowski's journeys to the East – in a narrow, literal sense, as well as broadly, metaphorically understood – it is obvious that it was the East of an artist rather than of an Orientalist scholar. This distinction signifies fundamentally different attitudes and goals. Certainly, Grotowski experienced India in a different way than Indologists; likewise, he experienced China in a different way than Sinologists; or Japan in a different way than Japanologists and so on. The key to his experience of the East were in all cases his revelations; the research he conducted in advance or during his trips served as preparation, and sometimes as inspiration. His first inspiration was Brunton's book read in childhood and then a two-month trip to Central Asia in the spring of 1956 taken during his studies in Moscow.

The second point is somewhat related: an artist, unlike an academic researcher, is not obliged to disclose the true source and the reasons for his/her creation. Artists often conceal their sources, inspirations, and reasons for their fascinations, or knowingly provide false clues. This was true also for Grotowski. For example, the officially given reason for his first trip to India was research for a book on classical Indian theatre. He knew very well that he did not have to write such a book and that he would not be kept accountable. He could even allow himself to give such information to the public as a joke. Certainly such behaviour would be unacceptable in the case of a researcher. And this is another difference between an artist and an academic scholar.

This book, by definition, is not principally addressed to academic researchers of the East. I lack that kind of competence and motivation. The book is intended for a variety of readers and, also in this sense – 'open'.

This does not mean, of course, that an Orientalist scholar cannot find in it something interesting, and perhaps new.

Chronicle

1941–1943

Nienadówka near Rzeszów
Jerzy Grotowski reads Paul Brunton's *A Search in Secret India*,
translated by Wanda Dynowska. He writes his 'Zapiski inicjacyjne'
[Notes on initiation] (kept in the Manuscript Archives at the
Ossolineum Library in Wrocław).

1956

April–May, Uzbekistan and Turkmenistan
Grotowski's route: on 1 April by plane from Moscow to Baku; on 1–2
April by plane from Baku to Ashgabat in southern Turkmenistan;
on 2 April by railway across the Kara Kum desert (along the
Soviet-Iranian border) to the Bayram-Ali Oasis (near Afghanistan);
beginning 2 April, a seven-week stay in the health resort of the
former emir's palace; c. 20 May, return by railway from Ashgabat
via Tashkent (near Himalayas) along the Syr Darya River; on 22
May, across the desert; on 23 May, Bukhara; on 24 and 25 May,
Samarkand; 25 May, Aral; 26 May, route across Kazakhstan; 29 May,
return to Moscow. He writes in his letters:

18 May 1956, to Romuald Farat:

> Many impressions, still too fresh to write about them succinctly.
> In short: architecture in Murgabu oasis: the ruins of ancient
> Antioch, a town of Alexander the Great – massive and symmetrical
> buildings, made of clay and unburned bricks, just as everything
> here, even today. The architecture of Bayramaly and the city of
> Merv is typical of Arabic traditions, filtered by Persia, something
> like *One Thousand and One Nights*. Mosques, domes, towers,
> Arabic inscriptions. People's clothes are original and beautiful,
> multicoloured; women who maintain tradition (i.e. faithful
> Muslims) wear veils and walk several metres in front or behind
> their husbands. Common means of locomotion and transportation
> besides bicycles and cars: camels, donkeys to ride and donkeys
> harnessed to two-wheel carts.
>
> Yesterday I was on an excursion to the ruins of ancient Antioch
> and Merv; tomorrow I am visiting a mausoleum of Sultan Sanjar,
> considered a holy place by Muslims.
>
> On my way back I want to visit Bukhara, Samarkand and
> Tashkent (Uzbekistan), cities of wonderful architecture (especially
> mosques) and several hundred years of history. For many centuries,

even millennia, they were unified with Iran, thus there are many monuments of pre-Arabic, Zoroastrian culture there.[260]

18 April 1956, to Alina Obidniak:

A Session of the Board of Cult[ure] is certainly an event. I do not overestimate its results. As far as my poems are concerned, I do not believe in the possibility of publication, unless [Artur] Sandauer and [Tadeusz] Kantor get their own magazine.[261] And this is obviously impossible. Yet the issue bothers me much less, as you can imagine. I am proud of my nationality; our artists are above mythology and the burning of witches.[262]

28 April 1956, to Anna Obidniak:

I am reading a lot – exclusively in Russian. Before my departure, I read only Russian fragments, and not without some effort. Here there was nothing else, so I plucked up my courage, and now there is almost no difference to me whether I read in Polish or in Rus[sian]. I surprised myself. I have read over two thousand p[ages] from, among other works, [Tolstoy's] *War and Peace*, Dostoyevsky's *The Idiot*, works of Lermontov, of Mayakovsky, Russ[ian] translations of Indian *Mahabharata* and Persian *Shahnameh*, various works on the Middle E[ast], etc. Read *War and Peace* and *The Idiot* one more time; the philosophical depths of these works are shocking.[263]

23 May 1956, to Irena Jun:

I am writing in a hotel. I am staying in a common room; my neighbours include Uzbeks, Russians, Turkmen, Kazakhs, Persians, Tajiks, Afghans, Kurds, Armenians. I am starting to believe that if you accost two passers-by one by one in Bukhara, they will certainly be of two different nationalities.[264]

1957

December, Kraków, Student Club Pod Jaszczurami

Jerzy Grotowski gives a series of 16 lectures on Eastern philosophy.[265] They are arranged in two sub-series: 'On the foundations

---

[260] Obidniak, *Pola energii*, pp. 202–03.

[261] Artur Sandauer (1913–1989), Polish literary critic, essayist, translator. In the 1950s he was an active opponent of Socialist realism, and his work was barred from publication.

[262] Obidniak, *Pola energii*, p. 205.

[263] Obidniak, *Pola energii*, p. 206.

[264] Osiński, Listy 'Jerzego Grotowskiego z ZSRR, 1955–1956', in Osiński, *Jerzy Grotowski. Źródła, inspiracje, konteksty*, pp. 46–47.

[265] 'Odczyty. "Pod Jaszczurami"', p. 6.

of Hindu philosophy', given between 15 December 1957 and 26 January 1958, and 'Oriental philosophical thought', given between 30 March and 1 June 1958.

The first sub-series included seven lectures: 'Basic systems of Hindu philosophy' (15 December 1957); 'Philosophy of Buddha' (22 December); 'Philosophical systems of Buddhism' (29 December); 'Philosophy of yoga' (5 January 1958); 'Philosophy of *Upanishads* – [Adi] Shankara's system' (12 January); 'Philosophy of *Upanishads* – Ramanuja's system' (17 January); 'Contemporary schools' (26 January).

The second sub-series included nine lectures, four of them on Chinese philosophy: 'Basic currents of Chinese philosophy' (30 March 1958); 'Confucius' (20 April); 'Taoism (general characteristics)' (13 April); 'Taoism (philosophical canon: Laozi, Zhuangzi, Lie Yukou)' (27 April); two on Japanese philosophy: 'Basic currents of Japanese philosophy' (4 April), 'Philosophy of Zen (Zen-Buddhism)' (11 May); two on Indian philosophy: 'Basic currents of Indian philosophy' (18 May); 'Philosophy of Advaita Vedanta' (25 May); the last lecture, given on 1 June 1958 was titled 'European Analogies'.[266]

1958

20 June
Polish Radio broadcasts *Shakuntalā*, a radio play based on fragments of the ancient Indian drama by Kalidāsa, with motifs from the *Upanishads*. Translated by Stanisław Schayer. Radio adaptation by Jerzy Grotowski. Directed by Jerzy Grotowski and Aleksandra Mianowska.

1959

C. 25 July – c. 22 August
Grotowski travels to several countries of the Middle East and Africa. In his letters to Alina Obidniak, he writes:

3 August 1959, Istanbul, Turkey: '[…] I am leaving Turkey today. My

---

[266] 'Pod Jaszczurami', *Dziennik Polski*, 6 February 1958; k, 'Ambitne plany Klubu "Pod Jaszczurami"' [Ambitious plans of Pod Jaszczurami Club], *Dziennik Polski*, 22 March 1958; Jerzy Huczkowski, 'Studencki Komitet Rewolucyjny w Krakowie i jego losy'; Huczkowski, 'Zwalisty', pp. 40–41.

proper "adventure" begins here: Syria, Lebanon, Egypt. Greece en route. Many impressions, and "surprises" – "to avoid boredom"...'

August [19]59, Egypt (the United Arab Republic), the Nile Delta: 'Here is a new stage of my wandering through cities of Asia and Africa. Exotica, tropical heat, "many adventures", many surprising impressions.'

29 August, Lanckorona [Poland]: 'One week ago I returned form my last strange journey of one thousand nights: the Balkans, Greece, Turkey (Istanbul) [until 3 August], Lebanon (Beirut), the United Arab Republic: Syria (Latakia) and Egypt (Port Said on the Suez Canal, Alexandria, the Nile Delta, Cairo, Giza, part of Libyan Sahara). Many days on sea, twice under "storm conditions". I survived the journey excellently, and returned drunk with impressions. To arrange everything internally, I went for a week to a hermitage (almost literally), in a dense forest near Lanckorona, a hut in the woods, 4 km from the nearest settlements, completely alone, without books, without newspapers. To post this letter I have to walk 8 km through the woods.

On 1 September I am beginning a new job as a director in Opole.'[267]

13 October, Kraków
Polish Radio broadcasts *Kredowe koło* [*The Circle of Chalk*], a radio play based on an old Chinese legend in Klabund's version. Translated by Michalina Szwarcówna and Józef Jedlicz. Literary and radio adaptation by Jerzy Grotowski. Directed by Jerzy Grotowski and Józef Grotowski.

1960

20 March
Polish Radio broadcasts *Nagarjuna*, a radio play based on old Tibetan tales. Edited and translated by Marian Bielicki. Written and directed by Jerzy Grotowski.

13 December, Opole, Theatre of 13 Rows
Premiere of *Shakuntalā*, an ancient Indian erotic tale in two acts, based on the drama by Kālidāsa. Translated by Stanisław Schayer. Adapted and directed by Jerzy Grotowski. The director's assistants: Rena Mirecka, Antoni Jahołkowski. Stage design by Jerzy Gurawski

---

[267] Obidniak, *Pola energii*, pp. 234–35.

(since then Grotowski's permanent collaborator until *The Constant Prince*). Costumes: children from the Fine Arts School in Opole. Forty-three performances, including eighteen outside Opole. Cast: Rena Mirecka as Shakuntalā; Zygmunt Molik as King Dushyanta; Antoni Jahołkowski as Joker; Barbara Barska as Anasuya; Ewa Lubowiecka as Prijamvada; Antoni Jahołkowski as Fisherman; Andrzej Bielski as Yogi 1; Adam Kurczyna as Yogi 2; 'many other people, animals, birds and plants, not to mention insects'.

1961

8–15 January, Kraków
Guest performances of *Shakuntalā* in Dom Plastyka, ul. Łobzowska 3.

21–22 January, Łódź
Guest performances of *Shakuntalā* in the venue of the Student Satirical Theatre Cytryna.

16–29 March, Wrocław
Guest performances of *Shakuntalā* in the mirror hall of the Student Club Pałacyk.

8–9 April, Kędzierzyn
Theatre of 13 Rows, the Voivodeship Committee of the Union of Socialist Youth (ZMS) and the Factory Council of the Azoty Chemical Plant organized a weekend event called the Workers' Theatre Fete in the Factory Community Centre. The programme included: 8 April, 6 p.m., lecture by Jerzy Grotowski, performance of *Mystery-Bouffe*, dancing party with revue shows of actors of the Theatre of 13 Rows; 9 April, 6 p.m., lecture by Jerzy Grotowski, performance of *Shakuntalā*, discussion on the artistic ideals of the Theatre of 13 Rows, dancing party.

8 May, 7 p.m., Błotnica
Rehearsal for *Shakuntalā* (preparation for the Village Theatre Fete).

9 May, Błotnica
The Village Theatre Fete, including a performance of *Shakuntalā*, one Estrada Publicystyczna and revue shows.[268]

---

[268] Estrada Publicystyczna [The journalistic platform], general term for several 'textual montages', or quasi-cabaret programmes performed by actors of the Theatre of 13 Rows, in Opole and on tours around the region in the early

12 May, Opole
Seminar of the Theatre of 13 Rows, 'Oni są naszą tradycją: Craig, Meyerhold, Artaud, Tairow, Witkacy' [They are our tradition: Craig, Meyerhold, Artaud, Tairov, Witkacy]. Participation in the Workers' Theatre Fete: revue shows at the party in the Opole Knitting Factory. In the evening, *Shakuntalā* was performed in the auditorium of the Theatre of 13 Rows.

21–22 May, Opole
The noted Polish poet Władysław Broniewski visits Opole and attends *Shakuntalā* and *Turyści* [Tourists]. He invites the group for dinner. He is to remain a faithful friend of the Theatre of 13 Rows till the end of his life. Broniewski's remarks were published in the programmes of *Forefathers' Eve* by Mickiewicz and *Pamiętnik Śląski* [Silesian diary]. The full text of his letter to the members of the Theatre of 13 Rows was published in the June 1974 issue of *Dialog*. The publication of the letter was preceded by the editors' commentary. I quote with some abbreviations:

> [...] Broniewski's letter to the Theatre of 13 Rows is not a private correspondence; it is rather a statement or an open letter. There is no header; it was written on the spot, in Opole, on 22 May 1961. [...] Broniewski wrote it in the period of increasing attacks by the press and theatre circles against the Theatre of 13 Rows that it was gibberish, odd, snobbish, 'suspiciously' experimental, and useless to 'us' in general. The small ensemble in provincial Opole was already a black sheep of Polish theatre. There was the threat of administrative decisions to melt the theatre. [...] Broniewski was among the first to defend Grotowski and his group, as it is confirmed by the present letter. It is also a beautiful testimony of Broniewski's honesty as an artist. His long-established lyrical imagination, style, even the problems he focused on in his work seem very distant from the proposals of Grotowski's theatre at that time. Yet Broniewski did not hesitate to risk his entire authority as a poet-revolutionary in defence of the young, almost unknown – but already infamous – ensemble from Opole, because he saw in it an authentic artistic phenomenon, Read: a phenomenon that should not only be respected but also protected.

1960s. Highly journalistic, raw and simple in form, they were intended to convince local authorities of the relevance of the Theatre, at that time often accused of political and moral appropriateness. Seth Baumrin, 'Ketmanship in Opole: Jerzy Grotowski and the Price of Artistic Freedom', *TDR: The Drama Review*, 4 (2009), 49–77.

Autumn, Warsaw, Society of Polish-Indian Friendship, Wierzbowa Street
Shakuntalā, scenes from the performance with Rena Mirecka[269], Antoni Jahołkowski, and Zygmunt Molik. Based on information provided by Jerzy Grotowski and Antoni Jahołkowski.

1962

12 February, Opole
Eugenio Barba, a young recipient of the UNESCO scholarship, an Italian citizen who came from Norway, writes a letter to the managers of the Theatre of 13 Rows:

> I would like to get professional qualifications in directing. Since I am particularly interested in unconventional theatre, I seek an assistant director position in your theatre, and eventually wish to work as an independent director under the guidance of director Jerzy Grotowski. At the same time I am going to continue appropriate studies in literature as advised by you. After receiving a positive answer, with your help, I would like to apply to the appropriate Polish authorities for an official diploma.

Appended to the letter is a curriculum vitae with some information in English, French, and Polish:

> August, September 1958: While in France, Barba carries out a sociological poll among coal miners in Lorraine.

> 1960: he receives a Magister Artium diploma in literary history from the University of Oslo.

> 1960: as a member of the Norwegian delegation at the Scandinavian Summer University, he participates in seminars on theatre and architecture.

> 1954–1960: he undertakes numerous journeys and research visits in many countries in Europe, as well as in Turkey, Israel, India, and the Far East.

> June 1961: he passes the entrance exam to the Department of Directing in the Warsaw drama school, with Professor Bohdan Korzeniewski as his tutor.

---

[269] Artistic pseudonym of Irena Kądziołka.

22 March – 10 April, Kraków, Krzysztofory Gallery and Teatr 38
Guest performances of *Forefathers' Eve* based on Mickiewicz: 23, 24 and 31 March, 4, 5 and 6 April, Krzysztofory; guest performances of *Kordian* based on Słowacki: 27–29 and 30 March, 1, 3, 7 and 8 April, Krzysztofory; guest performances of *The Idiot* based on Dostoyevsky: 23, 25, 27 and 28 March, 1 April, Teatr 38, 5 and 8 April, Krzysztofory.

One of the performances of *Forefathers' Eve* was attended by two Swiss journalists from *Journal de Genève*: the editor-in-chief Olivier Reverdin and the writer, playwright and translator Walter Weideli. In the 26 April issue of *Journal de Genève*, Weideli published an article titled *Essayer le pour, essayer le contre*; its extensive excerpts were published in Polish translation under the title *Próbować pro, próbować kontra* in the April 1963 issue of *Materiały – Dyskusje*. Grotowski always considered this text as one of the most important publications about the early activities of the Laboratory Theatre.

It is noteworthy that Grotowski drew knowledge of Noh theatre from two Swiss who also sent Zeami's book to him. (Published in 1960, by Gallimard, as *'La tradition secrète du noh' suivi de 'Une journée de Noh'*, translated and annotated by the world-famous Japanologist Renée Sieffert.[270]) In the letter dated 'Opole, 18 May 1962', Grotowski thanked Waideli for the book and for his text on the Theatre of 13 Rows: 'Je vous remercie cordialement pour le livre sur le théâtre Nō et pour votre chaleureuse description de notre theater.' [271] On 6 July 1962 Grotowski informed Waideli about his planned journeys to Finland and China and his expected return to Poland by the end of September: 'A la fin de juillet j'irai en Finlande et en suite en Chine d'où je rentrerai à la fin de septembre.'[272]

---

[270] Zeami, *'La tradition secrète du nō' suivi de 'Une journée de nō'*.

[271] A one-page letter, typed on white paper, A4 format, with a stamp reading 'Kierownik Artystyczny i Dyrektor Teatru 13 Rzędów Jerzy Grotowski' in the bottom right corner and a handwritten signature. Grotowski Institute Archive, Wrocław.

[272] A one-page letter, typed on white paper, A4 format, with a stamp reading 'Teatr Laboratorium "13 Rzędów", Opole, Rynek 4' in the top left corner, a stamp stating 'Kierownik Artystyczny i Dyrektor Teatru 13 Rzędów Jerzy Grotowski' (Artistic Director and Manager of the Theatre of 13 Rows Jerzy Grotowski), and a handwritten signature. Grotowski Institute Archive, Wrocław. Osiński, *Grotowski and His Laboratory*, pp. 65–66; Osiński, 'Mei Lanfang, legenda opery pekińskiej. Polska recepcja i konteksty', in Osiński, *Polskie kontakty teatralne z Orientem w XX wieku. II: Studia*, pp. 49–92, 255–63.

6 March, Warsaw
The Dean of the State Theatre Academy, Professor Bohdan Korzeniewski, writes a letter to Grotowski, informing him that Eugenio Barba had passed the entrance examination entitling him to study as an auditor and 'to undertake his theatrical practice in the Theatre of 13 Rows'.

10 May, Opole
Grotowski writes (in French) an evaluation letter to the Ministry of Foreign Affairs of Italy in Rome, about Eugenio Barba's apprenticeship in the Theatre of 13 Rows:

> His choice was dictated by the fact that our theatre is a theatre 'laboratory', and that Barba's interests coincide with our exploration. [...] At his personal request, he received a special permit from the Dean of the Department of Directing of the Warsaw's State Theatre Academy to conduct practical work in our theatre. On 1 February 1962 he started working as assistant director (under my guidance he leads independent practical exercises with our actors and, at the same time, he actively assists in regular directing work). He also effectively continues his theoretical studies of contemporary theatre, especially on the period of the Great Reform. Taking into consideration the special nature of our theatre, Barba also studies psychology of Carl Gustav Jung.
>
> My practical and theoretical research of contemporary theatre, also as a teacher at the State Theatre Academy in Kraków, allows me to recognize the work of Eugenio Barba as very promising.

17 August – 15 September, China
Grotowski visits the People's Republic of China as an official delegate of the Team for Theatre Issues of the Ministry of Culture and Art. His visit includes: Beijing (17–24 August); Nanjing (25–28 August); Shanghai (28 August – 2 September); Hangzhou (3–4 September); Shanghai (4 September); Beijing (5–9 September).

17 September, Opole
In his letter to the Ministry of Higher Education, Grotowski describes the courses taken by Eugenio Barba at the Laboratory Theatre of 13 Rows between 1 February and the end of July 1962:

> 1. Theoretical studies related to the direction of our theatre, thus covering mainly the traditions of the Great Reform, tragifarce, the issue of collective representations (Durkheim and Jung, among others). 2. Studying of published and unpublished theoretical materials of the Laboratory Theatre of 13 Rows (issues of staging and

working with actors), and regular seminars with Jerzy Grotowski and Ludwik Flaszen on the above issues. 3. Regular presence at rehearsals and practical exercises of the Theatre: a) Attendance at the daily training of actors: calisthenics, physical exercises, plasticity of gesture and movement, breathing and diction exercises, etudes. Barba's high degree of competence in these exercises allowed us to entrust him with conducting etude work with the actors. b) Presence at the current rehearsals of the Theatre: since April 1962 Mr Barba has worked as an assistant director on a new production titled *Akropolis*, based on Wyspiański (adapted and directed by Grotowski); Mr Barba's assistantship is active: he conducted several rehearsals with the actors by himself, within the guidelines of the director's general staging concept, and with good results. 4. After Mr Barba completes one more directing assistantship, the Theatre's management intends to entrust him with directing Dante's *Divine Comedy*. It will be an independent work (under the artistic supervision of Jerzy Grotowski). The Theatre's management hopes that this production will provide the basis for the final examination in directing for Mr Barba. 5. Mr Barba wrote (in French) a paper about our staging methods and ways of working with actors; he is currently preparing a more comprehensive work as a doctoral dissertation, to be defended in Poland.

28 September, Opole
The Theatre of Small Forms from the Voivodeship Community Centre organizes a talk with Jerzy Grotowski, the director of the Theatre of 13 Rows, on classical Chinese theatre.

1967

August, Iran
Grotowski visits Iran.

1968

The winter break of 1968, India
Grotowski's first visit to the Indian subcontinent.

1969

August 1969, India
Grotowski's second visit to the Indian subcontinent, described in detail in his letter to Eugenio Barba, dated Calcutta, 10 August 1969.

1970

C. 5 July – 23 August 1970, India
Grotowski's third visit to the Indian subcontinent, lasting six weeks. Preparations for this voyage are mentioned in his letter to Tadeusz Byrski and – indirectly – to his son, Maria Krzysztof Byrski, written on 15 April 1970 in Wrocław.[273] M. K. Byrski answered with a letter written on 27 April in Warsaw, to which Grotowski replied on 9 May in Wrocław. The last letter regarding that issue was written by M. K. Byrski on 4 June 1970.[274]

23 August, Shiraz
Returning from India, Grotowski meets with the members of the Laboratory Theatre at the airport in Shiraz.

23 August – 12 October, Middle East
The sixth foreign tour of the Wrocław-based Laboratory Theatre: Iran (Shiraz, Teheran) and Lebanon (Beirut). Performances of *The Constant Prince* based on Calderon/Słowacki: Shiraz: 28–31 August and 1, 3, 4 September (Shiraz-Persepolis Festival of Arts); Emir El-Amin near Beirut: 9, 10, 12–14 September; Teheran: 17 September – 11 October.

Publication of a Persian translation of *Towards a Poor Theatre*: Jerzy Grotowski, *Besuje teatre biczic*, translated by Hasan Marandi (Persepolis, Shiraz: 1970), shortened version.

1971

'Japońskie polonica' [Japanese polonica], an interview with Yukio Kudō, a lecturer at the University of Warsaw since 1967 and a great propagator of Polish literature in Japan, conducted by Andrzej Włodarczyk, *Tygodnik Kulturalny*, 3 October 1971, p. 5. Discussed are: the premiere of Witold Gombrowicz's *The Wedding* [*Ślub*], translated by Kazuo Yonekawa, planned for the end of September in the Tokyo-based theatre Bungakuza (1971); Jerzy Grotowski; and two plays by Witkacy, *The Mother* [*Matka*] and *The Shoemakers* [*Szewcy*].

---

[273] Osiński, *Nazywał nas bratnim teatrem*, pp. 209–10.
[274] Ibid., pp. 211–13.

Japanese translation of *Towards a Poor Theatre*: Jerzy Grotowski, *Jikken-engeki-ron*. *Motazaru engeki mezashite* [A treatise on experimental theatre: Towards a poor theatre], translated by Tsutomu Ōshima, commentary by Tetsuo Toshimitsu (Tokyo: Teatoro S.A., 1971).

1972

17–20 April, Paris
Jerzy Grotowski holds a seminar at the Theatre of Nations. On 20 April in Le Théâtre Recamier he takes part in a public debate with the seminar participants, among them Tadashi Suzuki, the founder of the Waseda-shōgekijō.

1973

12–15 August, Tokyo
'Jerzy Grotowski gives lectures on the work with the actor'. This was the official purpose of Grotowski's journey given to the media. The real course of his only stay in Japan was presented by Tadashi Suzuki in his text published in the October issue of *Shingeki*: 'Bunka – to engeki kōi no konkyo', *Shingeki*, 10 (1973), 36–41. Henryk Lipszyc comments:

> Jerzy Grotowski paid a short visit to Japan, a stopover, so to speak, on his way [home] after a trip across the United States, Canada, and Australia', write the editors in a preliminary note to the conversation with Suzuki. 'In Japan, I would like to meet with Tadashi Suzuki and Kayoko Shiraishi', Grotowski requested. He managed to do it, although his visit lasted only a day and a half. Accompanied by Suzuki, he also managed to visit the Shibuya district at night and watch a rehearsal in a Noh theatre. [The next day he flew to Bangkok].

• hl [Henryk Lipszyc], 'Japończyk o Grotowskim', p. 167. Osiński, *Grotowski i jego Laboratorium*, pp. 199–201; Osiński, *Grotowski wytycza trasy*, pp. 138–40.

1976

C. 20 December 1976 – 10 January 1977, India
Grotowski, with his mother, takes a trip to India.

1978

4–7 June, Warsaw and Grzegorzewice near Warsaw
The symposium 'Art of the Beginner', followed by a training of
the same name, under the guidance of Jerzy Grotowski. Among
the participants are Hideo Kanze, an eminent Japanese actor and
master of classical Noh theatre, and Krishnan Nambudiri, an actor-
dancer of Indian theatre Kathakali. It was the first official visit of
Noh and Kathakali actors to Poland. Hideo Kanze's translator was
Henryk Lipszyc, a scholar at the Faculty of Oriental Studies at the
University of Warsaw, who later became the ambassador of the
Republic of Poland to Japan.

• Jerzy Grotowski, 'L'art du débutant' [The art of the beginner],
text drawn up on the lines of Georges Banu's French version, from
the original consecutive translation of the conference by Mr Andre
Gregory, Warsaw, 4 June 1978, *International Theatre Information*
(Paris: ITI, 1978), pp. 6, 11; Anna Czekanowska, 'Teatr – muzyka
– człowiek', *Ruch Muzyczny*, 20 (1978), 15; Zbigniew Osiński,
'Symposium sur "l'Art du débutant" – Symposium: "The Art of the
Beginner"', *Le Théâtre en Pologne – The Theatre in Poland*, 9–10
(1978), 18–20.

1980

2–25 February, India
The seven-person international and intercultural team of Theatre
of Sources led by Grotowski travels to West Bengal. The group
includes: Micado Cadet (Haiti), Pierre Guicheney (France), Fran-
çois Liège (France), Marek Musiał (Poland), Catherine Seyferth
(West Germany), and Jacek Zmysłowski (Poland). The purpose of
the visit is 'to accomplish tasks leading towards opening the initial
phase of Theatre of Sources and carry out research among rural-
tribal groups in the Hindu cultural circle'. The group conducts
a brief workshop with the members of The Living Theatre at their
headquarters in Khardaha, near Calcutta, then (16–22 February)
another workshop, with eighteen participants, in Kenduli, in
Birbhum District. Grotowski invites five of the participants (Baul
Gaur Khepa, graduate student Dibyendu Gangipadhya (Gangali),
and three members of The Living Theatre: Abani Biswas, Prabir
Guha, and Ramakrishna Dhar) to take part in the work of the

international team of Theatre of Sources in Wrocław (between 7 May and 31 August 1980).[275]

1984

24–28 September, Rome
Università degli Studi di Roma La Sapienza Centro Teatro Ateneo organizes the International Congress 'Teatro Oriente/Occidente' (with Agostino Lombardo as president, and Ferruccio Marotti as director). Grotowski delivers a keynote in French, 'Orient/Occident', listed in the conference programme under the Italian title 'I malintesi fra le due culture. L'est nell'occhio dell'ovest e l'ovest nell'occhio dell'est' [Misunderstandings between two cultures: The East in the eyes of the West, and the West in the eyes of the East].[276]

Chinese and Korean translations of Grotowski's *Towards a Poor Theatre* are published: *Mai xiang zhipu xiju*, translated by Wei Shi, translation reviewed by Liu Anyi (Beijing: Zhongguo xiju chubanshe, 1984); and *Gananhan yeonkeuk*, translated by Go Seung Gil (Seoul: Gyobo Moongo, 1984).

1992

Tokyo
The third issue of the magazine *Polonica* is published in 1991 and 1992, under Professor Shōzō Yoshigami as the editor-in-chief. It includes a set of texts by and on Grotowski in Japanese: Jerzy Grotowski, 'Performer', translated by Tokimasa Sekiguchi, pp. 12–21; Peter Brook, 'Gurotofusuki, nakadachi toshite no geijutsu (Art as a Vehicle)', translated by Tokimasa Sekiguchi, pp. 22–26; Tetsuo

---

[275] *Chitrabani* magazine (Calcutta), January 1981, pp. 1–12, on Jerzy Grotowski and the Theatre of Sources.
[276] There is a multiplicated 20-page typescript of this speech in French (Roma: Istituto del Teatro e dello Spettacolo, 1984). Two years later it was translated into Italian by Luisa Tinti and published as 'Oriente/Occidente', in *Teatro Oriente/Occidente*, pp. 7–19. English translation: 'Around Theatre: The Orient – The Occident', trans. by Mauren Schaffer Price, in *Asian Theatre Journal* (University of Hawaii Press), vol. 6, no. 1 (1989), 1–11. First French edition: 'Orient/Occident', in *Confluences. Le dialogue des cultures dans les spectacles contemporains. Essais en l'honneur d'Anne Ubersfeld*, ed. by Patrice Pavis, prépublications du petit bricoleur de Bois-Robert, Saint-Cyr l'Ecole, 1990), pp. 231–43.

Toshimitsu, 'Motazaru engeki mezashite (Towards a Poor Theatre)', pp. 28–36; Zbigniew Osiński, 'Gurotofusuki no hiraita michi: obujekutibu dorama kara richuaru ātsu made (Grotowski Blazes the Trails: From Objective Drama to Ritual Arts)', translated by Shōzō Yoshigami, pp. 37–57; Hideo Kanze, 'Gurotofusuki to no deai (The Encounter with Grotowski)', pp. 60–61.

1993

15–16 December, Ankara, Department of Theatre, Ankara University
Zbigniew Osiński's lecture 'On the work of Jerzy Grotowski' for faculty and students, followed by a presentation of documentary films.[277]

• Zbigniew Osiński, 'Grotowski i Teatr Laboratorium wobec kultury Orientu', in Osiński, *Grotowski wytycza trasy. Studia i szkice*, pp. 113–46.

1996

14–20 April, Ankara, Ankara University
Symposium 'Polish Contemporary Theatre', organized by the Wrocław-based Grotowski Centre and the Ankara University. Papers are presented by: Stanisław Krotoski, 'Organization of Theatrical Life in Poland'; Janusz Degler, 'The Great Reform of Theatre in Poland'; Leszek Kolankiewicz, 'Ethnological Theatrical Explorations and Theatrical Concepts of Anthropology'; Ewa Zielińska, 'Reading Witkacy: A New Concept of Drama According to Witkacy'; Andrzej Zieliński, 'Witold Gombrowicz's Playing with Form'; Zbigniew Osiński, 'Grotowski Today'; Grzegorz Niziołek, 'Great Personalities of Polish Theatre: Kantor, Lupa, Grzegorzewski'; Agnieszka Koecher-Hensel, 'From Artistic Staging to the Theatre of Artists: From Wyspiański through Witkacy, Cricot 2, Szajna and Mądzik to the Theatre of Visual Artists: Szajna, Majewski'; Mukadder Yaycioglu, 'Kantor's "Theatre of Death"'; Danuta Kuźnicka 'Theatre of Movement and Body Expression (Henryk

---

[277] Zbigniew Osiński, 'Grotowski – dzisiaj' [Grotowski today], *Arkusz*, 9 (1996), 7.

Tomaszewski's Pantomime Theatre, Ewa Wycichowska's Dance Theatre, Wojciech Misiuro's Theatre of Expression)'; Małgorzata Komorowska, 'Contemporary Musical Theatre Explorations'; Marek Waszkiel, 'Twentieth-century Experiences of Polish Puppet Theatre'; Krystyna Miłobędzka, 'Artistic Theatre of Children and for Children'.

1997

24 March 1997 – 26 January 1998, Paris
In nine lectures given at the Collège de France, Jerzy Grotowski frequently mentions Peking opera as an important reference point in his artistic trajectory. During the second lecture, given in the Odéon-Théâtre de l'Europe on 2 June 1997, he uses excerpts from a documentary film presenting performances of Peking Opera in Paris in 1955.

1999

14 March, New Delhi, National School of Drama
The Conference of the Birds based on Farid ud-Din Attar. Stage adaptation: Jean-Claude Carrière and Peter Brook. Translation into Hindi: Sonalee Hardikar. Brook dedicates this work to the memory of Jerzy Grotowski, who dies on 14 January 1999.

2000

28–29 October, New Delhi, National School of Drama, Studio Theatre of NSD Repertory Company
'Jerzy Grotowski and His Theatre', lectures and video presentations. The programme included lectures by: Stanisław Krotoski, 'The Activities of the Centre of Studies on Jerzy Grotowski's Work and of the Cultural and Theatrical Research in Wrocław'; Zbigniew Osiński, 'Jerzy Grotowski and the Laboratory Theatre in Relation to the Culture of the Orient'; and Ludwik Flaszen, 'Grotowski from a Small Distance'; and presentations of documentary films: *A Letter from Opole*, *Akropolis* (two presentations), *Training at Grotowski's Laboratorium in Wrocław* (Ryszard Cieślak's exercises), and *'Pełen guślarstwa obrzęd świętokradzki'. O Teatrze Laboratorium Jerzego*

Grotowskiego ['This blasphemous ritual, full of sorcery': On Jerzy Grotowski's Laboratory Theatre].

30 November, Haridwar
Ambassador Jan Krzysztof Mroziewicz and other Polish participants pay homage to Jerzy Grotowski, placing a flowered wreath in the Ganges River.
The programme note published by the Polish Embassy, edited by Danuta Zasada and Piotr Rudzki, included a reprint of Grotowski's text 'Around Theatre: The Orient – The Occident', first published in *Asian Theatre Journal*, 1 (1989).

2002

Turkish translation of *Towards a Poor Theatre* by Jerzy Grotowski: *Yoksul Tiyatro*, translated by Çiğdem Genç, with Hakan Gürel and others, *MIMESIS*, special issue, 4 (1992); *Yoksul Tiyatro* (Istanbul: Boğaziçi Üniversitesi Yayınevi, 2002). Turkish edition differs from the original version.

2009

Shanghai
The magazine *Xiju yishu* [Theatre arts. Academic journal], 5 (2009), publishes a set of texts on Grotowski in Chinese: Richard Schechner, 'Geluotuofusiji he Geluotuofusijiren' [Grotowski and the Grotowskian], translated by Caoeng, pp. 4–11; Jerzy Grotowski, 'Zhixueshengde gaobie yanshuo' [A farewell speech to the pupils], translated by Yu Youming, pp. 12–25; Osiński, 'Geluotuofusiji yu Kai'ente' [Grotowski and Tadeusz Kantor], translated by Sun Manlin, pp. 26–33; Kermit Dunkelberg, 'Duikang, huofang, tuizun – wusite jutuande pinkun xiju' [Confrontation, simulation, admiration: The Wooster Group's poor theatre], translated by Lu Cheng, pp. 34–44; Wu Jingqing, 'Sitanni yu Geluotofusiji: liangzhong biaoyan xuntian xiangrong yu hubude kenengxing' [Stanislavski and Grotowski: The possibilities of mutual accommodating between the two training methods], pp. 45–52.

Author's Afterword

On 28 June 2007, in the house of Professor Kazimierz Grotowski in Tarnawa near Tarnów, I discovered a notebook belonging to his brother, Jerzy, containing notes taken during Jerzy's visit to China in the summer of 1962. I named it 'Dziennik chiński' [The Chinese diary]. I found it in one of eight big cardboard boxes filled with documents, notes, letters, photographs, and books never intended to be transferred to the archives of the Laboratory Theatre. This personal stash, probably unknown to anyone, Jerzy Grotowski passed to his brother after deciding to leave Poland. It was stored in a barn for twenty-five years. I also found in this stash Grotowski's 'Zapiski inicjacyjne' [Notes on initiation] from his childhood years in Nienadówka, a village near Rzeszów.

Indologist Koryna Dylewska is undoubtedly right in claiming that:

> There are still some gaps in the studies on Grotowski; one of the most acute is a lack of competent analysis of Indian motifs present in his work. [...] Many scholars emphasize the significance of the Orient, and particularly of India, in his life and artistic work, yet until now there has been no detailed account of theatrical, artistic or, more broadly, anthropological aspects of Grotowski's project in relation to Indian tradition.
>
> We have two types of scholarship at our disposal: on one hand, studies of Grotowski's biographical motifs focused on his direct contacts with India or Indian culture in general, and, on the other hand, attempts to interpret traces indicated by Grotowski himself. In his texts and statements we can find a series of recurring keywords referring to Indian philosophy and religion (especially to Hinduism and Buddhism). Emphasizing their significance, many scholars investigate sometimes-complex references and terms scattered throughout Grotowski's texts. We cannot speak about Grotowski while ignoring the points of view he indicated himself [...]. However, the starting point [of the study] must be a critical attitude towards both previous interpretations of Indian motifs in Grotowski's work and his own comments about India.
>
> What seems crucial, although sometimes forgotten by scholars, is the necessity of maintaining a distance from ready-made formulas offered to us by Grotowski. One must be extremely careful while following the tracks made by Grotowski, for they may turn out to be misleading. At first we must clearly realize that Grotowski's India does not necessarily correspond to the real India. Quite often it is only an artistic interpretation, a selective synthesis of inspiring and extraordinarily fertile religious and philosophical motifs, and – in terms of theatrical practice – artistic techniques. Their critical comparison with the Indian tradition

will reveal to us Grotowski's vision of India, emphasizing certain currents in the Indian world that were most important to him. We will then be able to ponder the reasons Grotowski so often referred to that tradition while explaining successive stages of his artistic work.

Grotowski's attitude towards India is actually not as obvious as one might assume. Certainly, it was not a result of a common fascination with the Orient, at least not in that sense in which other artists of the theatrical avant-garde so often succumbed to at that time. Rather, we would say that it was quite the opposite: Grotowski passes as an Expert, or maybe even as a Follower of the Indian tradition – to use Józef Kelera's words. Which of these two terms is more adequate in regard to his attitude towards India? Questioning the validity of both, we can gain a brand new interpretative perspective. For hasn't Grotowski interpreted, modified, subjectified, used to his own means, and perhaps appropriated the examples from the Indian tradition that he so willingly called upon?[278]

This question concerns an issue of fundamental significance for understanding Grotowski's artistic position, yet it primarily requires an Indologist with a background in cultural studies and anthropology to answer it competently. That seems obvious. Certainly areas of fascinating collaboration between Orientalist and theatre studies emerge here.

I learned a lot from my Orientalist colleagues, as well as from other scholars interested in the issues of intercultural dialogue whom I invited as lecturers to my seminars at the Faculty of Polish Studies of the University of Warsaw between 2004 and 2007. The participants of the seminars – students of various disciplines, such as Japanese studies, German studies, Polish studies, and philosophy – also taught me a lot.

One of the most significant consequences of my work on *Polskie kontakty teatralne z Orientem w XX wieku* was the need to reconsider many commonplace judgments and opinions, including some which I had already published.[279]

---

[278] Koryna Osuch [presently Dylewska, now Chair of South Asian Studies and faculty member of Oriental Studies at the University of Warsaw], *Grotowski a Indie* [Grotowski and India], from the digest of her doctoral thesis presented at a meeting of the Section for Theatre and Performance of the Institute of Polish Culture at the Faculty of Polish Studies at the University of Warsaw.

[279] For example, I was convinced that the classical Chinese opera first visited Poland in 1959, that the Peking Opera first performed in Poland in 1985, and that the first presentation of Kathakali in Poland occurred in 1979. However,

Substantial fragments of Kathakali were shown in Poland at least on seven different occasions between 1954 and 1972. They were performed by: the Indian Ensemble of Music and Dance (1954); the Indian Artistic Ensemble, which included a dance company from Shantiniketan (1956); the Darpana Dance Company led by Mrinalini Sarabhai (1960); Hindu Dance Company (1962–1963); Indian Song and Dance Ensemble led by K. Surabhamayan (1968); and Indian Music and Dance Ensemble (1972).

These performing groups typically accompanied official diplomatic visits, which reflected a 'warm' relationship of the People's Republic of Poland with China and India, or most importantly, the relationship of those countries with the USSR at that time. Consequently, most groups came to Poland (and other countries of the Soviet Bloc, such as Czechoslovakia, East Germany, Bulgaria, Romania, and Hungary) after their visit to the Soviet Union. A characteristic aspect of these performances was their collage form, in which next to the cantatas praising Joseph Stalin one could see, for example, sizable fragments (and sometimes entire pieces) of classical Chinese opera. A reviewer wrote in 1953:

> Wonderfully matched vocally, a mixed Chinese choir sang a few songs at the beginning of the performance. Next to the excerpts from Chinese operas one could hear songs about the heroic struggle of the Chinese nation and its leader Mao Tse-tung as well as 'Szła dzieweczka do laseczka' [a popular Polish folk song] performed in unaccented Polish.[280]

---

the source research revealed that I was wrong and that already between December 1951 and 1961 every year one could see entire productions or large excerpts of classical Chinese opera, on tour in several Polish cities. The companies, in chronological order, included: the Youth Artistic Ensemble of the People's Republic of China (1951); the Song and Dance Ensemble of the People's Republic of China (1953); the Song and Dance Ensemble of the Chinese People's Liberation Army (1954); the Chinese Youth Artistic Ensemble of Students of the Beijing Theatre School with teams from India and Indonesia during the Fifth World Festival of Youth and Students in Warsaw (1955); both the Indian Artistic Ensemble and the Puppet and Shadow Theatre of the People's Republic of China (1956); the Representative Theatre/Dance Ensemble of the People's Republic of China (1958); the Chinese Ensemble of the Sichuan Opera (1959); and both the Chinese Central Theatre of Opera and Ballet from Beijing and the Korean Song and Dance Ensemble from Pyongyang (1961).

280 Bohdan Hryniewiecki, 'Z pobytu Chińskiego Zespołu Pieśni i Tańca' [From the visit of the Chinese Song and Dance Ensemble], *Gazeta Białostocka*, 25 September 1953, p. 3.

In the opinion of another reviewer,

> The wonderful, unforgettable evening with the Chinese Song and Dance Ensemble consisted of performances that instantly won over the audience. Particularly mesmerizing with their charm, artistic taste, and unmatched technique were fragments of choreographies from classical operas [...].[281]

'Enchantment' was probably the most frequent word used in the numerous reviews. The performances were met with much greater interest than anticipated, and tickets were hard to obtain. Here is a representative excerpt from Witold Zechenter's review, published in a newspaper, *Echo Krakowa*:

> [...] the distribution of tickets raised objections. The battles that representatives of Kraków's art circles, singers, musicians, writers, painters, and actors had to fight to get into the Chinese artists' performances should cause serious reflection at appropriate cultural/social institutions [...].[282]

The performances of Indian ensembles met with a similar reception. One of the reviewers in Łódź states that the Teatr Nowy's 700-seat auditorium was filled, while 'it would be easy to sell ten times as many tickets, for that's how much interest there was'.[283] He continues:

> Frankly, some of the audience thought that the biggest attraction of the event would be its exoticism. However, it wasn't the 'otherness' of Indian art that turned the spectators' interest into enthusiasm, but rather the perfection and virtuosity of the performers.[284]

In a review titiled 'Wieczór niezapomnianych wrażeń' [An evening of unforgettable impressions], an *Echo Krakowa* reporter starts with the following paragraph:

> The only performance of the Indian Artistic Ensemble in Kraków, which took place yesterday in the Juliusz Słowacki Theatre, drew enormous interest, and it was undoubtedly an unusual cultural

[281]   Szymon Zakrzewski, 'Wielka sztuka wielkiego narodu' [Great art of a great nation], *Przyjaźń*, 13 September 1935, pp. 8–9.
[282]   Witold Zechenter, 'Z teatru. Występy zespołu pieśni i tańca Chińskiej Republiki Ludowej' [From the theatre: Performances of the song and dance ensemble of the People's Republic of China], *Echo Krakowa*, 24 September 1953, p. 3.
[283]   'Hinduscy artyści zdobyli serca łódzkiej publiczności. Wczorajszy występ w Teatrze Nowym' [Indian artists won over the hearts of the audience in Łódź], *Łódzki Express Ilustrowany*, 22–23 July 1956, p. 1.
[284]   Ibid.

event in our city. A crowd of people besieged the theatre before the beginning of the performance, hoping that they could somehow get desired tickets for this unusual show. Many people stayed outside the theatre until the end of the performance just to hear about it from the lucky spectators who would share their immediate impressions with them.[285]

Dance historian Irena Turska captures a deeper sense and meaning of these presentations in her article:

In China, for many years a vibrant folk culture had fought against the petrified official one, promoted by the feudal rulers [...]. The only surviving remnant of the golden past is theatre – the most conservative and conventional theatre in the world.

A theatre group of the Song and Dance Ensemble [of the Chinese People's Liberation Army], showed us an example of traditional theatre art in its painstakingly preserved form. It was an excerpt from a classical Chinese opera [*Havoc in the Dragon's Palace*] with the following plot: from a crack in the rock on Mount Hua Kuo jumps out a monkey who learns how to use weapons and proclaims himself the monkey king. He decides to get better weapons overseas at the dragon palace. The turtles and lobsters, which guard the palace, do not let the monkey king in, but, overpowered by his magic, take him to the king of the dragons. The king of the dragons presents the king of the monkeys with an extremely heavy needle of the sea kingdom, assuming that it would be too heavy for the monkey to lift. However, the king of the monkeys handles the needle with ease. Upset, the king of the dragons requests the needle back. He orders the storm at the sea and sends his army against the king of the monkeys. Yet despite his cleverness, the king of the dragons is defeated.

The short scene shows the essence of classical Chinese opera: convention-based symbolic use of costumes, makeup, props, gestures, and acrobatics, and a close connection between movement and music. Strange-to-our-taste, colourful, ornately decorated costumes, masterful makeup or expressive masks help to portray the type and function of the character. The props serve a particularly interesting function: on the stage a few crouching actors cover themselves with sheets of blue silk, putting the material into a steady wavy motion – a calm sea! When the king of the monkeys joggles the legendary needle with an incredible speed, on the order of the king of the dragons the sea becomes stormy – in the hands of one of the actors a huge blue flag starts waving while brave soldiers perform fierce somersaults through the flowing waves. The incredible

---

[285] (aż), 'Po wizycie hinduskiego zespołu artystycznego. Wieczór niezapomnianych wrażeń' [After the visit of an Indian artistic ensemble: An evering of unforgettable impressions], *Echo Krakowa*, 25 July 1956, p. 2.

precision and the microsecond synchronization of difficult stunts with the waves of the silk are the proof of high discipline in movement and the craft of operating the props. This entire fragment is not merely a showy effect, but is, rather, fundamentally connected with the text and the dramatic situation. For this is the purpose of acrobatics in Chinese theatre – acrobatics full of meaning, serving the text and the ideas presented in the performance. [...]

The masterful dance and acrobatic technique that charmed us so much is the result of painstaking exercises, mindfully developed over the centuries, which the actors practice from early childhood. [...]

When one looks at the company members moving 'privately' on the stage (for example when moving the set, which is done in plain view of the audience) one is struck by the odd elasticity, cat-like softness of each of their moves. Calmness and inner focus, masterful acting craft, fit and fully controlled bodies make each tiniest movement full of expression and meaning. No wonder that, not finding the foundation in European technique, the entire genre of expressionist dance that developed in Germany in the 1930s depended to such a degree on the elements of movement of the Far East dance!

We admired the absolute precision of the ensemble movement and its correlation with music. The Chinese dancers use all means of expression with unfailing confidence. And what about the means of expression themselves? They serve one artistic principle: simplicity and restraint. One of the greatest features of Chinese choreography is the masterful use of very simple means of expression. And all this can be captured in one phrase: high artistic culture.[286]

I must admit that I did not know about these performances while writing my books about Grotowski, even though all this had happened during his studies and initial years of practice as a director. Thus it is highly probable that he had seen classical Chinese theatre or Kathakali in Poland many years before his journeys to China and India. Yet, at least publicly, he never mentioned it and no one seems to have asked him about it.

I also was not aware of the great success of the Peking Opera at the International Theatre Festival in Paris in the spring of 1955.

Similarly, I did not know about frequent visits to China by many politicians, journalists, scholars, and artists. Among them were: Andrzej Braun, Tadeusz Breza, Kazimierz Budzyk, Ryszard Kapuściński, Jan Kott, Bohdan Korzeniewski, Zofia Lissa, Jerzy Pomianowski,

---

[286] Irena Turska, 'Chińscy tancerze w Polsce' [Chinese dancers in Poland], *Dziś i Jutro*, 28 November 1954, p. 6.

Jerzy Putrament, Jadwiga Siekierska, Roman Szydłowski, Wanda Wasilewska, Stefania Woytowicz. Some of them published articles and books, including *Notatnik chiński* [The Chinese notebook] by Putrament (1952), *Uroki Chin* [The charms of China] by Siekierska (1956), and *30 dni w Chinach* [30 days in China] by Wasilewska (1957).

Polish theatrical contacts with Korea and Vietnam have been rare. Contacts with Burma, Laos, Turkey, Iran, and other Muslim countries have also been sporadic. They have been usually limited to one or two visits of song and dance ensembles. The Shiraz-Persepolis International Festivals of Arts, organized since 1967 during the reign of Shahanshah Mohammad Reza Pahlavi, were undoubtedly important. Almost the entire artistic world attended the festival, including left-leaning artists such as the American Bread & Puppet Theater. Moreover, the *sama* ritual of the Mevlevi Sufi Brotherhood was of crucial importance for Grotowski. The Mevlevi Order (*maulawiyya* in Arabic, *Mevleviyye* in Turkish), whose members are known in Europe as the Whirling Dervishes, was founded in the thirteen century in the city of Konya, in southern Anatolia, by the followers of one of the greatest Persian mystic poets and scholars, Jalal ad-Din Muhammad Rumi (1207–1273), who was known as *maulana* (*mowlana*), or 'our lord'. It is also worthwhile to mention that two world-famous artists, Maurice Béjart and Robert Wilson, invoked the *sama* ritual in their performances.

In his book *O polityce. O sztuce. O sobie* [About politics. About art. About myself], published in 2000, Andrzej Wajda confesses:

> [...] I agree with Ryszard Kapuścinski's forecast that the world will head towards Asia. The spirit of the era is moving there. Europe is becoming a heritage park [...], it becomes sterile, boring and devoid of vital powers. I am afraid that one cannot expect much here anymore [...].[287]

In his lecture, 'Wojna czy dialog?' [War or dialogue?], inaugurating the founding of the Uniwersytet Latający Znaku [Znak's Flying University],[288] Kapuściński took a stance on the currently

[287] Andrzej Wajda, *O polityce. O sztuce. O sobie*, ed. by Maria Malatyńska (Warsaw: Prószyński i S-ka, 2000), p. 220.
[288] Delivered on 17 January, 2002, in the auditorium of the Collegium Novum of the Jagiellonian University in Kraków. Uniwersytet Latający Znaku is a series of open lectures organized by the Foundation of Christian Culture 'Znak' and the journal *Znak*. Editor's note: The name, 'Uniwerstytet Latający' [The Flying University], pays homage to past independent initiatives in Poland which provided education during the Partitions and later during the communist regime.

propagated notion of the 'war of civilizations', firmly opting for inter-civilizational and intercultural dialogue, and considering it a necessity.[289]

Jan Kieniewicz, a scholar who focuses on these issues, emphasizes that the encounter of the East with the West, like every real encounter, is not a hypothesis, but a relation. The personal aspect is of crucial importance here: a dialogue is an interpersonal relation. Any relation always takes place between particular persons. Only people can meet and engage in dialogue; civilizations cannot. Dialogue assumes two conditions: first, each person has to have a clear identity, or an ability to exist; second, both require the same communicational code, and a communicative space must be defined by shared values. Thus, to give someone the gift of oneself, one has to have identity – this is a preliminary condition for dialogue to happen. Yet one cannot give oneself outside of one's values, outside of the commonly accepted system of values. The most important aspect of European civilization is the ability to engage in dialogue. However, here 'dialogue' means the relation between people of two different civilizations. In the entire process, enormous energy is needed to break through the wall that each social system builds around itself.[290]

The issue has been studied from an anthropological perspective by one of the most eminent contemporary scholars, Clifford Geertz, who, besides such classic works as *The Interpretation of Cultures*[291] and *Local Knowledge: Further Essays in the Interpretive Anthropology*,[292] also wrote a study on the theatre of Bali, *Negara: The Theatre State in Nineteenth-Century Bali*.[293]

The name refers to the necessary nomadic style of this illegal operation, which was to assure that the authorities would not close it down.

[289] Ryszard Kapuściński, 'Wojna czy dialog?' [War or dialogue?], +*Plus –Minus* (weekly supplement to *Rzeczpospolita*), 2–3 March 2002. See: Kapuściński, 'Rabi śpiewa Upaniszady' [A rabbi sings the Upanishads], *Gazeta Wyborcza*, 4–5 October 2003, pp. 14–15.

[290] Jan Kieniewicz, *Wprowadzenie do historii cywilizacji Wschodu i Zachodu* [Introduction to the history of civilization of the East and the West] (Warsaw: Wydawnictwo Akademickie Dialog, 2003). Kieniewicz also gave lectures in the Centre of Studies on the Classical Tradition at the University of Warsaw (currently the Artes Liberales Institute for Interdisciplinary Studies).

[291] Clifford Geertz, *The Interpretation of Cultures: Selected Essays* (New York: Basic Books, 1973).

[292] Geertz, *Local Knowledge: Further Essays In Interpretive Anthropology* (New York: Basic Books, 1983).

[293] Geertz, *Negara: The Theatre State in Nineteenth Century Bali* (Princeton: Princeton University Press, 1980).

The impact of Eastern cultures on Grotowski and his ensemble is part of the theme that could be called 'the tradition of Jerzy Grotowski and the Laboratory Theatre'. On the other hand, the impact of Grotowski and his theatre on Eastern cultures might belong to 'Grotowski and the Laboratory Theatre as a tradition'. In my understanding, these are two complementary aspects of the same phenomenon or process. Only when we see it this way, can the process be portrayed in all its complexity.

I am aware of the risk inherent to my use of 'the East' as a general category. Let me justify myself by the fact that despite many various objections, this concept is still used when reflecting upon culture. Also Grotowski often used it in such a generalizing sense. As early as during his Theatre of Productions period, he repeatedly revealed his interest in classical Oriental theatre, especially Peking opera and Indian Kathakali.[294] Later, on 23 October 1971, when he and his closest collaborators carried out practical experiments with the Theatre of Participation, during a meeting of the Third International Student Theatre Festival in Wrocław, he said on that issue:

> There was a period when Oriental theatre was very exciting for me. This was at the time when I thought that it was possible to search for signs and build a work consciously. Today I am very far from thinking this way. And still, there is in the Oriental theatre I know, in the Peking opera before the Cultural Revolution or in the Kathakali theatre in India (I mention those theatres, for I have watched their work from behind the scenes), something magnificent, something very beautiful, which I could call the 'morality of work'. No, this term is probably not suitable; it is too stiff. They simply don't work only 'out of duty', or for their own benefit. Interesting and instructive in this context are the differences between traditional Oriental and European sports. What we try to do in our cultural sphere is to attain a certain special skill by systematic training, with an aim to beat the enemy, without relating that to the concept of man's existence as a complex whole. But, for example, for a Japanese person, judo could be a means of overcoming one's self, to meet life; in fact it is life itself, a way of existence. And there was something of that in Oriental theatre, in their classical theatre. And this I consider to be beautiful, unusual and unique in that theatre, although their aes-

---

[294] 'Z Jerzym Grotowskim o teatrze' [With Jerzy Grotowski about theatre], interview by J[erzy] F[alkowski], *Współczesność*, 1–30 December 1958, p. 8; 'Teatr – godzina niepokoju. Rozmowa z Jerzym Grotowskim' [Theatre: an hour of unrest. A conversation with Jerzy Grotowski], interview by Jerzy Falkowski, *Odra*, 6 (1964), 55–58; Grotowski, *Towards a Poor Theatre*, ed. by Eugenio Barba (Holstebro: Odin Teatrets Forlag, 1968).

thetic is completely alien to me. I do not think we can adopt from them any techniques, or that they could inspire us directly. [...]

I believe that an encounter with the East, not merely in the theatrical but in a broader, human sense, is a very important matter. Someone put it very nicely, I will quote: 'A European who never saw India is like a man who has been brought up in a boarding school for boys, and never saw a girl.' There is some danger in it, however: Europeans often go to the East because they want to become 'men of the East'. This is a misunderstanding and nonsense. It is the same as if somebody saw a girl and would like to become that girl. We are attracted by what is different. Thanks to the difference found in an 'other', man sees himself in a different light, more clearly; and eventually he finds himself.[295]

The change in Grotowski's attitude is obvious. He no longer accepts – in fact, he repudiates – any kind of imitation of Oriental theatre, considering such practices futile and uncreative.

By 'Oriental theatres' I primarily understand classic Asian theatres (Central and Eastern Asia, especially Tibet, China, India, Indonesia, Japan), although I do not exclude contemporary phenomena (such as Butoh, or avant-garde theatre, most of which were inspired by the cultures of the West).

I have been gathering materials on Oriental theatres for almost half a century, since 1959, when, as a sophomore in Polish Philology at the Adam Mickiewicz University in Poznań, I saw a team of Sichuan Opera performing at the Poznań Opera, and two years later, in the same venue, the Chinese Central Theatre of Opera and Ballet. My collection consists mainly of magazines, books, photographs, and various kinds of archival materials.

During that time I maintained contact with Jerzy Grotowski and Eugenio Barba, and, as much as possible, I watched productions of ensembles, actors and dancers from Bali, China, and Japan performing in Poland and other countries during successive sessions of the International School of Theatre Anthropology or Theatre Festivals in Nancy, France.

Why do I quote instead of replacing the quotation with a commentary? For me, quotation is a special kind of 'found object', resembling Tadeusz Kantor's *l'objet trouvé*. Quite often it is literally found in the depths of libraries and archives; found on audio or video tapes. For me, quotation is a real thing. It is a certain reality.

---

[295] 'Meeting with Grotowski', *Le Théâtre en Pologne/The Theatre in Poland*, 7 (1972), 10.

One can quote mechanically and meaninglessly – a quotation for the sake of quoting, resulting from lack of invention. However, there is also another kind of quotation: as a 'found object' with its whole reality, dirt, and charm. Sometimes a quotation can be a source – it can stimulate energy.[296] That is my case.

In his magnificent introduction to *Tybetańska księga umarłych* [*The Tibetan Book of the Dead*], Ireneusz Kania wrote:

> One of the dangers that accompanies the phenomenon of adopting values originating from completely different exotic cultural circles by European culture is a peculiar distortion of the perspective of reception. It is associated with the fact that the work of the human spirit (for example, a literary work) comes to us somehow 'alone', 'naked', often by accident. The loneliness of a merely interesting work (I mean deprivation of cultural, religious, philosophical etc. context) sometimes may trigger its great career and gain for it a rank of significance. If it is significant, it may pass as superb. Because of a lack of proper perspective (the knowledge of context), we tend to identify isolated examples of alien cultures as absolutely unique and project this appraisal onto the ground from which they stem (Would it be one more illusion of Eurocentrism *à rebours*?).[297]

I am aware that there are few answers in this book. There are many more questions than answers. Yet my main purpose is to initiate something and to show how much there still is to do. What I have managed to achieve I consider just a beginning. One has to start with something. This book is just to give an indication, not to suggest a solution.

We can find a good example of 'Polonocentrism', which is nothing else but a local variety of ethnocentric attitude, in an article by the well-known music critic and journalist Ludwik Erhardt. Reviewing a 1960 Warsaw performance by the Indian classical dance group led by Mrinalini Sarabhai (admired by the greatest dance experts and awarded for her achievements by the Archives Internationales de la Danse in Paris), Erhardt titled his text, 'O muzyce: Indie i europej-

---

[296] See: Ewa Rewers, 'Obsceniczna kultura cytatów: przyjemność i opór' [The obscene culture of quotations: pleasure and resistance], in *Dwudziestowieczność* [Twentieth-century-ness], ed. by Mieczysław Dąbrowski, Tomasz Wójcik (Warsaw: Wydział Polonistyki Uniwersytetu Warszawskiego, 2004), pp. 83–96.

[297] *Tybetańska księga umarłych*, trans. from Tibetan and ed. by Ireneusz Kania (Kraków: A, 2005), p. 28. See: Nicola Savarese, 'Incomprehensions and interventions: from the Silk Road to Seki Sano', in Eugenio Barba and Nicola Savarese, *A Dictionary of Theatre Anthropology: The Secret Art of the Performer*, trans. by Richard Fowler, 2nd edn (New York: Routledge 2011), p. 106.

ska megalomania' [About music: India and European megalomania] – although, in fact, megalomania and its reverse, the inferiority complex, are the core of all ethnocentrisms. He wrote:

> With a high degree of probability I can suppose that none of the readers of *Express* has ever heard her name, although she can be found in any encyclopedia of ballet, including the popular *A Dictionary of Ballet*, published by Penguin Books and available in our bookstores […].
>
> This lack of knowledge is a characteristic symptom of our ignorance towards Indian culture. It is even more – a manifestation of megalomania particular to the Europeans for whom the concept of 'art' has also a geographic meaning. We have become used to assuming that a dozen centuries of artistic activity in the space between Saint Petersburg and Paris, London and Rome is the essence of civilization and humanity.
>
> However, the twentieth century – which is not only the age of nuclear energy and space travel, but also the century of communication and communication-related discoveries – surprises us more and more often, forcing us to rethink commonly accepted opinions. The European monopoly on culture becomes more and more questionable. China, Japan, and India slowly reveal to us treasures of their centuries-old cultures, unknown to us for such a long time that they seem alien, incomprehensible, and exotic. We cannot understand these cultures. We cannot evaluate them. Confronted with their vastness of age, we are impressed and anxious. The feeling is similar to the one we experience while gazing into stellar space; its infiniteness makes us humble.
>
> People of the East are characterized by their calm. Their art also reveals a classical, philosophical calm, so needed in an era when illnesses of the nervous system are becoming a social plague. In our atmosphere of constant excitement, in the mood of hysteria […] the art of the East manifests an old truth – *ars longa, vita brevis*.
>
> Mrinalini Sarabhai, her partner Chathunni Panicker, and the whole group, Darpana, are bringing to Poland an art of classic dance cultivated in India for three thousand years. […] We are going to listen to music and songs accompanying the dances. We will certainly find them strange and incomprehensible. Then it will be worthwhile to realize that already three 'Millennia'[298] have passed since their beginning.[299]

[298] Author's remark about three 'Millennia' written with a capital letter is an allusion to the heavily publicized thousand-year anniversary of Polish statehood (celebrated by the government), coinciding with the thousand-year anniversary of the 'Baptism of Poland' celebrated by the Catholic Church.

[299] Ludwik Erhardt, 'O muzyce. Indie i europejska megalomania', *Express Wieczorny*, 6–7 January 1960, p. 8.

The author uses the term 'ethnocentrism' in the classic sense as 'a way of perception in which one's own group is in the centre of the world and everything around is evaluated and classified in reference to it'.[300] Erhardt refers to such attitudes and their results (such as negative stereotypes and ethnic prejudice), proving their limitations and anachronism.

The number of different ethnocentrisms seems to be inexhaustible. The almost total lack of basic materials documenting visits of Oriental artists and groups in Poland (not to mention studies on their reception) in publications, libraries, and archives strikes me as one of the symptoms of our local Polish ethnocentrism. A deficiency of pre-war resources may be explained by the fact that many archives and libraries were destroyed during WWII, yet the post-war ones are equally meager. It is as if our contacts with the cultures of China, India, Indonesia, Japan, and other Asian countries did not belong to the history of Polish culture. That precisely demonstrates ethnocentrism.

[300] A[leksander] Posern-Zieliński, 'Etnocentryzm' [Ethnocentrism], in *Słownik etnologiczny. Terminy ogólne* [Dictionary of ethnology. General terms], ed. by Zofia Staszczak (Warsaw and Poznań: Państwowe Wydawnictwo Naukowe, 1987), pp. 86–87; Aleksandra Jasińska-Kania, 'Etnocentryzm' [Ethnocentrism], in *Encyklopedia socjologii* [Encyclopedia of sociology] (Warsaw: Oficyna Naukowa, 1998), pp. 195–98.

APPENDIX

Jadwiga Rodowicz's path to the Tessenkai Theatre

THE WORLD PREMIERE of *The Piano Tuner* [*Stroiciel fortepianu*] by Jadwiga Maria Rodowicz-Czechowska, the first Polish Noh play, performed by the famous Tokyo-based Tessenkai Theatre on 17 February 2011 in the Stanisław Ignacy Witkiewicz Studio Theatre in Warsaw, became an artistic and diplomatic event at the same time. The author's contributions to the Polish reception of Noh have been discussed earlier. *The Piano Tuner* was translated into Japanese by Professor Tokimasa Sekiguchi of the Tokyo University of Foreign Studies (TUFS). The broadest overview of Jadwiga Rodowicz's creative path was presented in a conversation with Joanna Derkaczew, published in *Duży Format* of 17 February 2011:

As early as my first year of Japanese Studies at the University of Warsaw, I co-founded with several people a student theatre, Sigma. This group included, among others, Leszek Kolankiewicz and Jacek Zmysłowski. We made our only show titled *Porzućcie wszelką nadzieję* [Abandon all hope], but then Grotowski took Jacek Zmysłowski to Wrocław, and we lost a leader. At that time I was looking for a subject for my seminar paper. I found Grotowski's texts in which he described his unique concept of the actor's presence and the creative act. Following this trace, I unexpectedly discovered fourteenth-century theatrical treatises of Motokiyo Zeami, one of the founders and theorists of Noh theatre. At that time no one was interested in Noh. Perhaps there was one article about Noh theatre published in Polish, and Western publications were hardly available.

There was a single 16 mm film with a recording of Noh performance in the Embassy of Japan [in Warsaw]. Yet only institutions were allowed to borrow it. It seemed that Noh was nothing but some kind of a museum form: exotic, yet dead, and not worthy of attention. Japan in the 1970s was poorly known [...]. Meanwhile, burrowing in the Zeami's texts, I discovered how modern his concept was, and how close it was to the paratheatrical activities of the Laboratory Theatre in which I participated between 1974 and 1976. High ethical demands, the quest for self-knowledge, understanding, enlightenment. Since then, I have been dealing with Zeami virtually all my life. The only long break I took was between 1979 and 1989, when I was working with the Gardzienice Theatre. Yet even then it was a break in a practical sense only. The practice of Gardzienice was different than the one of Noh, yet it was in Gardzienice where I wrote my doctoral thesis on Noh, defended two years after the premiere of *Gusła* [Sorcery].

[...] The summer of 1976 [after the fourth year of my studies] I spent in France. I worked in a provincial factory, packing peaches. However, at the end of my stay I went to Paris. It turned out that the last European performance of Mr Kanze's Tessenkai group was taking place at Jean-Louis Barrault's Theatre d'Orsay. It is the same group that is now to perform the piece about Chopin. I had to try [to get in]. I went to the theatre without tickets (they had been, of course, sold out long ago), I sat on the steps next to the porter's lodge and waited for the artists. When they arrived, I roused up courage and in my modest Japanese asked them to show me the main actor. I explained that I was a student from Poland, interested in Noh, yet I still had had no opportunity to see it performed. Mr Kanze took me to the backstage and I sat in the main box. From there I saw a presentation that was not only thrilling, but, as it turned out, also historic. The professional literature described it later as exceptional in terms of experience and level of acting. I expected something hieratic, cold, but instead I was struck by the intensity of contact between the actors and musicians. People in the audience had tears in their eyes. One year later I went to Japan on a scholarship and went directly to Mr Kanze, who allowed me to participate in training sessions with the actors.

Usually no outsiders were accepted. But I was not only 'the friend from the stairs at the front of the d'Orsay', but also a holder of the Japanese government scholarship, a student at the prestigious University of Tokyo, under the care of a distinguished professor. I could watch freely. That did not mean I received special treatment in other matters. I was drilled and shouted at. In winter I was cold in unheated training rooms. Discipline was as if we were practising martial arts and held swords in our hands, so a small distraction could cause injury. Absolute focus, subordination. Instead of openness to the partner, focus on acquiring technique. And, at the same time, absolute peace of mind. I perfected the techniques at home, tripping on a mat in *tabi* socks, or hiding in the closet.

Joanna Derkaczew: And why the closet?

Jadwiga Rodowicz: I practised singing. If you put a quilt at the closet's door, you could scream in peace, without disturbing other roommates.

Joanna Derkaczew: Were some of these [experiences] useful in your work with Grotowski? He sought understanding between cultures, didn't he?

Jadwiga Rodowicz: These two worlds were totally different! My participation in Grotowski's actions was limited to a series of activities, which in general cannot be described today in theatre terms. I would play the guitar, sing, compose music. I would lead physical work. I would follow physical work. I would lead groups going blindly through groves. Maybe I was an assistant to the leaders? Or, perhaps, an accompanying musician? Contact with nature was perhaps the only aspect bringing us close to the Japanese culture. Yet besides that, we were doing things so separate, so elusive. At that time we functioned in the area Grotowski called the sphere of active culture. In these actions no one was only an observer, only a leader, or only a participant. This kind of creative ethos belonged to that specific time and the specific group of people in Poland. This time is somehow gone. I do not know if anyone needs such experiences. In any case, they are no longer initiated. The Laboratory Theatre dissolved. Groups that were close to it have changed the nature of their activities. Maybe it all continues somewhere invisibly, but there is no sign of this kind of sensitivity in the mainstream.[301]

Two years earlier I asked Jadwiga Rodowicz about her relationships with the Laboratory Theatre. In response, I received an email, dated 12 July 2009:

I began to work at the Laboratory Theatre in projects of Ryszard [Cieślak] and Jacek [Zmysłowski] in 1974, and between 1975 and 1977 I worked several times with Grot[owski] alone in Brzezinka. I signed a labour contract (the first in my life anyway, it should count for ZUS [Social Insurance]) in 1975. In 1979, after my return from Japan, Grot[owski] suggested that I participate in the Theatre of Sources, but I chose Gardzienice, mainly for family reasons, and because I simply wanted to work in theatre. After my Japanese experiences, Noh training, and research on traditional rural forms, Gardzienice seemed to me to be the perfect place.[302]

On the very same day Rodowicz wrote about her direct experience of Noh theatre and her work with Grotowski. It was her response to my information that Grotowski 'wanted to check if it is possible to create the equivalent of Noh theatre under the conditions of Western culture', as he had put it during one of our meetings in Italy in 1988 and 1996.[303] She said:

---

[301] 'Wykrojone serce Chopina. Okazało się, że moja wiedza w nowej Polsce może być przydatna. Zwłaszcza sztuki walki' [The cut-out heart of Chopin. It turned out that in the new Poland my knowledge can be useful. Especially [knowledge of] martial arts], Jadwiga Rodowicz, the Ambassador of the Republic of Poland and the author of the first Polish Noh play, interviewed by Joanna Derkaczew, *Duży Format*, weekly supplement to *Gazeta Wyborcza*, 17 February 2011, pp. 18–19.

[302] In the author's collection.

[303] Osiński, 'Japońskie inspiracje i zauroczenia: Jerzy Grotowski, Mieczysław Limanowski' [Japanese Inspirations and Enchantments: Jerzy Grotowski, Mieczysław Limanowski], *Didaskalia. Gazeta Teatralna*, 102 (2011), 113–23. Updated version in *Japonia w Polsce. W 90. rocznicę nawiązania stosunków*

The problem is that if someone has experienced Noh theatre, especially as an actor, it is unlikely that [...] he would find something 'strong' and true for himself in other forms, because Noh was developed with considerable emphasis on body techniques and concentration of the mind developed through martial arts (fencing, thus fighting to the death). It is precisely why Grot[owski] moved away from the imitative function of theatre (the function led to a certain kind of perfection by Stanislavski) in favour of the refined presence of the actor directed towards another actor or spectator. Paying attenttion to 'presence' has been brought to the extreme in martial arts, because, after all, it is a matter of survival on the battlefield. It was the conditioning in which the acting techniques of Noh, as we know them today, were developed. For over two centuries Noh was an art of the samurais, forbidden to other people, of course, with various exceptions to this absolute rule. In many plays the theme was 'undoing' someone's death, or evoking a spirit. Thus, besides gloominess, we are dealing with very strong concentration.

Just like Grot[owski] laboured (it is evident in his over-authoritative remarks on the language of translation, etc.) with technical and professional terminology ('our own working terminology'), the masters of the sword do, too. I have witnessed for several years how they explain techniques to foreigners attending their trainings. There are many ambiguities; the same phenomenon can be explained in several ways. I think that Grot[owski] gradually abandoned old terms in favour of the new ones, as he moved on his artistic path, and consequently, he did not want to hold on to concepts that were not useful to him anymore. Generally, such emphasis on the accuracy of terminology is exactly what hurts the living art of theatre. Personally, I cannot stand descriptions of body techniques. When I had to describe the sliding step *kamae*, a basic position in Noh, I almost convulsed, yet it was necessary to explain this world to the readers – a world so alien to them. When I first stood on the Noh stage and Kanze gave me instructions how I should look, how I should walk, I had an impression that I landed on the Moon, it was a speech out of this world. However, times have changed and now it is easy for me to describe these steps. Nevertheless, it seems to me that Grot[owski] did not want to go this route.

It is a pity that Poles did not get what they should have received right away – as soon as possible – the Polish text.[304] After a decade

oficjalnych między Polską i Japonią [Japan in Poland: On the 90th anniversary of the establishment of official relations between Poland and Japan], ed. by Beata Kubiak Ho-Chi, (Warsaw: Wydawnictwa Uniwersytetu Warszawskiego, 2012), pp. 245–74.
[304] Polish translation of Grotowski's *Towards a Poor Theatre*, trans. by Grzegorz Ziółkowski, ed. by Leszek Kolankiewicz (Wrocław: Instytut im. Jerzego

the book was no longer so 'sharp', so revealing, because it was as-sociated with a crucial period of the theatre, and AFTER the break-through it is always too late. That's life.[305]

In the programme for the production of *The Piano Tuner*, Rodowicz writes:

The stage action is accompanied by Noh music, based on the mys-terious drums and flute, accented with the shouts of musicians. It sounds a bit like jazz, and at the same time the piano playing a few pieces by Chopin can be heard. The unique sixteenth-century Noh mask, taken from the treasury of the Tessenkai theatre, was used to present Chopin's spiritual disposition.

Here is the cast of the performance: Kanze Tetsunojō (the *shite*, or principal actor, protagonist); Tonoda Kenkichi (the *waki*, or sec-ondary actor, deuteragonist); Shimizu Kanji (a *kōken*, or master assisting the *shite* on stage); Takao Nishimura (a *kōken*); Shibata Minoru, Umano Masaki, Nagayama Keizō, Tanimoto Kengo, Andō Takayasu (the *jiutai*, or choir); Uzawa Hikaru (*hataraki*, or stage as-sistant); Fujita Rokurobyōe (*hayashi kata*, or musician; *nōkan*, flute); Kamei Hirotada (*hayashi kata*; *ōtsuzumi*, big hand drum); Ōkura Genjirō (*hayashi kata*; *kotsuzumi*, small hand drum); Kodera Masato (*hayashi kata*; *taiko*, stick drum); Magdalena Lisak (piano player).

Director: Kasai Kenichi. Set designer, assistant director: Torakawa Eiji. Producer: Mukawa Yoshiki, Anna Galas (Instytut Te-atralny). Assistants of the director and the author of the play: James Karpoluk, Yoko Fujii-Karpoluk.

Three performances took place in the Studio Theatre – on 17, 18 and 19 February – as part of the project 'Chopin – Noh' marking the globally celebrated anniversary of Chopin, along with the book launch of Jadwiga Maria Rodowicz's *Boski dwumian* [The divine binomial] on 17 February, a theatre workshop for students of the Aleksander Zelwerowicz Theatre Academy (run by actors of the Tessenkai Theatre, and open to the public on 19 and 20 February), and an artistic homage paid to Chopin at St Cross Church (in the form of a twenty-minute presentation of fragments of the perform-ance in the nave, with Michał Dąbrowski playing the organ).[306] The

Grotowskiego, 2007), thirty-nine years after the first English edition.

[305] In the author's collection.

[306] Many opinion-making newspapers and magazines, especially those dedi-cated to music and theatre, published announcements and later reviews of the event: Paulina Gumowska, 'Japoński dramat pani ambassador' [A Japanese dra-ma of Madam Ambassadress], *Rzeczpospolita*, 5–6 February 2011, p. 2; Sandra

project was organized by the Embassy of the Republic of Poland in Tokyo, the National Noh Theatre in Tokyo, the Zbigniew Raszewski Theatre Institute, the Fryderyk Chopin National Institute, and the Stanisław Ignacy Witkiewicz Studio Theatre. Honorary patrons included the Minister of Foreign Affairs Radosław Sikorski, the Ministry of Foreign Affairs of Japan, Agency for Cultural Affairs, and the Embassy of Japan in Poland. The printed programme includes the author's 'special acknowledgments' to Waldemar Dąbrowski, a former Minister of Culture, 'who, as the President of the Chopin Year 2010 Celebrations Committee, provided great support to our project'. We also read there: '*The Piano Tuner* is a play that contains thirty years of my experience of Japanese culture and theatre, as well as many hours of reading about Chopin. In a sense, it is the project of my life.'

Wilk, 'Ważne spotkanie' [An important encounter], *Rzeczpospolita*, 11 February 2011; SZY, 'Polsko-japoński spektakl o Chopinie' [A Polish-Japanese show about Chopin], *Gazeta Wyborcza*, Warsaw edition, 14 February 2011; Joanna Derkaczew, 'Uwierz w ducha… Chopina' [Believe in the ghost… of Chopin], *Gazeta Wyborcza*, 19–20 February 2011; Małgorzata Komorowska, 'Chopin w teatrze nō' [Chopin in Noh theatre], *Ruch Muzyczny*, 3 April 2011, pp. 25–26; Tadeusz Kornaś, 'Chopin w teatrze nō' (Chopin in Noh Theatre), *Didaskalia. Gazeta Teatralna*, 102 (2011), 123–25; Jacek Dobrowolski, 'Duch Chopina w japońskim teatrze no' [The ghost of Chopin in Japanese Noh theatre], *Odra*, 5 (2011), 145–47.

ARTAUD, Antonin, *Teatr i jego sobowtór*, trans. and with an introduction by Jan Błoński, notes by Jan Błoński and Konstanty Puzyna (Warsaw: Wydawnictwa Artystyczne i Filmowe, 1966). Polish translation of the book *Le Théâtre et son Double*, originally published in 1938. English version: *Theatre and Its Double*, trans. by Mary Caroline Richards (New York: Grove Press, 1958).

ASLAN, Odette, and Béatrice Picon-Vallin, eds, *Butô(s)* (Paris: CNRS Éditions, 2002).

ATTISANI, Antonio, and Mario Biagini, eds., *Opere e sentieri* (Roma: Bulzoni Editore, 2007–2008), I: *Il Workcenter of Jerzy Grotowski and Thomas Richards*, texts by Thomas Richards, with Mario Biagini and others; II: Jerzy Grotowski: *Testi 1968–1998*; III: *Testimonianze e riflessioni sull'arte come veicolo*.

AWASTHI, Suresh C., and Maria Krzysztof Byrski, 'O teatrze w Indiach' [On theatre in India], General Secretary of Indian Academy of Music, Dance and Drama, Dr Suresh C. Awasthi, interviewed by Maria Krzysztof Byrski, *Teatr*, 7 (1971), 21–22.

BANACH, Andrzej, 'Bunraku, nō, kabuki i Grotowski' [Bunraku, Noh, Kabuki, and Grotowski], *Literatura*, 9 (1973), 3.

BANACH, Ela and Andrzej, *Cztery tygodnie w Japonii* [Four weeks in Japan] (Kraków: Wydawnictwo Literackie, 1973), pp. 195–211.

BANU, Georges, *L'acteur qui ne revient pas. Journées du théâtre au Japon*, rev. edn (Paris: Gallimard, 1993), postscript by Jean-Jacques Tschudin. 1st edn: Paris: Éditions Aubier, 1986.

BARBA, Eugenio, *Alla ricerca del teatro perduto. Una proposta dell'avanguardia polacca* (Padova: Marsilio Editori, 1965).

—, *Beyond the Floating Islands*, trans. by Judy Barba, with Richard Fowler and others (New York: PAJ Publications, 1986), postscript by Ferdinando Taviani.

—, 'The Kathakali Theatre', *Tulane Drama Review*, 4 (1967), 37–50. Polish translation: 'Indyjski teatr kathakali', trans. by Witold Kalinowski, *Dialog*, 12 (1979), 107–15.

—, *The Paper Canoe: A Guide to Theatre Anthropology*, trans. by Richard Fowler (London and New York: Routledge, 1995). Polish translation: *Canoe z papieru. Traktat o Antropologii Teatru*, trans. by Leszek Kolankiewicz and Dagmara Wiergowska-Janke (Wrocław: Instytut im. Jerzego Grotowskiego, 2005).

—, *La terra di cenere e diamanti. Il mio apprendistato in Polonia seguito da 26 lettere di Jerzy Grotowski a Eugenio Barba* (Milan: Società Editrice il Mulino, 1998). English translation: *Land of Ashes and Diamonds. My Apprenticeship in Poland. Followed by 26 Letters from Jerzy Grotowski to Eugenio Barba*, trans. from Italian by Judy Barba, Grotowski's letters trans. from Polish by Eugenio and Judy Barba (Aberystwyth: Black Mountain Press, Centre for Performance Research, 1999). Polish translation: *Ziemia popiołu i diamentów. Moje terminowanie w Polsce oraz 26 listów Jerzego Grotowskiego do Eugenia Barby*, trans. from Italian by Monika Gurgul, ed. by Zbigniew Osiński (Wrocław: Ośrodek Badań Twórczości Jerzego Grotowskiego i Poszukiwań Teatralno-Kulturowych, 2001).

—, *La terra di cenere e diamanti. Il mio apprendistato in Polonia seguito da 26 lettere di Jerzy Grotowski a Eugenio Barba*, new edn, with previously unpublished material (Milan: Ubulibri, 2004).

—, and Nicola Savarese, *The Secret Art of the Performer: A Dictionary of Theatre Anthropology* (London and New York: Routledge, 2005). Polish translation: *Sekretna sztuka aktora. Słownik antropologii teatru*, trans. by Jarosław Fret, with Grzegorz Godlewski and others, translation edited by Leszek Kolankiewicz (Wrocław: Ośrodek Badań Twórczości Jerzego Grotowskiego i Poszukiwań Teatralno-Kulturowych, 2005).

BOWERS, Faubion, *Theatre in the East: A Survey of Asian Dance and Drama* (London, Edinburgh, Paris, Melbourne, Toronto and New York: Thomas Nelson and Sons Ltd, 1956).

BRANDON, James R., *Brandon's Guide to Theater in Asia* (Honolulu: The University Press of Hawaii, 1976).

—, *The Cambridge Guide to Asian Theatre* (Cambridge: Cambridge University Press, 1993, 1999).

—, ed., *The Performing Arts in Asia* (Paris: UNESCO, 1971).

—, *Theatre in Southeast Asia* (Cambridge, Massachusetts: Harvard University Press, 1967).

BRECHT, Bertolt, 'Bemerkungen über die chinesische Schauspielkunst', in Bertolt Brecht, *Schriften zum Theater* (Berlin and Frankfurt: 1957), pp. 77–89. Polish translations: 'Efekty osobliwości w teatrze chińskim', trans. by Roman Szydłowski, *Trybuna Ludu*, 20 October 1957, p. 4, text preceded by a note from the translator; 'Efekty osobliwości w chińskiej sztuce aktorskiej', in Bertolt Brecht, *Wartość mosiądzu*, sel., ed. and annotated by Werner Hecht, collective translation (Warsaw: Wydawnictwa Artystyczne i Filmowe, 1975), pp. 124–34.

BROOK, Peter, 'Grotowski, Art as a Vehicle', *TDR: The Drama Review*, vol. 35, no. 4 (1991), 91–94; repr. in *The Grotowski Sourcebook*, ed. by Lisa Wolford and Richard Schechner (London and New York: Routledge, 1997), pp. 379–82 and in Brook, *With Grotowski: Theatre is Just a Form*, ed. by Georges Banu and Grzegorz Ziółkowski with Paul Allain (Wrocław: Grotowski Institute, 2009), pp. 31–35. Polish translation: 'Grotowski, sztuka jako wehikuł', trans. by Magda Złotowska, *Notatnik Teatralny*, 4 (1992), 27–29. Japanese translation: 'Gurotofusuki, nakadachi toshite no geijutsu', trans. by Tokimasa Sekiguchi, *Polonica* 3 (1992), 22–26.

BYRSKI, Maria Krzysztof, 'Grotowski a tradycja indyjska' [Grotowski and the Indian tradition], *Dialog*, 8 (1969), 86–91.

—, 'Miejsce teatru w kulturze indyjskiej' [The place of theatre in Indian culture], *Przegląd Orientalistyczny*, 3 (1979), 228–33.

—, 'Najstarszy teatr świata w Warszawie' [The world's oldest theatre in Warsaw], *Teatr*, 14 (1980), 7–8.

—, *Nāṭya. O kształcie indyjskiego teatru klasycznego* [Nāṭya: On the form of classical Indian theatre] (Wrocław: Biuro Wystaw Artystycznych, [1986]), series 'W kręgu kultur krajów Dalekiego

Wschodu' [Far East Cultures], ed. by Ryszard Łubowic, fasc. *Indie* 2.

—, 'O sakralności klasycznego teatru indyjskiego' [On the sacral aspects of classical Indian theatre], in *Dramat i teatr sakralny* [Sacral drama and theatre], ed. by Irena Sławińska, with Wojciech Kaczmarek and others (Lublin: Redakcja Wydawnictw Katolickiego Uniwersytetu Lubelskiego, 1988), pp. 25–31.

—, 'Taniec między bytem i nicością' [A dance between being and nothingness], in *Taniec bogów. Mit jako opis świata* [The dance of the gods: Myth as a description of the world], materials of the Faculty of Oriental Studies of the University of Warsaw, Festiwal Nauki, 26–28 September 1997, pp. 13–19.

—, 'Teatr a sprawa indyjska' [Theatre and the issue of India], *Dialog*, 12 (1979), 101–06.

—, 'Teatr indyjski' [Indian theatre], *Pamiętnik Teatralny*, 4 (1969), 597, corrections to the article 'Teatr najantyczniejszy' [The most ancient theatre].

—, 'Teatr i ofiara. Antyczny teatr indyjski a msza wedyjska' [Theatre and sacrifice: Ancient Indian theatre and Vedic mass], *Zeszyty Naukowe KUL*, 2 (1968), 27–31.

—, 'Teatr najantyczniejszy' [The most ancient theatre], *Pamiętnik Teatralny*, 1–2 (1969), 11–47.

—, 'Theatre – a mirror of nature of the world', in *Modern Theatre in Different Cultures*, ed. by Eleonora Udalska (Warsaw: Energeia, 1997), pp. 189–201.

Chopin – Polska – Japonia. Wystawa z okazji 80 rocznicy nawiązania stosunków oficjalnych między Polską a Japonią oraz Roku Chopinowskiego. 20 stycznia – 25 lutego 2000 r. Muzeum Literatury im. Adama Mickiewicza, Warszawa, oraz 6–31 marca 2000 r. Centrum Sztuki i Techniki Japońskiej 'Manggha', Kraków, 2000 [Chopin – Poland – Japan. The exhibition commemorating the 80th anniversary of the establishment of official relations between Poland and Japan, and the Year of Chopin. 20 January – 25 February 2000. Adam Mickiewicz's Museum of Literature, Warsaw, and 6–31 March 2000, the Manggha Centre of Japanese Art and Technology, Kraków, 2000], ed. by Henryk Lipszyc, with Ewa Pałasz-Rutkowska and others (Warsaw: Wydawca Komitet Organizacyjny Wystawy z okazji 80 rocznicy nawiązania stosunków oficjalnych między Polską a Japonią oraz Roku Chopinowskiego, 1999): Zbigniew Osiński 'Japońsko-polskie kontakty teatralne – dwudziesty wiek' [Theatrical contacts between Japan and Poland], pp. 222–25; Ōta Shōgo, 'Teatralne podróże do Polski' [Theatrical journeys to Poland], trans. by Henryk Lipszyc, pp. 228–29; Ueda Misako, 'Moje doświadczenia z teatrem polskim w Japonii' [My experiences with Polish theatre in Japan], trans. by Krystyna Okazaki, pp. 233–35. Catalogue in Japanese and Polish.

CIECHOWICZ, Jan, 'Siakuntala Kalidasy w Polsce' [Kālidāsa's Shakuntalā in Poland], Roczniki Humanistyczne, XXI, 1 (1973), 151–81.

—, 'Teatr polski wobec tradycji indyjskiej' [Polish theatre and Indian tradition], Przegląd Orientalistyczny, 3–4 (1982), 127–34.

—, 'Z dziejów recepcji teatru staroindyjskiego w Polsce' [From the reception history of ancient Indian theatre in Poland], Pamiętnik Teatralny, 2 (1974), 245–60.

CUESTA, Jairo, 'W drodze z Grotowskim' [On the road with Grotowski], trans. by Katarzyna Kacprzak, Pamiętnik Teatralny, 1–2 (2001), 232–40.

CZEKANOWSKA, Anna, Kultury muzyczne Azji [The musical cultures of Asia] (Kraków: Polskie Wydawnictwo Muzyczne, 1981).

—, Kultury tradycyjne wobec współczesności. Muzyka, poezja, taniec [Traditional cultures and contemporaneity: Music, poetry, dance] (Warsaw: Trio, Collegium Civitas, 2008).

—, 'Teatr, muzyka, człowiek' [Theatre, music, man], Ruch Muzyczny, 20 (1978), 15–16.

CZERMIŃSKI, Adrian, 'Współczesność i Nō' [Contemporaneity and Noh], Teatr, 12 (June), 16–18.

DEGLER, Janusz, 'Pierwsza podróż Jerzego Grotowskiego na Wschód' [Jerzy Grotowski's first journey to the East], *Notatnik Teatralny*, 20–21 (2000), 9–13; repr. in Alina Obidniak, *Pola energii. Wspomnienia i rozmowy* [Fields of energy: Recollections and conversations], introduced by Janusz Degler, appendix: *Listy Jerzego Grotowskiego do Aliny Obidniak (2 kwietnia 1956 – 12 lutego 1995)* (Wrocław: Instytut im. Jerzego Grotowskiego, 2010), pp. 192–97.

—, and Grzegorz Ziółkowski, eds., *Misterium zgrozy i urzeczenia. Przedstawienia Jerzego Grotowskiego i Teatru Laboratorium* [The mystery of horror and enchantment: Jerzy Grotowski and the Laboratory Theatre's performances] (Wrocław: Instytut im. Jerzego Grotowskiego, 2006).

EISENSTEIN, Sergei Mikhailovich, 'Театр Мэй Лань-фана/Teatr Mei Lan-fana' [Theatre of Mei Lanfang], 'Чародею грушевого сада/ Charodeyu grushevogo sada' [The magician of the pear orchard], trans. from English by Tadeusz Szczepański, *Dialog*, 10 (1979), 108–16; trans. from English by Ewa Guderian-Czaplińska, in *Mei Lanfang. Mistrz opery pekińskiej* [Mei Lanfang: The master of Peking opera], pp. 151–65.

FLASZEN, Ludwik, 'Dostojewski – Wielki Inkwizytor – teatr' [Dostoyevsky – The Grand Inquisitor – theatre], Ludwik Flaszen interviewed by Leszek Kolankiewicz, *Didaskalia. Gazeta Teatralna*, 95 (2010), 113–19.

—, *Grotowski & Company*, trans. by Andrzej Wojtasik with Paul Allain, ed. and introduced by Paul Allain with the editorial assistance of Monika Blige and with a tribute by Eugenio Barba (Holstebro, Malta and Wrocław: Icarus Publishing Enterprise, 2010).

—, 'Po śmierci Jerzego Grotowskiego. Świat żegna proroka' [After Jerzy Grotowski's death: The world bids the prophet farewell], *Gazeta Wyborcza*, 18 January 1999, p. 12.

—, *Teatr skazany na magię* [A theatre condemned to magic], ed. and introduced by Henryk Chłystowski (Kraków and Wrocław: Wydawnictwo Literackie, 1983).

—, *Trzewik Montaigne'a* [Montaigne's shoe], Ludwik Flaszen, co-founder of the Laboratory Theatre and collaborator of Jerzy Grotowski, interviewed by Tadeusz Sobolewski, *Gazeta Wyborcza*, 14 January 2010, pp. 14–17.

—, and Carla Pollastrelli, eds, with the editorial assistance of Renata Molinari, *Il Teatr Laboratorium di Jerzy Grotowski 1959–1969. Testi e materiali di Jerzy Grotowski e Ludwik Flaszen con uno scritto di Eugenio Barba* (Pontedera: Fondazione Pontedera Teatro, 2001).

GROTOWSKI, Jerzy, 'L'art du debutant' [The art of the beginner], text drawn up on the lines of Georges Banu's French version, from the original consecutive translation of the conference by Mr André Gregory, Warsaw, 4 June 1978, *International Theatre Information* (Paris: ITI, 1978), pp. 7–11.

—, 'Ćwiczenia' [Exercises], ed. by Leszek Kolankiewicz, *Dialog*, 12 (1979), 127–37; repr. in Grotowski, *Teksty z lat 1965–1969. Wybór* [Texts, 1965–1969: A selection], sel. and ed. by Janusz Degler and Zbigniew Osiński, 2nd edn, revised and extended (Wrocław: Wiedza o kulturze, 1990), pp. 111–44.

—, 'From the Theatre Company to Art as Vehicle', in Thomas Richards, *At Work with Grotowski on Physical Actions* (London and New York: Routledge, 1995). Originally in Richards, Thomas, *Al lavoro con Grotowski sulle azioni fisiche* (Milano: Ubulibri, 1993). French translation: *Travailler avec Grotowski sur les actions physiques*, trans. from English by Michel A. Moos (Actes Sud/Académie Expérimentale des Théâtres, 1995). Polish translation: *Pracując z Grotowskim nad działaniami fizycznymi*, trans. by Magda Złotowska, Andrzej Wojtasik (Kraków: Homini, 2003).

—, 'Korespondencja z świątyni Ahura Mazdy' [Correspondence from the temple of Ahura Mazda], *Argumenty*, 22 March 1959, 6.

—, 'Listy do Aliny Obidniak z oazy Bajram Ali (2 IV – 20 V 1956)' [Letters to Alina Obidniak from the Bayram-Ali oasis (2 April – 20 May 1956)], ed. by Janusz Degler, *Notatnik Teatralny*, 20–21 (2000), 14–28.

—, 'Między Iranem a Chinami (1). Prorok odchodzi z trzech pustyń' [Between Iran and China (2). The prophet leaves three deserts], *Dziennik Polski*, 9–10 September 1956, pp. 3–4; 'Między Iranem a Chinami (2). Wieża Babel' [Between Iran and China (2). The Tower of Babel], *Dziennik Polski*, 22 November 1956, pp. 2–3; repr. in *Notatnik Teatralny*, 20–21 (2000), 29–35.

—, 'Mim i świat' [The mime and the world], *Ekran*, 8 March 1959, p. 9.

—, 'Od zespołu teatralnego do sztuki jako wehikułu' [From the Theatre Company to Art as Vehicle], trans. from Spanish by Magda Złotowska, *Notatnik Teatralny*, 4 (1992), 31–43.

—, 'O praktykowaniu romantyzmu' [About practising romaticism], ed. by Leszek Kolankiewicz, *Dialog*, 3 (1980), 112–20.

—, *Rozmowa z Grotowskim* [A conversation with Grotowski], Jerzy Grotowski interviewed by Andrzej Bonarski, *Kultura*, 11, 1975; repr. in *Instytut Laboratorium. Teksty* (Wrocław: Instytut Aktora – Teatr Laboratorium, 1975), pp. 3–38; and Andrzej Bonarski, *Ziarno* [The seed] (Warsaw: Czytelnik, 1979), pp. 19–44. An abbreviated version of the interview is available in English in Jennifer Kumiega, *The Theatre of Grotowski* (London: Methuen, 1985), pp. 217–23, as 'Conversation with Grotowski', trans. by Boleslaw Taborski.

—, 'Sympozjum "Sztuka debiutanta"' [The symposium 'The Art of the Beginner'], in the programme *Międzynarodowe Spotkania Teatralne. Warszawa 1978: 23 V – 9 VI 1978* (Warsaw: Komitet Organizacyjny MST, 1978), p. 60.

—, 'Teatr a rytuał' [Theatre and ritual], *Dialog*, 8 (1969), 64–74, repr. in *Teksty z lat 1965–1969. Wybór* (Wrocław: Wiedza o kulturze, 1990), pp. 61–86.

—, 'Teatr Laboratorium po dwudziestu latach. Hipoteza robocza' [The Laboratory Theatre after twenty years. A working hypothesis], *Polityka*, 26 January 1980, pp. 1, 10. Available in English as 'The Laboratory Theatre 20 Years After: A Working Hypothesis', *Polish Perspectives*, 5 (1980), 35.

—, 'Teatr Źródeł' [Theatre of sources], ed. by Leszek Kolankiewicz, *Zeszyty Literackie*, 19 (1987), 102–115.

—, *Teksty zebrane* [Collected texts], ed. by Agata Adamiecka-Sitek, with Mario Biagini and others (Wrocław and Warsaw: Instytut im.

Jerzego Grotowskiego, Instytut Teatralny im. Zbigniewa Raszewskiego, Wydawnictwo Krytyki Politycznej, 2012).

—, *Teksty z lat 1965–1969. Wybór*, sel. and ed. by Janusz Degler, Zbigniew Osiński, 2nd edn, corrected and extended (Wrocław: Wiedza o kulturze, 1990); 3rd edn: Wrocław 1999.

—, *Towards a Poor Theatre*, ed. by Eugenio Barba, preface by Peter Brook (Holstebro: Odin Teatrets Forlag, 1968). Polish version: *Ku teatrowi ubogiemu*, ed. by Eugenio Barba, trans. from English by Grzegorz Ziółkowski, Polish version ed. by Leszek Kolankiewicz, preface by Peter Brook, editorial annex by Leszek Kolankiewicz (Wrocław: Instytut im. Jerzego Grotowskiego, 2007).

—, 'Wędrowanie za Teatrem Źródeł' [Wandering after the Theatre of Sources], ed. by Leszek Kolankiewicz, *Dialog*, 11 (1979), 94–103.

—, 'Wschód – Zachód' [East – West], trans. from French by Ludwik Flaszen, *Didaskalia. Gazeta Teatralna*, 27 (1998), 6–10, text based on the lecture given in Istituto dello Spettacolo in the University of Rome; seminar on the East and the West, 24 September 1984. Italian original: 'Teatro Oriente/Occidente', trans. from French by Luisa Tinti, in Antonella Ottai, ed., *Teatro Oriente/Occidente* (Rome: Bulzoni Editore, 1986), pp. 7–19. English translation: 'Around Theatre: The Orient – The Occident', trans. by Mauren Schaffer Price, in *Asian Theatre Journal*, vol. 6, no. 1 (1989), 1–11.

—, *Z Jerzym Grotowskim o teatrze* [With Jerzy Grotowski on theatre], Jerzy Grotowski interviewed by J[erzy] F[alkowski], *Współczesność*, 1–30 December 1958), 8.

GROTOWSKI, Kazimierz, 'On poprzez teatr bada świat. Rozmowa z Kazimierzem Grotowskim, profesorem Uniwersytetu Jagiellońskiego, fizykiem jądrowym, himalaistą' [He studies the world through theatre: A conversation with Kazimierz Grotowski, Profesor of the Jagiellonian University, nuclear physicist, and Himalaya-mountaineer], Kazimierz Grotowski interviewed by Teresa Błajet-Wilniewczyc, *Notatnik Teatralny*, 4 (1992), 85–93.

—, 'Podróż w biografię. Spotkanie z Kazimierzem Grotowskim, 17 października 1999' [A journey into a biography: An encounter with

Kazimierz Grotowski, 17 October 1999], transcribed and ed. by Maria Hepel, *Notatnik Teatralny*, 22–23 (2001), 8–25.

—, 'Portret rodzinny' [A family portrait], *Pamiętnik Teatralny*, 1–4 (2000), 9–36.

—, and Andrzej Michał Kobos, 'Wędrowałem za fizyką' [I wandered following physics], in *Po drogach uczonych. Z członkami Polskiej Akademii Umiejętności rozmawia Andrzej M. Kobos* [On the paths of scientists: Conversations of Andrzej M. Kobos with members of the Polish Academy of Knowledge] (Kraków: Polska Akademia Umiejętności, 2007), pp. 247–80.

Grotowski – narracje, introduced and ed. by Leszek Kolankiewicz (Warsaw and Wrocław: Uniwersytet Warszawski, Instytut im. Jerzego Grotowskiego, 2013)

GUDERIAN-CZAPLIŃSKA, Ewa, and Grzegorz Ziółkowski, eds. *Mei Lanfang. Mistrz opery pekińskiej* [Mei Lanfang: The master of Peking opera] (Wrocław: Ośrodek Badań Twórczości Jerzego Grotowskiego i Poszukiwań Teatralno-Kulturowych, 2005).

HÜBNER, Zygmunt, 'Sztuka debiutanta' [The Art of the Beginner], *Dialog*, 10 (1978), 147–49.

KALVODOVÁ, Dana, *Čínské divadlo* [Chinese theatre] (Prague: Panorama, 1992).

KANZE, Hideo, 'Gurotofusuki to no deai' [The encounter with Grotowski], *Polonica*, 3 (1992), 60–61.

KANZE, Hideo, 'Po występach teatru japońskiego. Rola na całe życie' [After performances of a Japanese theatre: A role for the entire life], Hideo Kanze interviewed by Roman Pawłowski, *Gazeta Stołeczna*, 13 July 1994, p. 6.

KASAREŁŁO, Lidia, and Gao Xingjian, 'Pielgrzym Gao Xingjian' [Pilgrim Gao Xingjian], *Więź*, 11 (2000), 10–12.

KOLANKIEWICZ, Leszek, *Święty Artaud* [Saint Artaud], 2nd edn, revised and extended (Gdańsk: słowo/obraz terytoria, 2001).

KOTT, Jan, 'Nō, albo o znakach' ['Noh, or about signs'], in *Pisma wybrane* [Selected texts], sel. and ed. by Tadeusz Nyczek, III: *Fotel recenzenta* [The reviewer's armchair] (Warsaw: Krąg, 1991), pp. 317, 319, 321. English translation: Jan Kott, 'Noh, or About Signs', in *The Theater of Essence* (Evaston: Northwestern University Press, 1986).

LIMANOWSKI, Mieczysław, *Był kiedyś teatr Dionizosa* [There once was Dionysus' theatre], selected, ed. and introduced by Zbigniew Osiński (Warsaw: Instytut Sztuki Polskiej Akademii Nauk, 1994).

—, and Juliusz Osterwa, *Listy* [Letters], ed. and introduced by Zbigniew Osiński (Warsaw: Państwowy Instytut Wydawniczy, 1987).

LIPSZYC, Henryk, 'Japończyk o Grotowskim' [A Japanese on Grotowski], *Dialog*, 11 (1974), 167–73.

—, 'Obecność teatru japońskiego w powojennej Polsce' [The presence of Japanese theatre in post-war Poland], in *Moi bitelsi. Wybór dramatów japońskich* [My Beatles: A selection of Japanese plays] (Warsaw: Wydawnictwo Akademickie Dialog, 1998), pp. 197–206.

ŁABĘDZKA, Izabella, 'Artaud, Yeats, Brecht i teatry Wschodu' [Artaud, Yeats, Brecht, and theatres of the East], *Dialog*, 5 (1997), 142–49.

—, *Obrzędowy teatr Dalekiego Wschodu* [Ceremonial theatre of the Far East] (Poznań: Wydawnictwo Naukowe UAM, 1999).

—, *Teatr niepokorny* [Rebellious theatre] (Poznań: Wydawnictwo Naukowe UAM, 2003).

ŁUBIEŃSKI, Stefan, *Między Wschodem a Zachodem. Japonia na straży Azji (Dusza mistyczna Nipponu)* [Between the East and the West: Japan guarding Asia (A mystical soul of Nippon)] (Kraków: Gebethner i Wolff, 1927).

—, 'Teatr Nipponu' [Nippon's theatre], *Scena Polska*, 3–4 (1926), 57–90.

MEI LAFANG, *Сорок лет на сцене/Sorok let na stsene* [Forty years on the stage] trans. from Chinese by E. Rozhdestvensky and V. Taskin (Moscow: Iskusstvo, 1963).

'Nasze zderzenie z kathakali' [Our clash with Kathakali], abridged record of a debate organized on 19 June 1979 in the Adam Mickiewicz Room of the Auditorium Maximum of the University of Warsaw by the Institute of Indology of the Faculty of Oriental Studies of the University of Warsaw, the 'Akademia Ruchu' Theatre, and the editors of *Dialog* monthly magazine on the occasion of the performances of the group Kerala Kala Kendram, directed by Krishnan Nambudiri, the debate was introduced by Maria Krzysztof Byrski and moderated by Konstanty Puzyna, *Dialog*, 12 (1979), 116–26.

OBIDNIAK, Alina, *Pola energii. Wspomnienia i rozmowy* [Fields of energy: Recollections and conversations], introduction by Janusz Degler (Wrocław: Instytut im. Jerzego Grotowskiego, 2010). Appendix: *Listy Jerzego Grotowskiego do Aliny Obidniak (2 kwietnia 1956 – 12 lutego 1995)* [Jerzy Grotowski's letters to Alina Obidniak (2 April 1956 – 12 February 1995)].

ORTOLANI, Benito, and Samuel L. Leiter, eds., *Zeami and the Nō Theatre in the World*, consulting editor Daniel Gerould (New York: CASTA/Center for Advanced Studies in Theatre Arts, The City University of New York, 1998).

OSIŃSKI, Zbigniew, '"Dancer"-Actor of Jerzy Grotowski', trans. by Justyna Rodzińska, in *Theatrum Mirabiliorum Indiae Orientalis: A Volume to Celebrate the 70th Birthday of Professor Maria Krzysztof Byrski*, ed. by Monika Nowakowska and Jacek Woźniak, *Rocznik Orientalistyczny*, vol. 60, no. 2 (2007), 394–412.

—, 'Grotowski and Tadeusz Kantor', trans. from Polish and English by Sun Manlin, *Theatre Arts Academic Journal*, 5 (2009), 26–33, text in Chinese (journal in Chinese and English).

—, 'Grotowski and the Reduta Tradition', trans. from Polish by Kris Salata, in *Grotowski's Empty Room*, ed. by Paul Allain (London, New York and Calcutta: Seagull Books, 2009), pp. 19–54.

—, 'Grotowski Blazes the Trails: From Objective Drama to Ritual Arts', trans. by Ann Herron and Halina Filipowicz, ed. by Halina Filipowicz, *TDR: The Drama Review* vol. 35, no. 1 (1991), 95–112. Later version, with a changed title: 'Grotowski Blazes the Trails: From Objective Drama to Art as Vehicle', trans. by Ann Herron and Halina Filipowicz, ed. by Halina Filipowicz, in *The Grotowski Sourcebook*, ed. by Lisa Wolford and Richard Schechner (London and New York: Routledge, 1997), pp. 383–98. Japanese translation: 'Grotowski – no hiraita michi: Objective Drama – kara Ritual Arts made (1985-)', trans. by Shōzō Yoshigami, *Polonica*, 3 (1992),37–57.

—, *Grotowski i jego Laboratorium* (Warsaw: Państwowy Instytut Wydawniczy, 1980). American edition: *Grotowski and His Laboratory*, trans. and abridged by Lillian Vallee and Robert Findlay (New York: PAJ Publications, 1986).

—, 'Grotowski i Teatr Laboratorium wobec kultury Orientu' [Grotowski, the Laboratory Theatre and the culture of the Orient], *Przegląd Orientalistyczny*, 3 (1979), 218–27. Edited and extended version in *Grotowski wytycza trasy. Studia i szkice* (Warsaw: Pusty Obłok, 1993), pp. 113–46.

—, 'Grotowski i jego Teatr Laboratorium wobec kultury Orientu – po dwudziestu pięciu latach' [Grotowski, his Laboratory Theatre and the culture of the Orient – after twenty five years], Part 1: *Didaskalia. Gazeta Teatralna*, 59/60 (2004), 58–67, Part 2: *Didaskalia. Gazeta Teatralna*, 61/62 (2004), 90–98.

—, 'Grotowski w Chinach (lato 1962) i znaczenie tego pobytu' [Grotowski in China (Summer 1962) and the importance of his visit], in *Sztuka Chin*, ed. by Joanna Wasilewska (Warsaw: Neriton, 2009), pp. 137–48. In English: 'Jerzy Grotowski in China', trans. by Joanna Klass and Artur Zapałowski, in *Poland-China. Art and Cultural Heritage*, ed. by Joanna Wasilewska (Kraków: Jagiellonian University Press, 2011), pp. 259–67. In Chinese: Zibieniefu Aoxinsiji (Zbigniew Osiński) 'Yeshi Geluotuofusiji Zhongguo zhi xing ji qi yiyi', in *Poland-China: Shiyan yu xingshi. Gu-jin Bolan yishu yu Zhong-Bo yishu jiaoliu, Poland-China: Art and Cultural Heritage*, ed. by Mading Yagubi (Marcin Jacoby), Chen Shujun, Polish Institute of World Art Studies, the Adam Mickiewicz Institute (Shanghai: Shanghai jinxiu wenzhang chubanshe, 2012), pp. 191–98.

—, *Grotowski wytycza trasy. Studia i szkice* [Grotowski blazes the trails: Studies and drafts] (Warsaw: Pusty Obłok, 1993).

—, 'Japońskie inspiracje i zauroczenia: Jerzy Grotowski, Mieczysław Limanowski' [Japanese inspirations and enchantments: Jerzy

Grotowski, Mieczysław Limanowski], *Didaskalia. Gazeta Teatralna*, 102 (2011), 113–23. Expanded version in *Japonia w Polsce. W 90. rocznicę nawiązania stosunków oficjalnych między Polską a Japonią* [Japan in Poland. On the 90th anniversary of the establishment of official relations between Poland and Japan], ed. by Beata Kubiak Ho-Chi (Warsaw: Wydawnictwa Uniwersytetu Warszawskiego, 2012), pp. 245–74.

—, 'Japońsko-polskie kontakty teatralne – dwudziesty wiek – 20 seiki – iu okeru Nihon-to Pōrando – no engeki – kōryū' [Japanese-Polish theatrical contacts: The twentieth century], trans. by Nagisa Rządek, in the catalogue to the exhibition 'Szopen – Polska – Japonia', wystawa z okazji 80. rocznicy nawiązania stosunków oficjalnych między Polską a Japonią oraz Roku Chopinowskiego 1919–1999 ['Chopin – Poland – Japan': An exhibition celebrating the establishment of official relations between Poland and Japan, and the Chopin Year 1919–1999] (Tokyo and Warsaw: Komitet Organizacyjny Wystawy, 1999), pp. 218–21, 222–25.

—, 'Jerzego Grotowskiego podróże do Indii' [Jerzy Grotowski's journeys to India], in: *Estetyka pośród kultur*, ed. by Krystyna Wilkoszewska (Kraków: Universitas, 2012), pp. 67–93.

—, *Jerzy Grotowski e il suo Laboratorio. Dagli spettacoli a L'arte come veicolo*, ed. and trans. by Marina Fabbri, introduction by Eugenio Barba (Cronistoria di una ribellione/Chronicle of rebellion) and Marina Fabbri (Cercare l'acqua), postscripti by Zbigniew Osiński (L'opera di Jerzy Grotowski come oggetto di studi) and Franco Ruffini (I libri di Jerzy Grotowski) (Florence: Bulzoni, 2011).

—, *Jerzy Grotowski. Źródła, inspiracje, konteksty* [Jerzy Grotowski: Sources, inspirations, contexts] (Gdańsk: słowo/obraz terytoria, 1998).

—, *Jerzy Grotowski. Źródła, inspiracje, konteksty* (Gdańsk: słowo/obraz terytoria, 2009), I: 2nd edn, changed, II: *Prace z lat 1999–2009* [Works from the period 1999–2009].

—, 'Mei Lanfang, legenda opery pekińskiej. Polska recepcja i konteksty' [Mei Lanfang, the legend of Peking opera: Polish reception and contexts], in *Mei Lanfang. Mistrz opery pekińskiej* [Mei Lanfang: The master of Peking opera], ed. by Ewa Guderian-Czaplińska and Grze-

gorz Ziółkowski (Wrocław: Ośrodek Badań Twórczości Jerzego Grotowskiego i Poszukiwań Teatralno-Kulturowych, 2005), pp. 89–149.

—, 'Mei Lanfang w Warszawie, 1935' [Mei Lanfang in Warsaw,
1935], *Notatnik Teatralny*, 1 (1997), 159–75; repr. in *Teatr Orientu*,
papers from the academic session, ed. by Przemysław Piekarski
(Kraków: Uniwersytet Jagielloński, Instytut Filologii Orientalnej,
1998), pp. 155–173.

—, *Nazywał nas bratnim teatrem. Przyjaźń artystyczna Ireny i Tadeusza Byrskich z Jerzym Grotowskim* [He used to call us a sister
theatre: Artistic friendship of Irena and Tadeusz Byrski with Jerzy
Grotowski] (Gdańsk: słowo/obraz terytoria, 2005).

—, *Pamięć Reduty. Osterwa, Limanowski, Grotowski* [Memories of
Reduta: Osterwa, Limanowski, Grotowski] (Gdańsk: słowo/obraz
terytoria, 2003).

—, *Polskie kontakty teatralne z Orientem w XX wieku* [Polish theatrical contacts with the Orient in the 20th century], I: *Kronika* [The
chronicle], II: *Studia* [The studies] (Gdańsk: słowo/obraz terytoria,
2008).

—, 'Reduta dzisiaj' [Reduta today], *Konteksty. Polska Sztuka
Ludowa*, 1 (2008), 148–56.

—, 'Returning to the Subject: The Heritage of Reduta in Grotows-
ki's Laboratory Theatre'. trans. and ed. by Kris Salata, *TDR: The
Drama Review*, vol. 52, no. 2 (2008), 52–74. From *Pamięć Reduty.
Osterwa, Limanowski, Grotowski* [Memories of Reduta: Osterwa,
Limanowski, Grotowski] (Gdańsk: słowo/obraz terytoria, 2003).

—, *Spotkania z Jerzym Grotowskim. Notatki, listy, studium* [En-
counters with Jerzy Grotowski: Notes, letters, and a study] (Gdańsk:
słowo/obraz terytoria, 2013).

—, 'Symposium sur "l'Art du debutant"/Symposium: "The Art of
the Beginner"', *Le Théâtre en Pologne/The Theatre in Poland*, 9–10
(1978), 18–20.

—, *Szlakiem Grotowskiego: Od Teatru Źródeł ku Nienadówce* [In
Grotowski's Footsteps: From Theatre of Sources toward Nienadów-

ka], in: *Źródła pamięci. Grotowski, Kantor, Szajna*, ed. by Anna Jam-rozek-Sowa and Anna Adamska (Rzeszów: MITEL, 2013), 2nd edn, corrected and extended, pp. 9–64.

—, *Teatr Dionizosa. Romantyzm w polskim teatrze współczesnym* [The theatre of Dionysus: Romanticism in contemporary Polish theatre] (Kraków: Wydawnictwo Literackie, 1972).

—, 'Występy gościnne Teatru Laboratorium 1959–1984. Kronika działalności 1978–1984' [Guest performances of the Laboratory Theatre 1959–1984. Chronicle of activities 1978–1984], *Pamiętnik Teatralny*, 1–4 (2000), 627–90.

OSTERWA, Juliusz, *Listy Juliusza Osterwy* [Juliusz Osterwa's letters], introduction by Jerzy Zawieyski (Warsaw: Państwowy Instytut Wydawniczy, 1968).

OTTAI, Antonella, ed. *Teatro Oriente/Occidente* (Rome: Bulzoni Editore, 1986).

PAVIS, Patrice, *Słownik terminów teatralnych* [A dictionary of theatrical terms], trans., ed. and supplemented by Sławomir Świontek, introduction by Anne Ubersfeld (Wrocław, Warsaw and Kraków: Zakład Narodowy im. Ossolińskich, 1998). English version: *Dictionary of the Theatre: Terms, Concepts, and Analysis*, trans. by Christine Shantz (Toronto: University of Toronto Press, 1999).

—, *Le Théâtre au croissement des cultures* (Paris: J. Corti, 1990).

PAWELCZYK, Joanna Eliza, 'Mieczysław Limanowski – prekursor polskich "Dziadów kulturowych"' [Mieczysław Limanowski: A precursor of Polish 'cultural Forefathers'], *Konteksty. Polska Sztuka Ludowa*, 1 (2008), 84–89.

PIEKARSKI, Przemysław, ed., *Teatr Orientu* [Theatre of the Orient] (Kraków: Uniwersytet Jagielloński, Instytut Filologii Oriental-nej, 1998).

POLLI, Giovanni, ed., *Mostra del Trentennio del Festival (1934–1964), Catalogo ufficiale*, La Biennale di Venezia, XXIII Festival Internazionale del Teatro di Prosa – 1964.

PRONKO, Léonard C[abell], *Theater East and West* (Berkeley and Los Angeles: University of California Press, 1974).

PUZYNA, Konstanty, 'Nie takie dalekie' [Not so distant], in the programme for the production of *You Are Beautiful* by Yukio Mishima. A premiere of three one-act plays from the collection *Kindai-nō gaku-shū* (1956): *Fan*, *You Are Beautiful* and *The Damask Drum*, directed and adopted by Tadeusz Łomnicki (his directing debut), Warsaw, Teatr Współczesny, 9 March 1965.

RASZEWSKI, Zbigniew, *Raptularz 1968–1969* [Diary 1968–1969] (Kraków: Znak, 1997).

REGULSKA, Katarzyna, 'Reduta Juliusza Osterwy i Mieczysława Limanowskiego a Vieux Colombier Jacques'a Copeau' [Juliusz Osterwa's and Mieczysław Limanowski's Reduta and Jacques Copeau's Vieux Colombier], *Konteksty. Polska Sztuka Ludowa*, 1 (2008), 90–94.

REKLEWSKA, Zofia, and Konstanty Puzyna, 'Copeau i słowa "trzeba stąd iść"' [Copeau and the words 'One must leave'], in Jacques Copeau, *Naga scena*, sel. and ed. by Zofia Reklewska, trans. by Maria Skibniewska (Warsaw: Wydawnictwa Artystyczne i Filmowe, 1972, pp. 5–33.

RENIK, Krzysztof, 'Czam – taniec buddyjskich mnichów' [Cham: The dance of Buddhist monks], in *Taniec bogów. Mit jako opis świata* [The dance of the gods: Myth as a description of the world], materials of the Faculty of Oriental Studies of the University of Warsaw, Festiwal Nauki, 26–28 September 1997, pp. 36–39.

—, *Kathakali, sztuka indyjskiego teatru* [Kathakali: The art of Indian theatre] (Warsaw: Wydawnictwo Akademickie Dialog, 1994).

—, *Śladem Bharaty* [Following Bharata] (Warsaw: Wydawnictwo Akademickie Dialog, 2001).

RODOWICZ, Jadwiga M., ed., *Aktor doskonały. Traktaty Zeamiego o sztuce nō* [A perfect actor: Zeami's treatises on the art of Noh] (Gdańsk: słowo/obraz terytoria, 2000).

—, 'Aktor w teatrze nō' [The actor in Noh theatre], *Dialog*, 11 (1980), 115–23.

—, *Boski dwumian. Przenikanie rzeczywistości w teatrze nō* [The divine binomial: Interpenetration of realities in Noh theatre] (Wrocław: Instytut im. Jerzego Grotowskiego, 2009).

—, 'Nō, czyli umiejętność' [Noh; or, a skill], *Didaskalia. Gazeta Teatralna*, 45 (2001), 42–45.

—, *Pięć wcieleń kobiety w teatrze nō* [Five incarnations of woman in Noh theatre] (Warsaw: Pusty Obłok, 1993).

SAVARESE, Nicola, *Eurasian Theatre: Drama and Performance Between East and West from Classical Antiquity to the Present*, trans. from Italian by Richard Fowler, updated version revised and ed. by Vicki Ann Cremona (Holstebro, Malta and Wrocław: Icarus Publishing Enterprise, 2010).

—, 'Giappone: combiamenti e interferenze nella vita dello spettacolo dal 1853 al 1970. Le anse del fiume Sumida. A cura di Nicola Savarese' [Japan: Changes and interference in the life of performance arts from 1853 to 1970. The loops of the Sumida River, ed. by Nicola Savarese], *Sipario*, 406 (1980) ('L'Oriente per l'Occidente').

—, *Paris/Artaud/Bali. Antonin Artaud vede il teatro balinese all'Esposizione Coloniale di Parigi del 1931. Conferenza-spettacolo* (L'Aquila: Textus, 1997).

SCHAYER, Stanisław, 'Klasyczny teatr indyjski' [Classical Indian theatre], *Scena Polska*, 1 (1924), 5–24.

SCHECHNER, Richard, *Performative Circumstances from the Avant Garde to Ramila* (Calcutta: Seagull Books, 1983).

—, *Performatyka. Wstęp*, trans. by Tomasz Kubikowski, ed. by Marcin Rochowski (Wrocław: Ośrodek Badań Twórczości Jerzego Grotowskiego i Poszukiwań Teatralno-Kulturowych, 2006), Polish version of *Performance Studies: An Introduction* (New York and London: Routledge 2002, 2006).

—, *Przeszłość rytuału*, trans. by Tomasz Kubikowski (Warsaw: Oficyna Wydawnicza Volumen, 2000), Polish version of *The Future of Ritual: Writings on Culture and Performance* (London and New York: Routledge, 1993).

—, and Lisa Wolford, eds., *The Grotowski Sourcebook* (London and New York: Routledge, 1997).

SCHINO, Mirella, *Alchemists of the Stage: Theatre Laboratories in Europe*, trans. from Italian and French by Paul Warrington (Holstebro, Malta and Wrocław: Icarus Publishing Enterprise, 2009).

SEROVA, Svetlana A., *Театральная культура серебрянного века в России и художественные традиции Востока (Китай, Япония, Индия)/Teatralnaya kultura serebryannogo veka v Rossii i khudozhestvennye traditsii Vostoka (Kitai, Yaponiya, Indiya)* [Theatrical culture of the Silver Age in Russia and the artistic traditions of the East: China, Japan, India] (Moscow: Институт востоковедения РАН/ Institute of Oriental Studies of the Russian Academy of Sciences, 1999).

SHAKHMATOVA, Elena V., *Искания европейской режиссуры и традиции Востока/Iskaniya evropeiskoi rezhissury i traditsii Vostoka* [Quest of European stage direction and the traditions of the East] (Moscow: Эдиториал УРСС/Editorial URSS, 1997).

SLOWIAK, James, and Jairo Cuesta, *Jerzy Grotowski* (New York: Routledge, 2007).

TEMKINE, Raymonde, *Grotowski* (Lausanne: La Cité, 1968).

TOKARSKI, Stanisław, *Jogini i wspólnoty. Nowoczesna recepcja hinduizmu* [Yogis and communes: A modern reception of Hinduism] (Wrocław, Warsaw, Kraków, Gdańsk and Łódź: Zakład Narodowy im. Ossolińskich, 1987).

—, *Orient i kontrkultury* [The Orient and counter-cultures] (Warsaw: Wiedza Powszechna, 1984).

TUBIELEWICZ, Jolanta, *Kultura Japonii. Słownik* [Japan's culture: A dictionary] (Warsaw: Wydawnictwa Szkolne i Pedagogiczne, 1996).

ZEAMI, *'La tradition secrète du nō' suivi de 'Une journée de nō'*, trans. and ed. by Renée Sieffert (Paris: Gallimard/Unesco, 1960).

ZIÓŁKOWSKI, Grzegorz, *Guślarz i eremita. Jerzy Grotowski od wykładów rzymskich (1982) do paryskich (1997–1998)* [The Sorcerer and the hermit: Jerzy Grotowski from the Rome lectures (1982) to the Paris lectures (1997–1998)] (Wrocław: Instytut im. Jerzego Grotowskiego, 2007).

INDEX OF PHOTOGRAPHS

INDEX